FISH & SHELLFISH GRILLED & SMOKED

FISH & SHELLFISH GRILLED & SMOKED

300 FOOLPROOF RECIPES FOR EVERYTHING FROM AMBERJACK TO WHITEFISH, PLUS REALLY GOOD RUBS, MARVELOUS MARINADES, SASSY SAUCES, AND SUMPTUOUS SIDES

KAREN ADLER & JUDITH M. FERTIG

The Harvard Common Press
Boston, Massachusetts

To our families:
Sarah and Nick;
Dick and daughters Ellen and Jill,
and their families

THE HARVARD COMMON PRESS
535 ALBANY STREET
BOSTON, MASSACHUSETTS 02118
WWW.HARVARDCOMMONPRESS.COM

Printed in the United States of America
Printed on acid-free paper

Library of Congress Cataloging-in-Publication Data

Adler, Karen.
    Fish & shellfish, grilled & smoked : 300 foolproof recipes for everything from amberjack to whitefish, plus really good rubs, marvelous marinades, sassy sauces, and sumptuous sides / Karen Adler and Judith Fertig.
       p. cm.
    ISBN 1-55832-180-2 (cl : alk. paper) — ISBN 1-55832-181-0 (pbk. : alk. paper)
      1. Cookery (Seafood) 2. Barbecue cookery. 3. Cookery (Smoked foods) I. Fertig, Judith M. II. Title.

TX747.A315 2002
641.6'92—dc21

                                                  2001051538

Special bulk-order discounts are available on this and other Harvard Common Press books. Companies and organizations may purchase books for premiums or resale, or may arrange a custom edition, by contacting the Marketing Director at the address above.

10 9 8 7 6 5 4 3 2 1

JACKET & INTERIOR DESIGN BY RENATO STANISIC
Jacket photograph © Rita Maas/Envision
Illustrations by Chris Van Dusen

CONTENTS

ACKNOWLEDGMENTS

We thank the following home cooks, restaurateurs, chefs, cookbook authors, seafood aficionados, and barbecue friends for recipe inspiration: Jody Adams, Darina Allen, Georgiana Baer, Terry Barkley, Todd Baron, Brenda Burns, Steve Cole, Shirley Corriher, Norm Crisp, Ardie Davis, Brooke Dojny, Larry Forgione, Lila Gault, the late Jane Grigson, Sharon Tyler Herbst, Geraldene Holt, Monique Jamet Hooker, Paul Kirk, Susan Herrmann-Loomis, Michael McLaughlin, J.J. Mirabile, Joyce Molyneux, Laura O'Rourke, Louis Osteen, James Peterson, Patrick Quillec, Steve Raichlen, Chris Schlesinger, Guy Simpson, Michael Smith and Debbie Gold, Nancy Stark, Elizabeth Terry, the late Barbara Tropp, Carolyn Wells, and Patricia Wells.

Many thanks to the following for special assistance in the research of this book: the Chef's Cellaborative, the Catfish Institute, the National Audubon Society, Nick Nicholas, and Traeger Industries.

To all of our food friends from the International Association of Culinary Professionals, Les Dames D'Escoffier, the National Barbecue Association, and the Kansas City Cookbook Club, we thank you for your ongoing support.

The Harvard Common Press, our publisher, has a remarkable list of people that we work with, including Bruce Shaw, Pam Hoenig, Skye Stewart, Sunshine Erickson, Abbey Phalen, Beatrice Wikander, and many others.

Last but not least, our closest friends and family are the dear ones who put up with our cranky moods when deadlines are upon us, cheer us on when wonderful things happen, and do the grunt work of everyday life when our plates get too full. They also are the ones who help us clean our plates when we need thoughtful tasters. Our warmest thanks to: Dick Adler, Dee Barwick, Mary Ann Duckers, Nick Fertig, and Sarah Fertig.

INTRODUCTION

Why are two women from the landlocked Midwest writing a fish and shellfish cookbook? Good question.

First of all, new technology has made fresh fish available all over North America. In larger cities, just-caught fish is flown in daily. Frozen-at-sea halibut or cod and flash-frozen catfish, trout, and shrimp are also in supermarkets and seafood shops.

"But that's not fresh!" some might say. But we maintain that "fresh" is in the flavor and texture, and frozen-at-sea and flash-frozen fish and shellfish can often be delicious. In a recent seminar and blind fish and shellfish tasting by the Chef's Collaborative, many food professionals (including the two of us) preferred some of the previously frozen to the "fresh" fish and shellfish because the flavor and texture were superior.

To enjoy and cook from *Fish & Shellfish, Grilled & Smoked*, you don't have to live on a coast. You can live anywhere and just select the best and freshest-tasting fish and shellfish you can find. We are very careful to offer substitute varieties in our recipes and in an informative chart, as fish and shellfish in the wild have definite seasons when they are and aren't available. Overfishing has also caused depletion of some varieties, and you'll have to substitute others. Farm-raised fish and shellfish are generally available all year long.

Secondly, we live in a part of the country that takes grilling and smoking very seriously. Kansas City has been known as the "melting pot" of barbecue—where all of the many regional styles come together. So, we are in the perfect spot to grill and smoke fish and shellfish of all kinds, using many different techniques.

We have caught fresh fish, then grilled and smoked our catch far away from Kansas City as well. Karen and her husband, Dick, often go fly-fishing in Colorado and Idaho and deep-sea fishing around Baja, California. Judith grew up vacationing and fishing with her father and grandfather on the Great Lakes, lived and fished in New England, and now vacations with her family off the coast of the Carolinas. We know how delicious fresh-caught mackerel can be on the grill or in the smoker, but it is a fish that just doesn't travel well. Take our book with you when you go on a coastal vacation and enjoy grilling and smoking some of the fish varieties you can't get at home.

The two of us also belong to an all-women barbecue team—the tiara-topped, beauty queen sash–wearing Barbeque, or 'Que, Queens. In yearly Battle of the Sexes Barbeque contests for charity, the 'Que Queens usually beat the all-men's team. We have a costume, a special "secret ingredient" barbecue sauce known as "Love Potion for the Swine," and a song to go with it. For this book, we've set aside our 'Que Queen barbecued baby back ribs for amberjack and yellowfish, cherrystone clams, and Olympia oysters. But we haven't set aside the fun.

When we teach our fish and shellfish classes at culinary schools across the country, we like for everyone to laugh and learn. We have tried to include our two favorite concepts—big flavor and big fun—in every recipe. After all, when you're standing outside and smelling something wonderful on the grill or smoker, doesn't that put you in a good mood?

Because grilling and smoking fish and shellfish are fairly simple when you follow our guidelines, you'll feel accomplished when you turn out a perfectly grilled salmon fillet or moist and delicious smoked trout. When you taste the delicious grilled and smoked recipes you can easily prepare, along with sassy side dishes and sumptuous sauces, your taste buds will be ready to rumba. And so will your guests. Just be prepared.

PART 1

GRILLING FISH & SHELLFISH

When you're in the mood for a meal of fish or seafood, grilling is your quickest, easiest, and tastiest cooking option. Because fish has no tough connective tissue, it's perfect for the fast, hot nature of the grill.

Buy the Freshest Fish and Shellfish

Rule number one is to always use the freshest ingredients. When selecting and buying fish, go to a reputable fish and seafood market. The manager of this market, known as a fishmonger, will help you select the best catch of the day to sizzle on your grill. So be flexible—if your recipe calls for halibut but the salmon is the freshest, change your plans. The fishmonger also can suggest similar fish when you need to substitute, or use the Fish and Shellfish Substitution Guide for the Grill on pages 12 and 13. Choose fish with bright, clear eyes if you are buying whole fish, make sure the flesh is fresh and moist, and beware of an overpowering fishy or ammonia odor.

Sometimes "freshest" might mean frozen! Halibut and cod, fished in Alaskan waters, are processed on board with "Frozen at Sea," or FAS, technology. Likewise, Mississippi Delta catfish often go from pond to frozen package in less than 30 minutes. Shrimp farmed in Guatemala or Venezuela also go from pond to plant for Individual Quick Frozen, or IQF, processing.

Another hook to buying fish is farm-raised fish and shellfish, a safe and economical angle (pardon the puns). Farm-raised options got a boost when the federal government began regulating certain species that were overfished. For example, Gulf redfish surged in popularity during the heyday of Cajun blackened redfish recipes. Authorities banned commercial fishing of it until stocks were replenished. Now it's available again. New England cod catch quotas have been cut by half in the past, but it too is available again. Chilean sea bass, not really a sea bass at all, but rather the Patagonian toothfish, has been overfished and is now under the scrutiny of fish regulators. So although aquaculture may seem just a forced alternative to maintaining stocks, it has actually raised the quality and often lowered prices because of abundance of harvest. When a certain fish becomes protected from overfishing, a new find comes on the market like tilefish. In addition, new "faces," like tilapia, are appearing on the American fish market, thanks to farm-raising. Farm-raised catfish, a whole new taste and texture experience compared to the "wild," and tiger shrimp (farm-raised in Asia) are both plentiful, interesting choices.

Not all kinds of aquaculture are equal, however. Catfish farming is one of the most advanced, having been improved and perfected since the late 1960s. Shrimp and salmon farms are still working out the kinks in producing healthy products with good flavor. Aquaculture is a dynamic field of frequent change, however, with new advances and techniques every year. Your best bet is to rely on your fishmonger to help you select the best among wild and farm-raised fish and seafood.

Healthy Grilling

Health-conscious chefs are choosing fish and shellfish to grill because, overall, they are lower in fat and calories than other meat options. In fact, grilling itself is a very lowfat way to prepare any kind of food. The process is as simple as seasoning the fish and lightly brushing it with a low cholesterol oil to prevent sticking. The average calorie count for an uncooked seven-ounce serving of fish ranges from 160 to 200 calories for haddock and catfish to 400 calories for a "fatty" fish like trout or salmon. (The fish with higher fat content are easier to grill because they don't dry out as fast and their meat holds together better on the grill.)

FISH—FOR A HEALTHY THRILL OF THE GRILL

Grill aficionados and avid barbecuers don't like to hear about potential cancer risks from HCAs (heterocyclic amines created by cooking meat at high temperatures) or PAHs (polycyclic aromatic hydrocarbons deposited on food by flare-ups created by fat dripping onto hot coals). Although scientists have not yet determined how much exposure to these chemicals poses a cancer risk for people, the good news is that marinating, grilling, and smoking fish is a healthier approach.

Marinating, even briefly, appears to cut down on the formation of cancer-causing substances. Coating foods with "a thick oily mixture was enough to greatly reduce the formation of the heterocyclic amines," says Mark Knize of the Lawrence Livermore National Laboratory. Fish grills so quickly that HCAs and PAHs don't have much time to build up. And the cooking temperatures used in indirect cooking or smoking are too low to form HCAs or PAHs. Slow smoking also adds flavor without fats or sugars.

Add to that the Omega-3 benefits found in oilier fish like salmon, mackerel, and bluefish, and you've got even more reason—besides great taste—to grill and smoke fish.

Preparing Fish and Shellfish for the Grill

As you begin exploring the fish and seafood recipes in this book, follow these simple preparation guidelines with each. Always rinse fish in cold water to remove any bacteria and pat it dry with paper towels before marinating, seasoning, or cooking it. When a recipe calls for brushing oil on the fish or shellfish, make sure that you do so lightly; fire flare-ups can occur when excess oil drips on hot coals. A spray bottle of olive oil is an excellent way to get a light coating.

Preparing the Grill, Grill Equipment, and Utensils

The grill should be clean and the grill rack(s) lightly oiled (use any vegetable oil and a long-handled brush, and take care again to avoid dripping oil). Oil the inside or underside of all grill equipment and utensils that will directly touch the fish or seafood. This will keep the fish from adhering to the grill equipment and it will make cleanup of the equipment easier, too. Have all of your equipment handy, and your grilling experience will be relaxing and enjoyable.

The Utensils

Several basic tools make grilling fish easier. A local restaurant supply store or a barbecue and grill shop will be a good source for finding the items listed, and professional utensils are superior in quality and durability. Long handles are preferable on everything, to keep you a safe distance from the fire.

- A stiff wire brush with a scraper makes cleaning the grill a simple job (tackle this while the grill is still warm).
- Use a natural-bristled basting brush to oil the grill and use a second brush to baste the fish during grilling.
- Grill toppers or perforated grill racks are grates placed on top of the grill to accommodate small or delicate-textured items, such as fish fillets, scallops, shrimp, and vegetables. Always oil the grill topper on both sides before using so fish won't stick.
- Hinged grill baskets or fish baskets hold foods in place and make turning an easy process. They need to be oiled on all sides, too.
- Kabob baskets can save time in recipes that call for using skewers. They are more expensive than skewers, but the fish, shellfish, or vegetables are simply dropped into the oiled basket rather than threaded onto a skewer. Sometimes it is hard to pull food off of wooden or metal skewers; with the kabob basket, the food is easily emptied into an attractive serving bowl or onto individual dinner plates.
- Grill woks make "stir-grilling" possible. The wok has holes to let in smoky flavor and it sits directly on top of the grill. Oil both sides on the wok. Stir-grill marinated fish and vegetables by tossing with wooden paddles. The grill wok enables totally oil-free cooking and has become a staple with health-conscious grill chefs. There are 12- and 15-inch models to choose from. We recommend the larger 15-inch model. Make sure it fits on your grill, though, before purchasing it.
- The Nordicware fish boat is a porcelain-coated metal container shaped like a fish. It comes with a perforated half and a solid half. The solid half holds in liquids or sauces. Or if more heat and smoke are desired, the fish or

shellfish can be placed in the perforated side, much like a grill wok. Oil the inside and the outside of this fish boat before using.

• Disposable aluminum pans are particularly handy for grilling delicate-textured fish or small shellfish that would otherwise fall though the grill grate. They are also a great container for holding a mélange of small-cut vegetables to serve alongside your seafood supper.

• Heavy-duty aluminum foil, which can be crimped to make a pan or folded to make a packet, aids in grilling fish and shellfish. Dry wood pellets can be placed in a foil packet with holes poked in the top to place on the fire for smoke flavor, too.

• Heat-resistant oven or grill mitts offer the best hand protection, especially when you need to touch any hot metals during the grilling process. These will also provide good protection in our flambé recipes.

• Long-handled, spring-loaded tongs are easier to use than the scissors type. They are great for turning shrimp, scallops, sliced vegetables, and skewers. However, there is a set of fish-shaped scissor tongs that we like. The ends of the tongs are shaped like a six-inch fish and can be used like a metal spatula to scoop underneath a small fish fillet to turn it.

• Skewers—wooden or metal—allow smaller items to be threaded loosely together and then placed on the grill to cook. Wooden or bamboo skewers should be soaked in water for 20 to 30 minutes before using so the ends won't char during grilling. Flat metal skewers are preferred, so that cubed food doesn't spin while it is being turned.

• A long, wooden-handled, metal offset spatula with a five- to six-inch blade is essential for turning fish fillets. Oil it well to avoid sticking.

• Keep a spray bottle or pan filled with water handy to douse flare-ups.

• A garden hose within quick reaching distance can substitute, but make sure the water is turned on!

For the novice fish griller, firm-fleshed fish steaks (salmon, tuna, swordfish, shark) will be the easiest to grill. They require the least amount of special equipment because their firmness allows cooking them directly on the regular grill rack. They're also easier to turn. Shrimp will be the easiest shellfish to begin with. You'll need a perforated grill rack or skewers so they don't fall through the grill grates. As your confidence grows, so will your food and cooking-style options. Invest in some of the new grill toppers—racks and woks—that make handling delicate foods and even stir-grilling possible on the grill. And don't forget a set of skewers; they make grilling small chunks and items like shrimp and scallops a breeze. Buy several so you can skewer vegetables on the grill, too. Or for even more ease of preparation, buy several kabob baskets, one for each person you will be entertaining. That way you don't have to skewer the foods to have a kabob. Or place all the food in a hinged grill basket.

The Grill

Grilling is defined as cooking over a direct heat source. The kind of grill you choose will be determined by the space you have, the kind of fuel you want to use, the amount of cooking surface you need, and how much money you want to spend. The fuel choices are gas, electricity, and charcoal/hardwood. Gas and electric grills are quick to start and easy to clean; their prices, though, may be higher than a comparable-sized charcoal grill. When grilling on a gas or electric grill, follow the manufacturer's directions.

Charcoal grills come in all sizes and shapes, with or without covers. The most popular grill "rig" for home use is the kettle-shaped grill. New wood pellet grills combine the ease of an electric starter with the flavor of compressed wood pellets as fuel and flavoring. Whatever you choose, it's a sure thing that you'll be able to grill great fish!

Starting the Fire

The primal art of cooking over a fire is what outdoor grilling is all about. It's a Neanderthal root thing. And food that is grilled or smoked outside simply tastes better, too. Before you start your fire, make sure that the grill grates are clean and lightly brushed with oil to avoid flare-ups and prevent items from sticking.

CHARCOAL

Charcoal fires can be started in any of several safe, ecologically sound ways. We recommend using real hardwood charcoal, not chemically treated and compressed charcoal, the ubiquitous briquette. Hardwood charcoal, available at grill shops and select grocery stores, gives a better flavor and is better for the environment. We also discourage the use of charcoal lighter fluid, as it can infuse your food with an unpleasant chemical flavor. Instead, start your fire and charcoal in a metal charcoal chimney or with an electric starter, available at hardware, discount, and home improvement stores.

The charcoal is always mounded onto the lower fire grate of the grill except when using a charcoal chimney. When the fire is hot, spread the coals out in an even layer on the fire grate. This is the direct cooking area. The following items will aid you in easy fire starting:

Charcoal chimney: This is an upright cylindrical metal canister, which you will fill with 15 to 20 hardwood briquettes. Place it on a nonflammable surface, such as concrete or the top of the grill, and put crumpled paper in the bottom. Light the paper. After about 15 minutes, the coals will be hot. Empty the coals onto the lower fire rack of the grill.

Electric starter: This is the easiest way to start a fire. You'll probably need an outdoor electrical outlet or extension cord. Place the coil on the lower rack of the grill and stack charcoal on top of it. Plug it in and the fire will start in about 10 minutes. Remove the coil and let the starter cool on a nonflammable surface, out of the reach of children and pets.

Solid starter: This is a compressed wood block or stick treated with a flammable substance, such as paraffin. It is easy to ignite and doesn't give off a chemical odor.

10 TIPS AND TECHNIQUES FOR GREAT GRILLED FISH AND SHELLFISH, EVERY TIME

1. Select only the freshest fish and shellfish. Fresh fish has a glistening, dewy look, a sweet or briny smell of the sea, and a somewhat firm texture. Shellfish has a sweet or briny smell of the sea, too. If you buy flash-frozen fish or shellfish, make sure it is still frozen when you buy it. If it has thawed at the fishmonger's or grocery store, who knows how long it has been sitting there.

2. Handle fish and shellfish carefully. Buy fresh fish and shellfish, preferably the day you are going to cook it or the day before. Always keep it chilled until ready to grill or smoke. Rinse it thoroughly under cold running water, then pat dry. Discard any shellfish with cracked or open shells.

3. Marinate fish and shellfish for only 30 to 60 minutes in the refrigerator before grilling. Marinating longer could mean that the flavor of the marinade will dominate the flavor of the fish or shellfish. Also, there are no connective tissues in fish, so overmarinating can cause it to become mushy. There are exceptions to this rule; some shellfish can marinate overnight.

4. It is preferable to leave the fish skin on when grilling. Always place the fillet flesh side down first, then turn halfway through grilling onto the skin side (or the flesh side that had the skin on). The skin side is fattier and holds together better, so it makes for easier removal with the spatula when finished. Just as the skin protects fish, so too the shell on shellfish can help to keep it moister.

5. Grill just about any fish you like.

6. Grill over a hot fire. Hold your hand 5 inches above the heat source. If you can only hold it there for about 2 seconds, your fire is hot.

7. The general rule for grilling fish is 10 minutes per inch of thickness. Exceptions are shark and shellfish (see specific recipes for exact cooking times).

8. Test for doneness by making sure the fish and shellfish are opaque and somewhat firm. Fish that is done will just begin to flake when tested with a fork.

9. Grill gadgets that rule: two long-handled wide metal spatulas for fish steaks or fillets and long-handled tongs for shellfish. For delicate fish and small shellfish, it is best to use a perforated grill rack, disposable aluminum pans, Nordicware fish boat, or aluminum foil as a base so that the fish won't fall through the grill grates.

10. Substitute any of the fish or shellfish recommended in each recipe or use our Fish and Shellfish Substitution chart on pages 12 and 13.

Two or three will easily light the charcoal; set them on top of or beside the briquettes and ignite.

Gel fire starter: This is a nonpetroleum fire starter that you squeeze onto your charcoal according to manufacturer's directions and then light.

Grilling Temperature

Fish and shellfish are usually grilled directly over a hot to medium-hot fire, depending on the distance your grill rack sits from the fire. The fire is ready when the flames have subsided and the coals are glowing red and just beginning to ash over. The fire is medium-hot when the coals are no longer red, but ashen. Another test to gauge the temperature is to hold your hand 5 inches above the heat source. If you can only hold it there for about 2 seconds, your fire is hot; 3 to 4 seconds is a medium-hot fire, and 5 to 6 seconds is a low fire.

Grilling Time

Estimating grilling times is a challenge, because the time required to cook fish and shellfish is affected by the heat of the fire, the type of coals used, and the distance your heat source is from the grill rack. Use the suggested cooking times given in each recipe as guidelines but also watch your fish while it's cooking.

- *Fish fillets and steaks:* They're done when the color turns opaque and the flesh just begins to flake when tested with a fork. We would rather under-cook than overcook fish. You can always finish it in the microwave. Grill steaks and fillets over a hot fire quickly. The general rule of thumb is to cook 10 minutes per inch of thickness.
- *Whole fish:* We recommend cooking over a medium-hot fire. Sear the whole fish directly over the fire for 3 or 4 minutes on each side, then move the fish to the indirect side of the grill, close the lid, and continue to cook for about 20 minutes more. Check for doneness by carefully lifting the tail of the fish to see if the flesh falls away from the bones. You can also insert a fork into the thickest part of the fish and see if it flakes away from the bone. Whole fish takes 5 to 10 minutes longer than the 10 minutes per inch of thickness rule because of the bones. So cook a whole fish a little more slowly over a medium-hot fire, and a little bit longer so that the middle gets done.
- *Shellfish on the grill:* The rule is, grill it hot and fast. Most shellfish will get tough and rubbery if overcooked. Shrimp will grill over a hot fire in 5 to 6 minutes. It will turn a pinkish opaque color. Scallops need to be seared over a hot fire, too. Depending on their size, they will turn opaque and be done in 4 to 5 minutes. Small octopus and squid will take only a couple of minutes on each side. Their texture will firm up and the color becomes opaque when they are done. Lobster in the shell will take 10 to 15 minutes to grill, depending on the size. Cook it half the time with the cut flesh side down and the other half with the shell toward the fire; the flesh will be a pretty opaque white color when done. Grill clams and mussels over a hot fire in a single layer. They should pop open in 4 to 5 minutes.

FOR additional herb flavor, gather several stalks of your favorite herbs and tie them together with florist wire or twist ties to make an herb brush. Apply your baste or marinade with this fragrant brush.

Flavor Enhancements

Fish and shellfish pick up marinade flavors quickly. Marinating for 15 minutes to an hour should be sufficient. Be careful not to overmarinate or fish flesh will break down and become mushy—the juice of pineapples and papayas contains an enzyme that will reduce your fish to mush in record time. At their simplest, marinades and bastes can be a light application of oil with salt and pepper seasoning. The recipes in this book have accompanying bastes or marinades, but also see the chapter beginning on page 271 to experiment and find your favorite flavoring for fish on the grill.

Woods and herbs added to the grill fire offer another means of flavor enhancement. Fish cooks so quickly over a hot fire that your addition of soaked wood chips or herbs will not penetrate as effectively as will slow smoking with a closed-lid grill. But the heavenly odor in your backyard is worth giving it a try. So choose hardwoods that burn hot, such as mesquite or oak. Fruitwoods are also nice; try cherry, apple, or grapevines. Wood chips are best for quick cooking. Soak them in water for about 30 minutes prior to grilling or keep a plastic container filled with wood chips in water, then throw a handful on the fire when you need them.

Wood pellets do not require soaking, but need to be enclosed in a packet made from heavy-duty aluminum foil left partially opened or with holes poked in it to let the smoke escape. If you want more smoke flavor while you're grilling the fish, simply close the lid for a few minutes.

Dried herbs also can be thrown onto the fire, but soak them in water first. Try thick-stalked varieties such as fennel, mint, rosemary, sage, lavender, or basil. Soak them in water for 15 to 20 minutes before throwing them on the fire. Again, this is more an aromatic experience for the grillers than it is for the fish, but it's fun and adds to the outdoor atmosphere. So if it pleases you, do it!

To get more wood smoke flavor using a gas or electric grill, place the moistened wood chips, wood pellets, or herbs in a packet made from heavy-duty aluminum foil, poke holes in it, and place it directly over the lava rock. Do not put the wood chips or herbs directly on the lava rock, as the residue could block the holes in the gas burner.

Fish and Shellfish Substitution Guide for the Grill

Use this guide to help you select the freshest fish and shellfish at the market. If your choice is not available, substitute another from the same category, or one category over. Some recipes will work with almost any kind of fish, so experiment, if you like.

This guide helps you choose your fish and shellfish by flavor—mild to pronounced—and by texture—firm to delicate. Many of our delicate-texture fish recipes include grilling with a perforated grill rack, disposable aluminum pans, the Nordicware fish boat, or heavy-duty aluminum foil. This is so the delicate fish doesn't flake and fall between the grill grates onto the fire. Keep this in mind when choosing from this category.

Names of fish can be confusing. There's the fish family name, the local or regional name, and possibly a Hawaiian, Spanish, or French name commonly used. The most common usage is included to aid you in your fish shopping.

FIRMNESS	MILD FLAVOR	MODERATE FLAVOR	FULL FLAVOR
FIRM TEXTURE	Sea Bass/Loup de Mer	Black Drum	Bigeye Tuna/Ahi
	Blackfish	Clams	Chilean Sea Bass
	Halibut	Cobia/Sargentfish	Cuttlefish
	John Dory/St. Peter's Fish	Drum/White Sea Bass	Escolar
	Kinklip	Moonfish/Opah	Garfish/Needlefish
	Lingcod/Greenling	Salmon	Marlin/A'u
	Lobster	Shark	Mussels
	Monkfish	Shortbill Spearfish/ Hebi	Octopus
	Oreo Dory	Skate	Oysters
	Prawns	Striped Marlin/ Nairagi	Sailfish
	Red Drum/Redfish	Sturgeon	Squid
	Sea Robin	Swordfish	Triggerfish
	Shrimp	Yellowfin Tuna	Tuna
	Soft-shell Crab		

FIRMNESS	MILD FLAVOR	MODERATE FLAVOR	FULL FLAVOR
MODERATELY FIRM TEXTURE	Striped Bass Canary Rockfish/ Pacific Red Snapper Catfish Grouper Haddock Ocean Perch/ Rockfish/Redfish Orange Roughy Pompano Porgy Scup/Porgy Sea Scallops Sheepshead/ Convictfish Snapper Tilefish Walleye Whitefish Wolffish	Arctic Char Barracuda Bonito Mahimahi/Dorado Sablefish/Black Cod Sea Bream/Daurade Sea Trout/Weakfish Tilapia Trout	Amberjack Kingfish King Mackerel Mackerel Mullet Permit Yellowtail Jack/ Hamachi Yellowtail Snapper Wahoo/Ono
DELICATE TEXTURE	Bass (Freshwater) Crayfish Cod Flounder Fluke Hake/Whiting Hoki/Blue Hake Pink Snapper/ Opakapaka Red Snapper Sand Dab Turbot	Butterfish Herring Pomfret/Dollar Fish Shad Smelts/Whitebait	Anchovies Bluefish Buffalofish Sardines

SIMPLY GRILLED FISH

In its simplest and purest form, fish on the grill needs little more than oil, salt, and pepper. The oil adds moisture to the fish so that it won't dry out as easily. It also helps to prevent sticking. The rule of thumb is to grill over a hot fire for thin fillets and steaks. Grill over a medium-hot fire for whole fish, so that the middle gets done.

MAKES 1 SERVING

One 8-ounce fish fillet or
  steak about 1 inch thick
1 tablespoon oil
1/4 teaspoon salt
1/4 teaspoon freshly ground
  black pepper

1. Brush or spray the fish with oil and season with salt and pepper.

2. Prepare a hot fire.

3. When ready to grill, place the fish on an oiled grill rack over the fire and grill for 5 minutes on one side. Turn the fish and continue to cook until it is opaque and just begins to flake when tested with a fork, about an additional 5 minutes.

Anglers Norm Crisp and Georgiana Baer of Stream Side Adventures in Kansas City take groups of neophyte fly-fishermen to the best trout streams, almost every weekend. "Missouri trout fishing is one of those undiscovered secrets," says Norm. "You can catch a trophy trout, somewhere in Missouri, 365 days a year!" That's a lot of trout.

Norm and Georgiana have developed a method of preserving their extra catch. "With our way of preserving trout, even if you have to freeze them, they are still at their peak when you cook them," says Norm. Here's what they do:

FRESHWATER FISH PRESERVATIVE

1/4 cup fresh lemon juice
1 3/4 cups water
One 1-ounce package unflavored gelatin
Whole trout, gutted and cleaned

1. In a small saucepan, combine the lemon juice and water. Remove 1/2 cup of the mixture and set aside. Bring the remaining lemon juice mixture in the saucepan to a boil. Meanwhile, sprinkle the gelatin over the reserved 1/2 cup of lemon water until it softens. When the gelatin has softened, whisk it into the boiling lemon juice mixture and remove from the heat. Whisk until the gelatin has dissolved and set the saucepan aside to cool.
2. Dip each cleaned fish into the lemon juice/gelatin mixture, then wrap individually in plastic wrap and place in resealable plastic bags and freeze. Whole trout treated in this way can be frozen for up to a year.

FISH ON THE GRILL

MESQUITE-GRILLED AMBERJACK

The flavor of mesquite with grilled fish is perfect. Serve this with Avocado-Corn Salsa (page 332).

MAKES 4 SERVINGS

Four 6- to 8-ounce amber-jack fillets about 1 inch thick
1 to 2 tablespoons olive oil, as needed
Sea salt to taste
Freshly ground pink, green, and black peppercorns to taste
1 cup wood chips or ⅓ cup wood pellets

1. Thirty to 60 minutes before grilling, lightly brush the fillets with the oil and season with salt and the peppers. Place the wood chips in water to soak or wood pellets in a heavy-duty aluminum foil packet with holes poked into it.

2. Prepare a medium-hot fire.

3. When ready to grill, place the drained wood chips or foil packet on the fire. Place the fish on an oiled grill rack and grill for 5 minutes, then turn and grill until it is opaque and just begins to flake when tested with a fork, about another 5 minutes. Cover the grill for smokier flavor while the fillets are cooking.

Also good with: mackerel, permit, pompano, or yellowtail

Suggested wood smoke: maple, mesquite, mulberry, oak, or pecan

TAPAS-STYLE GRILLED ANCHOVIES

Anchovies and sardines are not often available in the United States but the Mediterranean coast teems with them. So either enjoy them when abroad or scour the Eastern seaboard fish markets for them. According to James Peterson, author of *Fish and Shellfish* (William Morrow, 1996), "A sardine should be eaten like corn on the cob—the rich fillets nibbled off the sides—or eaten whole, head and all."

MAKES 6 APPETIZER SERVINGS

3 dozen fresh anchovies, cleaned, with heads removed
2 tablespoons olive oil
Freshly grated zest and juice of 1 lime
1 tablespoon chopped fresh cilantro leaves
1/4 teaspoon sea salt
1/4 teaspoon freshly ground black pepper

1. Pat the anchovies dry with a paper towel and place in a shallow glass dish.
2. Combine the olive oil, lime zest, lime juice, cilantro, salt, and pepper and mix well. Brush over the anchovies and let stand for 5 to 10 minutes.
3. Prepare a hot fire.
4. When ready to grill, set an oiled perforated grill rack over the fire. Place the anchovies on the rack and grill for 2 to 3 minutes each side.
5. Serve the anchovies on a platter tapas–style.

Also good with: herring, sardines, or other small baby fish

THREE-PEPPER BARRACUDA

Found in American markets as Pacific or California barracuda, this is a firm-fleshed fish with moderate fat content that grills beautifully. Pair this fish with bittersweet Arugula, Spinach, and Berry Salad (page 345), serving the fish over it or on the side.

MAKES 6 SERVINGS

*3 tablespoons coarsely
    ground pink peppercorns
3 tablespoons coarsely
    ground green peppercorns
2 tablespoons coarsely
    ground black peppercorns
1 teaspoon kosher salt
Six 6-ounce barracuda
    fillets*

1. In a small bowl, combine the peppers and salt and apply to both sides of the fish fillets.

2. Prepare a hot fire.

3. When ready to grill, place the fillets on the hot oiled grill rack and grill about 10 minutes per inch of thickness, turning only once halfway through cooking time, until the fish is opaque and just begins to flake when tested with a fork.

Also good with: mahimahi, marlin, shark, swordfish, tuna, or wahoo

BARBECUED BASS FILLETS

Freshwater bass is very tender and will fall apart if placed directly on the grill grates. Use an aluminum pan, aluminum foil or foil packets, or the Nordicware fish boat for this recipe. Spicy Cauliflower (page 354) complements the bass, but add some color to this meal with a tomato salad.

2 pounds freshwater bass fillets
1 small red onion, sliced thinly into rings
Juice of 2 lemons
Sea salt and freshly ground black pepper to taste
Paprika to taste
1 cup wood chips or 1/3 cup wood pellets

1. Place fillets in a single layer in a disposable aluminum pan and cover them with the onion slices. Generously sprinkle the lemon juice over the top and season with salt, pepper, and paprika.

2. Place the wood chips in water to soak or wood pellets in a heavy-duty aluminum foil packet with holes poked into it.

3. Prepare a hot fire.

4. When ready to grill, place the drained wood chips or foil packet on the fire. Place the fillets on the hot oiled grill rack and grill for 10 minutes per inch of thickness, until the fish is opaque and just beginning to flake when tested with a fork. For smokier flavor, cover the grill while the fillets are cooking.

Also good with: catfish, salmon, or trout

Suggested wood smoke: alder, mesquite, oak, or pecan

GRILLED SEA BASS
FLAMED OVER DRIED FENNEL

This most intriguing presentation caught our attention in British cookbook author Geraldene Holt's *Recipes from a French Herb Garden* (Conran Octopus, 2000). We've adapted it for the grill. The giant sea bass is the king of Mediterranean fish and can weigh up to 550 pounds. It is known as *loup de mer* in France, translating to "sea wolf."

MAKES 4 SERVINGS

One 1½- to 2-pound
   whole sea bass, scaled
   and cleaned
5 or 6 sprigs fresh fennel
Grated zest and juice of 1
   lemon
1 to 2 teaspoons sea salt, to
   your taste
2 tablespoons olive oil
6 to 8 dried fennel twigs
3 tablespoons Pernod or
   other anise-flavored
   liqueur

1. Make 3 or 4 diagonal cuts on each side of the fish. Tuck a few fronds of fennel in the slits and the remaining fennel inside the fish. Sprinkle the lemon zest, juice, and half the salt inside the fish, too. Brush the outside of the fish with the olive oil and sprinkle with the remaining salt. Let it sit for 10 to 15 minutes before grilling.

2. Prepare a medium-hot fire.

3. When ready to grill, place the fish on the grill and cook until opaque and just beginning to flake when tested with a fork, 8 to 10 minutes per side, turning only once.

4. Arrange the dried fennel on a long flameproof dish or tray and lay the cooked sea bass on top. Before proceeding, read the section How to Flambé—Safely, right. In a small saucepan, warm the Pernod and set light to it. Carefully and immediately pour the flaming liquid over the fish so that the dried fennel catches fire and burns to give the fish a lovely distinctive aroma. Serve once the flames have extinguished themselves.

Also good with: grouper or mullet

HOW TO FLAMBÉ—SAFELY!

As a wonderful flavor note to grilled fish, sometimes we suggest flambé-ing, as in Stir-Grilled Scallops and Mushrooms Capri (page 152) or Grilled Sea Bass Flamed over Dried Fennel (left). This involves warming a liqueur like cognac or Pernod in a saucepan, then setting it alight in the pan and finishing the rest of the sauce or pouring the flaming liquid over the fish or shellfish.

If you don't want to flambé yourself or your kitchen, take these precautions:

• Use a long-handled, deep metal saucepan to heat—not boil—the liqueur on the stove.

• Turn off the ventilation fan above the stove, if you have one, as it could draw up the flames.

• Use a match with a long stick or a lighter with a long end (the same types you use for lighting a charcoal or gas grill).

• Protect your hands with ovenproof mitts.

• Point the match or lighter down into the saucepan, but not into the liqueur. The flame will ignite the fumes from the liqueur and then ignite the liqueur.

• As you light the warm liqueur, stand away from the sauce-pan. Do not bend over the saucepan. To that end, make sure long hair and scarves are tied back and that dangling sleeves are rolled up.

• Let the flames die down naturally, which takes only a few seconds. If, for some reason, the flames do not die down in a minute or two, place the bottom of a baking sheet over the pan to smother the flames.

GRILLED SEA BASS WITH BLACK BEAN SAUCE

Traditionally a sauce for steamed fish, Chinese Black Bean Sauce is also delicious with grilled fish. Serve with Chinese Grilled Asparagus (page 346) and steamed rice.

MAKES 4 SERVINGS

1 1/2 pounds sea bass fillets
Salt and freshly ground
     black pepper to taste

BLACK BEAN SAUCE:

2 cloves garlic, minced
2 tablespoons fermented
     black beans (available at
     Asian markets), rinsed
     and drained
1 tablespoon rice wine or
     dry sherry
1 tablespoon dark soy sauce
1 tablespoon light soy sauce
1 tablespoon vegetable oil
1 teaspoon toasted sesame
     oil
1 teaspoon sugar
One 2-inch piece fresh
     ginger, peeled and grated
2 green onions, cut on the
     diagonal into 1/4-inch
     pieces

1. Season the fish with salt and pepper and place in a baking dish. In a small bowl, whisk together the black bean sauce ingredients. Spoon half the sauce over the fish and let marinate, covered, for 30 minutes in the refrigerator. Reserve the remaining sauce.

2. Prepare a hot fire.

3. Grill the fish until opaque and just beginning to flake when tested with a fork, 4 to 5 minutes per side.

4. Serve hot with the remaining bean sauce on top.

Also good with: haddock, halibut, or salmon

GRILLED STRIPED BASS IN SAOR

In the Venetian dialect, *saor* simply means "sour," but this is really more of a fragrant, sweet-and-sour sauce that pairs well with grilled striped bass. We could just eat the *saor* by the spoonful before the fish is even finished grilling, but somehow we restrain ourselves.

MAKES 4 SERVINGS

1 cup wood chips or 1/3 cup
   wood pellets

SAOR:

1/3 cup extra virgin olive oil
2 large red onions, thinly
   sliced
2 tablespoons red wine
   vinegar
1/3 cup dry white wine
2 teaspoons sugar
2 tablespoons pine nuts,
   toasted
2 tablespoons golden raisins
2 teaspoons freshly grated
   orange zest
Salt and freshly ground
   black pepper to taste

FISH:

Four 8-ounce striped bass
   fillets, with skin on
Olive oil for brushing or
   spraying
Salt and freshly ground
   black pepper to taste
Chopped fresh Italian
   parsley leaves for
   garnish

1. Place the wood chips in water to soak or wood pellets in a heavy-duty aluminum foil packet with holes poked into it.

2. Prepare a hot fire.

3. Meanwhile, make the *saor*. In a large skillet, heat 1/3 cup of the olive oil over medium-low heat, add the onions, and cook, stirring, until very soft, about 20 minutes. Stir in the vinegar, wine, sugar, pine nuts, raisins, and orange zest. Season with salt and pepper and set aside.

4. When ready to grill, place the drained wood chips or foil packet on the fire. Brush or spray both sides of the fish with olive oil and season with salt and pepper. Place in an oiled hinged grill basket or on a perforated grilling rack. Grill until the fish is opaque and just beginning to flake when tested with a fork, about 5 minutes per side, or 10 minutes per inch of thickness.

5. To serve, place a spoonful of *saor* on each plate and top with a grilled fillet. Sprinkle with parsley and serve.

Also good with: bluefish, grouper, or mackerel

Suggested wood smoke: alder, fruitwood, oak, or pecan

MARINATED STRIPED BASS STEAKS

The sweet-and-hot marinade brings out the best in striped bass, also known as rockfish. Serve this with Skewered Scallions (page 362) and additional Pickapeppa sauce on the side, if you like.

MAKES 4 SERVINGS

Four 6- to 8-ounce striped bass steaks about 1 inch thick
1/3 cup olive oil
1/3 cup fresh lemon juice
3 tablespoons dry sherry
3 tablespoons Pickapeppa sauce
2 cloves garlic, minced
Sea salt and freshly ground black pepper to taste

1. Place the steaks in a shallow glass dish. Combine the remaining ingredients and pour half of the marinade over the fish. Reserve the other half for basting. Marinate the fish, covered, in the refrigerator for 30 minutes to 1 hour.
2. Prepare a hot fire.
3. When ready to grill, remove the fish from the marinade and discard the liquid. Place the steaks on the hot oiled grill rack and grill for 5 minutes, turn, and grill until the fish is opaque and just beginning to flake when tested with a fork, about another 5 minutes, basting frequently with the reserved marinade.

Also good with: catfish, orange roughy, sheepshead, or snapper

FISH TALES: ANGLING FOR STRIPED BASS

Striped bass (*Morone saxatilis*) were originally found only in coastal waters along the Atlantic seaboard. But then the sport of surf casting for "stripers," as the fish are still known as, became popular. In the late 1800s, businessmen in New York and Boston set up "bass clubs" where the stripers were teeming—in and around the Elizabeth Islands off the coast of Massachusetts. In those early days before Palm Pilots, FedEx, fax machines, and e-mail, these vacationing businessmen used carrier pigeons to stay in touch with their offices. That way, they could get down to the serious work of fishing and then drinking—their liquor bills were more than equal to their food bills.

In 1886, sportsmen brought the striped bass to the coastal waters around San Francisco Bay. Although the fish thrived in its new habitat, it developed behaviors different from its East Coast cousins. Atlantic striped bass migrate three times during the year: up freshwater streams to spawn in spring, then they take long-distance trips to southern Canada and New England, then back south to winter in the Chesapeake and Delaware Bays. Pacific stripers migrate only once—to spawn in freshwater streams, after which they return to the San Francisco Bay.

Serious fishermen keep tabs on the "Where's Waldo" antics of the stripers. When fish are in the area, they can be caught by casting or trolling from a boat, surf casting, or fly-fishing from the beach. The Orvis Cape Cod Ocean Fly Fishing School offers lessons in fly casting—ten-foot rods with heavy reels and 15-pound test line—for these challenging game fish. Veteran surf casters know about fishing the tides and the big visual clue as to where the fish are: seagulls hovering over the water. Although the recommended lures include the Lead-headed Jig with its flowing mane, the Rebel Swimmer, the Rebel Popper, and the Redfish Swimmer, experienced anglers prefer "swimmer" lures, which go deeper, rather than "popper" lures, which stay close to the surface.

If you're fishing for stripers, you might also snag a few bluefish, which are oilier and not as delicate as stripers, but are still delicious grilled. When cleaning a striped bass, it's important to be careful when cutting off the pointy and slightly venomous dorsal fin on the upper back side of the fish. You lift it up carefully, then use scissors to cut it off as close to the skin as possible.

Although striped bass were once plentiful, like other fish, their numbers vary from year to year. That's why chefs like Elka Gilmore (of Liberte in San Francisco) and Gordon Hamersley (of Hamersley's Bistro in Boston) serve both wild and farm-raised striped bass. The chefs appreciate the smaller size and cleaner, less briny flavor of the farm-raised trout, while still extolling the virtues of the sweeter flavor and firmer texture of the wild variety.

CAPE COD BLACKFISH

Mild-flavored yet firm and meaty, New England blackfish is a favorite with sport fishermen, who appreciate the fight that this fish puts up. Serve this with Warm New Potato and Watercress Salad (page 369).

MAKES 4 SERVINGS

Four 6- to 8-ounce black-
  fish fillets
1 tablespoon extra virgin
  olive oil
1 teaspoon sea salt
1/2 teaspoon freshly ground
  black pepper

1. Prepare a medium-hot fire.
2. Brush the fish fillets with the olive oil and season with the salt and pepper.
3. When ready to grill, place the fish on an oiled perforated grill rack or grill basket and grill until opaque and just beginning to flake when tested with a fork, about 5 minutes per side or 10 minutes per inch of thickness, turning once.

Also good with: haddock, pollock, or snapper

FISH TALES: THE CHILEAN SEA BASS CONTROVERSY

Will the real Chilean sea bass (or Chilean seabass) please stand up? No one stands up. From a corner you can see the smirks on several clever seafood marketers' faces. The delicious fish they've renamed Chilean sea bass is the market name for what biologists call the Patagonian toothfish.

On a more serious note, according to the National Audubon Society, the majority of Chilean sea bass we eat is illegally caught. From 1998 to 1999, the illegally caught fish flooded the market in excess of 100,000 tons. The legal limit was 10,500 tons. The fish is from the sub-Antarctic, an area remote and seldom policed. Scientists predict the commercial extinction of the fish in just a few years.

Because of the changing ecological climate in which we live, we have tried to offer important information in our Fish and Shellfish Substitution chart on pages 12 and 13. Please use it to help buy fresh and safe fish at the market.

CIDER-MARINATED BLUEFISH WITH SPICY SLICED TOMATOES

Bluefish has a medium-strong fish flavor and cider marinade is a tasty way to tone down the fishiness. Plus, its spiciness is a tart foil to sweet garden tomatoes. If you can't get skin-on fillets, then place the fillets in an aluminum pan or a Nordicware fish boat so that the fish doesn't flake and fall through the grill grates.

MAKES 6 SERVINGS

*6 bluefish fillets, with skin
  on (about 2 pounds)*
*6 large, ripe tomatoes,
  sliced medium thick*
*1 large green bell pepper,
  seeded and sliced into
  thin rings*
*1 large sweet onion, sliced
  into thin rings*
*1/2 cup chopped fresh
  Italian parsley leaves or
  Gremolata (page 283)
  for garnish*
Cider Marinade (page 288)

1. Place the fillets in a shallow glass dish. Pour 1 cup of the marinade over the fish and refrigerate for up to 1 hour. Reserve the remaining marinade for the tomatoes.

2. Prepare a hot fire.

3. When ready to grill, place the fish on the hot oiled grill rack and grill until opaque and just beginning to flake when tested with a fork, about 10 minutes per inch of thickness, turning halfway through the cooking time.

4. On each dinner plate, alternate the tomato slices with the green pepper and onion rings. Place a fillet on each plate beside the tomatoes and spoon the marinade over everything. Garnish with the parsley and serve.

Also good with: striped bass, mackerel, or trout

BONITO BOCADILLOS

Simple grilled bonito becomes a gourmet tuna fish sandwich when paired with aioli, capers, chopped tomato, and sliced egg.

MAKES 4 SERVINGS

*Four 6- to 8-ounce bonito
    fillets*
1 tablespoon olive oil
*Sea salt and freshly ground
    black pepper to taste*
4 Italian buns, toasted
1/2 cup Aioli (page 311)
*2 hard-boiled eggs, shelled
    and sliced*
*1 large, ripe beefsteak
    tomato, chopped*
2 teaspoons capers, drained
*1/4 cup shaved Parmesan
    cheese*

1. Lightly brush the fillets with the olive oil and season with salt and pepper.

2. Prepare a hot fire.

3. When ready to grill, place the fillets on the hot oiled grill rack and grill until they are opaque and just begin to flake when tested with a fork, 4 to 5 minutes per side.

4. To assemble the sandwich, spread each bun with aioli, add a fillet of bonito, top with slices of egg, chopped tomato, capers, and cheese shavings.

Also good with: amberjack, catfish, halibut, salmon, or tilapia

BLUEBERRY BUTTERFISH

Nicknames for the delicate sweet butterfish include dollarfish and pumpkinseed fish because of its round silver coin shape. The blueberry sauce is an adaptation of a recipe from Chef Patrick Quillec of Hannah Bistro Cafe in Kansas City. He recommends spooning this sauce over white-fleshed fish for a beautiful contrast.

MAKES 4 SERVINGS

Four 14-ounce whole
   butterfish, cleaned
1 cup plus 1 tablespoon
   olive oil
Sea salt and freshly ground
   black pepper
1 pint fresh blueberries,
   picked over for stems
   and rinsed
1/2 cup balsamic vinegar
Juice of 1 lemon
1/4 cup sugar, or more if
   berries are very tart
1 to 2 tablespoons water (if
   necessary for thinning)

1. Place the fish on a platter. Lightly coat with 1 tablespoon of the olive oil and season with salt and pepper. Set aside.

2. Prepare a hot fire.

3. Meanwhile, in a food processor, combine the blueberries, vinegar, lemon juice, and sugar and process together until smooth. With the machine running, add the remaining 1 cup olive oil through the feed tube in a slow stream until the mixture thickens. (If the mixture becomes too thick, thin it with the water.) Season with salt and pepper. Adjust the sugar to taste. Set aside.

4. When ready to grill, place the fish on the hot oiled grill rack and grill until it just begins to flake when tested with a fork, about 5 minutes per side.

5. Transfer the fish to serving plates, spoon the sauce over each fish, and serve.

Also good with: halibut, pomfret, trout, or other flat fish

SALSA CATFISH

Catfish and cornmeal go together usually as fried catfish with hushpuppies. But try this catfish with Parmesan Grits (page 377) for a new twist—the piquant flavor of the salsa makes for a delicious contrast.

MAKES 6 SERVINGS

Six 6- to 8-ounce farm-raised catfish fillets
1/2 teaspoon freshly ground white pepper
3/4 teaspoon garlic salt
2 cups favorite salsa or Fresh Garden Relish (page 336)

1. Sprinkle the fillets with the pepper and garlic salt.
2. Prepare a hot fire.
3. When ready to grill, place the fish on an oiled perforated grill rack over the fire. Grill until the fish is opaque and just beginning to flake when tested with a fork, about 10 minutes per inch of thickness, turning once halfway through the cooking time.
4. Serve the fish topped with the salsa.

Also good with: cod, grouper, porgy, or snapper

STIR-GRILLED CATFISH WITH
RED WINE SHALLOT VINAIGRETTE

Stir-grill recipes are easily varied by substituting different medium- to firm-fleshed fish and colorful chunked or sliced vegetables. Eye appeal is key, so let color as well as taste be your guide. For catfish, we prefer to buy skinless fillets and cut them into strips versus catfish nuggets, which often have pieces of unsavory skin on them. We also prefer perforated grill woks, which allow more wood or charcoal flavor to permeate.

Four 3- to 5-ounce farm-
raised catfish fillets
12 cherry tomatoes
1 red onion, cut into 8
wedges
1 green bell pepper, seeded
and cut into strips
8 ounces mushroom caps
1 cup Red Wine Shallot
Vinaigrette (page 292)
1 cup wood chips or 1/3 cup
wood pellets

1. Slice the catfish fillets into 1/2-inch-wide strips and place with the vegetables in a large bowl. Pour 3/4 cup of the vinaigrette over all and marinate for 1 hour, covered, in the refrigerator. Reserve the remaining 1/4 cup vinaigrette.

2. Place the wood chips in water to soak or wood pellets in a heavy-duty aluminum foil packet with holes poked into it.

3. Prepare a hot fire.

4. When ready to grill, place the drained wood chips or foil packet on the fire. Set an oiled grill wok on the rack above the fire. Transfer the ingredients to the grill wok, using a slotted spoon to drain the excess marinade. Stir-grill in the wok until the fish is opaque and the vegetables are crisp-tender, 12 to 15 minutes, using two long-handled wooden spoons to toss the mixture. Close the grill lid during the last 5 minutes of cooking to heat through.

5. Serve on a plate and drizzle with the reserved vinaigrette.

Also good with: sea bass, haddock, orange roughy, or tilefish

Suggested wood smoke: mesquite, oak, or pecan

The broad, flat, virtually treeless expanse of the Mississippi Delta extends for miles on either side of the Mississippi River, south from Memphis down to New Orleans. Even in April, the humid weather can make you feel as if you're walking inside a warm blanket. Here you'll find the blues and B. B. King, cotton and catfish.

Belzoni, Mississippi, a quiet Delta town where everything seems to happen on the county courthouse grounds, is the center of the farmed catfish universe. Since the late 1960s when catfish farming first began, this enterprise has helped to put Belzoni on the map. Here is where the Catfish Institute is located and where the annual Catfish Festival, held during the first week of April, lures top chefs in celebrity cook-offs featuring, of course, catfish.

Chefs and catfish? If your first thought is "not a good combo," then you need to forget memories of muddy-tasting, bottom-dwelling river cat. Firm-fleshed yet tender and mild-tasting, farm-raised catfish is delicious. Raising these culinary charmers has become a science, with larger farms even employing fish biologists to monitor the water quality of the ponds and the condition of the fish.

From a high vantage point, you can see thousands of rectangular catfish ponds in every direction in farms spread out on either side of the Mississippi. For example, Tackett Farms, not far from Belzoni, has 5,800 acres in water with 495 catfish ponds and harvests 700,000 pounds of catfish every week.

Farm ponds of up to several acres in size are dug to a depth of 5 to 6 feet in the heavy clay soil and filled with spring water. Young catfish "fry" only 2 inches long will grow in these ponds for about 18 months. They're fed every day with an extruded mixture of puffed wheat, corn, and soy meal that looks like popcorn, which is blown out onto the water from the top of a truck. The fish rise to the surface of the pond to eat.

Catfish farms use other unusual equipment. Large paddlewheels keep the water aerated during the hottest and most humid months. When it's time to harvest—when the catfish have reached sizes from 1 to 2 pounds—a seine encloses the fish in a small area in the pond. Sort of a catfish roundup. Then a net is dropped from a crane attached to the harvesting truck on the bank nearby, and the fish are taken live from the pond to the water-filled container on top of the truck. From there, it's a short distance to the processing plant, where a live fish is processed in minutes, using Individual Quick Frozen (IQF) technology. That's about 30 minutes from pond to package. No wonder catfish tastes fresh.

Many catfish farmers also own their own feed mills and processing plants, alone or with other farmers in a cooperative. That way, they have total quality control from start to finish.

GRILLED WHOLE CATFISH

Fish fillets and steaks should be grilled over a hot fire fast. A whole fish should be grilled over a medium to medium-hot fire so that it has time to cook all the way through. Close the grill lid to hold in the heat so that the fish "bakes" more evenly.

MAKES 4 SERVINGS

1 lemon, sliced
1 medium-size onion,
    thinly sliced into rings
Four 2/3-pound catfish,
    dressed and skinned
1/2 cup extra virgin olive oil
1/4 cup fresh lemon juice
Sea salt and freshly ground
    black pepper to taste
1 cup wood chips or 1/3 cup
    wood pellets

1. Place the slices of lemon and onion in the cavity of each fish.
2. In a small bowl, combine the olive oil, lemon juice, salt, and pepper.
3. Place the wood chips in water to soak or wood pellets in a heavy-duty aluminum foil packet with holes poked into it.
4. Prepare a medium-hot fire.
5. When ready to grill, place the drained wood chips or foil packet on the fire. Place the fish on an oiled perforated grill rack or in a disposable aluminum pan over the fire. Grill until the fish just begins to flake when tested with a fork, about 10 to 15 minutes per inch of thickness for whole fish (30 to 40 minutes altogether), turning once halfway through the cooking time and basting often with the olive oil and lemon juice.

Also good with: whole salmon or trout

Suggested wood smoke: alder, mesquite, oak, or pecan

TERIYAKI CATFISH WITH
WASABI CUCUMBER SALAD

"Unpretentious, yet unforgettable" is one critic's description of the fare at Elizabeth's on 37th in Savannah, Georgia. It's also a very apt description of chef/owner Elizabeth Terry herself—and this recipe that she developed (and we adapted) for a recent Celebrity Chef Cook-Off at the annual Catfish Festival held in Belzoni, Mississippi. Terry is an advocate of New Southern Cuisine, elegant and lighter fare that she calls "company cooking, Southern style." The light, clear, brilliant flavors of this dish should convert us all—and it's low in fat! Terry suggests serving this with steamed green beans.

MAKES 4 SERVINGS

3 tablespoons teriyaki
   sauce
1 1/2 teaspoons wasabi
   powder (available in
   Asian markets)
1 teaspoon rice vinegar
   (available in the Asian
   section of grocery stores)
2 medium-size cucumbers,
   peeled, seeded, and
   chopped
1/3 cup nonfat sour cream
Four 3- to 5-ounce farm-
   raised catfish fillets
Fresh cilantro leaves for
   garnish

1. Prepare a hot fire.

2. Meanwhile, in a small bowl, stir together the teriyaki sauce, wasabi powder, and vinegar to make a marinade. Set aside for 10 minutes to let the flavors blend.

3. In a medium-size bowl, stir together 1 tablespoon of the teriyaki marinade and the cucumbers; stir in the sour cream.

4. When ready to grill, brush both sides of the catfish fillets with the remaining marinade and place on an oiled grill rack. Grill until the fish is opaque and just beginning to flake when tested with a fork, 2 to 3 minutes per side.

5. To serve, top the catfish with the cucumber salad and garnish with cilantro.

Also good with: char, salmon, or trout

GRILLED CATFISH SMOTHERED WITH SPRING ONIONS AND MORELS

Louis Osteen, the chef/owner of Louis's Restaurant & Bar in Charleston, South Carolina, is "celebrated as one of the chief proponents of Low Country cuisine," according to *Nation's Restaurant News*. Osteen has long been an advocate of regional cuisine, his own part of the country's in particular. In this dish, which we have adapted to grilling, he uses regional catfish and the old Southern technique of "smothering" it in a chopped vegetable sauce. There is no better salute to spring, no matter where you live.

MAKES 4 SERVINGS

10 tablespoons (1 1/4 sticks)
  unsalted butter
2 cups fresh morels or other
  wild mushrooms,
  stemmed and cleaned
3 cups spring or green
  onions cut on the bias,
  white part and some of
  the green
1 cup shallots, thinly sliced
1 cup peeled, seeded, and
  chopped fresh tomatoes
3/4 cup dry vermouth
1 cup fish stock or bottled
  clam juice
Four 3- to 5-ounce farm-
  raised catfish fillets
1/3 cup finely minced fresh
  chervil
Salt and freshly ground
  black pepper to taste

1. Prepare a hot fire.

2. Meanwhile, in a large saucepan or sauté pan, melt 1/2 cup (1 stick) of the butter over medium-high heat. When the butter foams up, then begins to die down, toss in the morels, green onions, and shallots and cook, stirring, until the green onions have softened, about 4 minutes. Stir in the tomatoes, vermouth, and fish stock, reduce the heat to medium, and simmer for 5 minutes, then set aside to keep warm.

3. Melt the remaining 2 tablespoons butter in a small saucepan. When ready to grill, brush both sides of the catfish fillets with the melted butter and season with salt and pepper. Place on an oiled grill and grill until the fish just begins to flake when tested with a fork, 2 to 3 minutes per side.

4. To serve, stir the chervil into the hot sauce, then top the catfish with the spring onion and morel sauce and serve immediately.

Also good with: sea bass, haddock, halibut, or salmon

GRILLED CHAR WITH ZUCCHINI SPAGHETTI

Moist and tender char is fished from the waters around Admiralty Island on the southern tip of Alaska. The simply grilled char is delicious served with an aioli, a beurre blanc, or a fresh herb garnish. Pair this with Savory Risotto Cakes (page 381).

MAKES 4 SERVINGS

4 small zucchini, ends trimmed and sliced lengthwise into 1/8-inch-thick ribbons
2 tablespoons olive oil
1 clove garlic, minced
Salt and freshly ground black pepper to taste
Four 6-ounce char fillets
Olive oil
1 tablespoon chopped fresh basil leaves

1. Prepare a hot fire.

2. Meanwhile, place the zucchini ribbons on a flat surface. With a paring knife, cut them lengthwise into 1/4-inch-wide strips.

3. In a large skillet, heat the olive oil over medium heat. Add the garlic and cook, stirring, for 2 minutes. Add the zucchini strips and cook, stirring, using a metal spatula to move the zucchini around the pan. Cook until the zucchini is crisp-tender but not browned. Remove from the heat and season with salt and pepper. Keep warm.

4. When ready to grill, brush both sides of the char fillets with olive oil, season with salt and pepper, and place on an oiled grill rack. Grill until the fish is just beginning to flake when tested with a fork, 3 to 4 minutes per side.

5. Plate the zucchini first and lay a fish fillet on top.

Also good with: barracuda, bonito, catfish, or mahimahi

GRILLED COBIA

A south Atlantic sportsman's fish, cobia is delicious grilled. Serve this with Low Country Black-Eyed Peas and Shrimp (page 349).

(page 349)

MAKES 4 TO 6 SERVINGS

1 cup wood chips or 1/3 cup
   wood pellets
6 cobia fillets (3 pounds)
1/3 cup olive oil
1/3 cup fresh lemon juice
1 1/2 teaspoons dry mustard
1 clove garlic, minced
1 teaspoon salt
1/2 teaspoon freshly ground
   black pepper

1. Place the wood chips in water to soak or wrap the wood pellets in a heavy-duty aluminum foil packet with holes poked into it.

2. Prepare a hot fire.

3. Place the cobia fillets in a deep bowl or baking dish. In a small bowl, whisk together the olive oil, lemon juice, mustard, garlic, salt, and pepper. Pour three-quarters of this mixture over the fish and let marinate for 15 minutes. Reserve the remaining marinade for basting.

4. When ready to grill, place the drained wood chips or foil packet on the fire. Remove the fish from the marinade and place in an oiled grill basket or on an oiled perforated grill rack. Grill until opaque and just beginning to flake when tested with a fork, about 4 minutes per side, turning once and basting several times with the reserved marinade.

Also good with: grouper, mullet, or redfish

Suggested wood smoke: alder, mesquite, oak, or pecan

LEMON-PEPPER CRUSTED COD

A zesty dish to revitalize the taste buds, serve this with Grilled Potato Wedges (page 367) and a simply dressed green salad or steamed spinach drizzled with balsamic vinegar.

MAKES 4 SERVINGS

Four 6- to 7-ounce cod fillets or steaks

Juice and finely grated zest of 2 lemons

3 tablespoons black peppercorns

3 slices stale bakery-style white bread, crusts removed

1 tablespoon anchovy paste

1/2 teaspoon salt

2 tablespoons chopped fresh Italian parsley leaves

2 tablespoons olive oil

Lemon wedges for garnish

1. Place the cod in a shallow dish and drizzle with the lemon juice. Let marinate for 30 minutes, covered, in the refrigerator.

2. Prepare a hot fire.

3. Meanwhile, place the lemon zest, peppercorns, bread, and anchovy paste in a blender or food processor and process until the mixture resembles fine bread crumbs. Spread the mixture over a large plate. Pour the olive oil into another dish. Dip each cod steak or fillet into the olive oil, on both sides, then dredge in the bread crumb mixture, coating it evenly.

4. When ready to grill, place the breaded cod steaks on an oiled perforated grill rack and grill until opaque and just beginning to flake when tested with a fork, 3 to 4 minutes per side.

5. Serve hot with lemon wedges on the side.

Also good with: catfish, grouper, moonfish, salmon, or swordfish

ONION-BUTTER BASTED COD

Parsleyed new potatoes would make an excellent side dish with this onion-flavored baste. The cod stays moist and flavorful during grilling.

MAKES 4 SERVINGS

Four 6-ounce cod fillets or
  steaks
1 tablespoon extra virgin
  olive oil
1 teaspoon sea salt
1/2 teaspoon freshly ground
  black pepper
Onion Butter Baste (page
  295)
1 lemon, cut into 4 wedges,
  for garnish

1. Brush the cod on both sides with olive oil and season with the salt and pepper.
2. Prepare a hot fire.
3. When ready to grill, brush the fish with the baste and place on an oiled perforated grill rack above the fire. Grill until opaque and just beginning to flake when tested with a fork, about 10 minutes per inch of thickness, turning once halfway through the cooking time and brushing frequently with the baste.
4. Serve with the lemon wedges.

Also good with: catfish, char, grouper, halibut, or wahoo

TANDOORI STIR-GRILLED COD

Cool, refreshing yogurt is a perfect foil for a hot summer day. This meal is fresh, fast, and fabulous. To serve along with Peppery Couscous (page 378), grill a couple of tomato slices per person for a few minutes while you're stir-grilling the cod. Make a double recipe of the yogurt mixture to dollop on the tomatoes. Your meal is complete.

MAKES 8 SERVINGS

1 cup plain yogurt

1/4 cup extra virgin olive oil

4 or 5 cloves garlic, to your taste, minced

One 2-inch piece fresh ginger, peeled and grated

1 teaspoon cayenne pepper

2 teaspoons ground cumin

2 teaspoons ground coriander

1 teaspoon salt

3 pounds cod fillets, cut into chunks

1. In a medium-size bowl, combine the yogurt, olive oil, garlic, ginger, cayenne, cumin, coriander, and salt. Add the fish chunks and let marinate for 30 minutes, covered, in the refrigerator.

2. Prepare a hot fire.

3. When ready to grill, set an oiled grill wok on a rack above the fire. Transfer the fish to a grill wok, using a slotted spoon to drain the excess marinade. Stir-grill in the wok until the fish is opaque, 12 to 15 minutes, using two long-handled wooden spoons to toss the fish. Cover the grill the last 5 minutes of cooking to heat through. Serve immediately.

Also good with: sea bass, catfish, haddock, or halibut

TWO chefs were competing to produce the city's Finest Fish Recipe. Their talents were about equal and their culinary training was similar, so it was a close race until, at the last minute, one chef covered his entry with a balsamic herb glaze. He won the title.

"Alas!" said the other chef. "There but for the glaze of cod go I."

COD WITH CAPER-PARSLEY SAUCE

The delicate, mild flavor of cod is a favorite the world over. The texture is delicate, too. It's best to grill cod on aluminum foil, in a disposable aluminum pan, or on an oiled perforated grill rack. The Nordicware fish boat works well, too.

MAKES 4 SERVINGS

Four 6-ounce cod fillets or
   steaks
1 tablespoon extra virgin
   olive oil
Sea salt and freshly ground
   pepper to taste
Caper-Parsley Sauce (page
   323)

1. Brush the fish lightly with the olive oil and sprinkle with salt and pepper.
2. Prepare a hot fire.
3. When ready to grill, place an oiled perforated grill rack above the fire. Place the fish on the grill rack and grill until opaque and just beginning to flake when tested with a fork, about 10 minutes per inch of thickness, turning once halfway through the cooking time.
4. Serve with the sauce, either spooned over the cod or spooned onto a plate, with the cod placed over it.

Also good with: freshwater bass, flounder, fluke, hake, hoki, or turbot

FISH TALES: THE STORY OF COD

Over a thousand years and four continents, the story of cod unfolds in Mark Kurlansky's remarkable *Cod: A Biography of the Fish That Changed the World* (Walker & Co., 1997). A biography of a fish, you might ask? *Boring.* But this fish tale has all the elements of a great drama.

The story of *Gadus morhua* begins with murder and intrigue. After the Viking thug/explorer Erik the Red was banished from both Norway and Iceland for murder, he set sail in an open boat for parts unknown. In 985, he reached the barren, icy land he called Greenland, a notable early example of untruth in advertising. From there, Erik's son Leif headed even farther west to what is now Newfoundland. During five expeditions between 985 and 1011, the Viking crews survived on wind-dried cod, fished from cold Old and New World waters and hung out to freeze dry in the winter air until it lost most of its weight.

The cod story then travels to a remote region of southwestern France and northwestern Spain, where the unique Basque culture has flourished for more than a thousand years. Speaking a language—Euskera—that is not related to any other language in the world, the Basques raise sheep on remote mountainsides and fish the Atlantic. Because they had access to Mediterranean salt, the Basques also traveled thousands of miles to fish for cod on the Grand Banks off the coast of Newfoundland, salting their catch to preserve it.

During the Middle Ages, when Catholic doctrine mandated meatless Fridays and other days of fasting, the Basques did a brisk business in salted cod. Even today, European cultures have a name for it: *bacaloa* (Spanish), *baccalà* (Italian), *bacalhua* (Portuguese), *morue* (French), *stockfisk* (Scandinavia). Like Microsoft and computer software today, the Basques had a virtual lock on the salt cod trade until 1497, when explorer John Cabot sailed to the mouth of the St. Lawrence River in Canada and claimed the region for England. He saw hundreds of Basque ships docked in Newfoundland and the St. Lawrence. In trying to keep their secret, the Basques had not thought to claim the shores and waterways they had been visiting for hundreds of years, and they lost out to the savvy English.

Other explorers followed. In 1602, British explorer Bartholomew Gosnold dubbed a land mass "Cape Cod" because his boat was "pestered" by so many. In 1851, Henry David Thoreau visited Cape Cod and noted that, "Salt fish were stacked on the wharves, looking like corded wood, maple and yellow birch with the bark left on. I mistook them for this at first, and such in one sense they were—fuel to maintain our vital fires—an eastern wood which grew on the Grand Banks."

The most recent chapter has been about overfishing. In a thousand years, the story of cod has been a progression from unbelievable abundance to unbelievable scarcity. Easy to catch, the cod likes to swim in the cold waters of the north Atlantic or—on the Pacific side—the Bering Sea and the Gulf of Alaska to a depth of only 120 feet. But now cod numbers have dwindled from billions to thousands. Conservation measures, strict limits on fishing, and alternative methods like cod raised on fish farms will hopefully help the wild cod recover. Meanwhile, the consumer can still enjoy cooking and eating farm-raised cod, appreciating what French chef Alain Senderens describes as "the way the flesh unfolds in white leaves."

FOIL PACKET FLOUNDER
WITH ARTICHOKE SAUCE

Foil packets are perfect for all of the delicate-textured fillets of fish. Serve this with Grilled Corn in the Husk (page 356) and grilled French bread.

MAKES 6 SERVINGS

6 flounder fillets
1/2 cup (1 stick) butter
1/4 cup chopped green
    onions
2 tablespoons chopped fresh
    Italian parsley leaves
3 cloves garlic, minced
Freshly grated zest and
    juice of 1 lemon
One 14-ounce can arti-
    choke hearts, drained
    and sliced
1 teaspoon sea salt
1/2 teaspoon cayenne
    pepper

1. Pat the fish fillets dry with paper towels and place each fillet on a large square of heavy-duty aluminum foil. (You may also use a disposable aluminum pan.)
2. Melt the butter in a medium-size saucepan over medium heat, then cook the green onions, parsley, and garlic, stirring, until softened. Add the lemon zest and juice, artichoke hearts, salt, and pepper and cook a few minutes, until heated thoroughly.
3. Prepare a hot fire.
4. Crimp the foil around the fish to hold sauce. Pour equal amounts of the sauce mixture over each fillet. Close the foil around the fish and place the packet on a baking sheet to transfer to the grill.
5. When ready to grill, place the foil packet or pan on the grill rack and grill until the fish just begins to flake when tested with a fork, 12 to 15 minutes. Do not turn the fish.

Also good with: cod, hake, hoki, or turbot

TEQUILA-ORANGE GLAZED FLUKE

Chef Terry Barkley grew up in the Kansas City restaurant business and worked with Karen at the original Houlihan's Old Place on the Country Club Plaza. He shares this lowfat barbecue glaze, which is great with fish, poultry, beef, or pork.

MAKES 6 SERVINGS

*1/4 cup frozen orange juice
    concentrate, thawed*
1/4 cup tequila
*2 cups KC Masterpiece
    barbecue sauce*
*1/4 cup whole-grain
    mustard*
*Sea salt and freshly ground
    black pepper to taste*
*Six 6- to 8-ounce fluke
    fillets*
2 tablespoons olive oil

1. Combine the orange juice concentrate and tequila in a large saucepan and cook over medium-high heat until reduced by half. Stir in the barbecue sauce. Bring to a boil, then reduce the heat to low, stir in the mustard, and simmer for 5 minutes. Season with salt and pepper. Pour 1/2 cup of glaze into a small bowl for basting. Reserve the rest of the glaze for serving.
2. Prepare a hot fire.
3. Place the fluke on a platter and drizzle both sides with the olive oil.
4. When ready to grill, place the fluke on an oiled perforated grill rack and place on the grill. Grill until it just begins to flake when tested with a fork, about 5 minutes per side. Baste with the glaze several times while grilling.
5. Serve the fluke with additional glaze on the side.

Also good with: freshwater bass, cod, hake, hoki, or plaice

FLORIBBEAN GROUPER WITH THAI GREEN CURRY SAUCE

Great seafood, tropical produce, and Caribbean seasonings inspire this dish with the sunny flavors of south Florida.

MAKES 4 SERVINGS

1 cup wood chips or 1/3 cup
    wood pellets
2 pounds grouper fillets
Salt and freshly ground
    black pepper to taste

FLORIBBEAN PASTE:

1 clove garlic, minced
2 tablespoons Thai green
    curry paste (available at
    Asian markets)
1 tablespoon toasted sesame oil
1/2 teaspoon honey
1 teaspoon soy sauce
1 tablespoon fresh lime juice

SAUCE AND GARNISH:

Thai Green Curry and
    Coconut Sauce (page
    327)
1 tablespoon seeded and
    diced red bell pepper
1 tablespoon seeded and
    diced green bell pepper
1 tablespoon chopped fresh
    cilantro leaves
2 tablespoons sweetened
    flaked coconut

1. Place the wood chips in water to soak or wood pellets in a heavy-duty aluminum foil packet with holes poked into it.

2. Prepare a hot fire.

3. Meanwhile, place the fillets on a large plate and season with salt and pepper.

4. In a food processor, process the Floribbean paste ingredients together until you have a smooth paste. Brush the paste on both sides of each fillet and place them on an oiled perforated grill rack.

5. Combine all the garnish ingredients together in a small bowl.

6. When ready to grill, place the drained wood chips or foil packet on the fire. Place the fish on the oiled grill rack and grill until the fish is opaque and just beginning to flake when tested with a fork, about 10 minutes per inch of thickness, turning once halfway through the cooking time.

7. Serve drizzled with the sauce and sprinkled with the garnish.

Also good with: striped bass, catfish, mahimahi, tilapia, or wahoo

Suggested wood smoke: apple, mesquite, oak, or pecan

HERB-GRILLED GROUPER

A light, fresh way to enjoy the mild flavor of grouper. Serve with Cheddar-Romano Potato Slices (page 367).

MAKES 4 SERVINGS

Four 6-ounce grouper fillets
1 lemon, cut into wedges,
    for garnish

LEMON-HERB MARINADE:

1/3 cup olive oil
1/4 cup minced fresh herbs
    (any combination of
    parsley, thyme, mar-
    joram, and/or Greek
    oregano)
3 1/2 tablespoons fresh
    lemon juice
3 large cloves garlic, crushed
    into a paste
1 tablespoon minced shallot
    or green onion
Salt and freshly ground
    black pepper to taste

1. Place fish fillets in a resealable plastic bag. In a small bowl, combine the marinade ingredients. Pour the marinade into the bag with the fish. Let marinate for 1 hour in the refrigerator.
2. Prepare a hot fire.
3. When ready to grill, remove the fish from the marinade and set on a plate. Pour the marinade into a small saucepan and let boil for about 5 minutes to use as a baste. Place the fish on an oiled grill rack. Grill until opaque and just beginning to flake when tested with a fork, 4 to 5 minutes per side, turning once and basting frequently.
4. Serve with the lemon wedges on the side.

Also good with: striped bass, cobia, cod, or redfish

Both inhabitants and vacationers who summer in coastal Virginia, the Carolinas, Georgia, Florida, and Alabama find rare treats offered at seafood shops and restaurants—game fish like cobia and grouper.

Cobia (*Rachycentron canadum*) is a long, slim fish with a bad underbite and a dark lateral stripe that extends from the eye to the tail. What sportsmen love about cobia is the hard-fighting, battling nature of this game fish—and the reward of a great-tasting prize afterwards. Cobia are generally about 30 pounds, but the record catch is a 103-pound fish. Cobia winter (December through March) around wrecks and reefs off the south Florida Keys, where they eat crabs, squid, and other small fish. Gradually, they migrate northwards to spawn and feed in the Chesapeake Bay area. So when cobia are seen in local waters, anglers pay attention. They know to troll or cast around buoys, pilings, and wrecks in inlets, bays, and among mangroves from May until September up the south Atlantic coast to the Chesapeake Bay, and along the Gulf Coast. The recreational catch of cobia is federally managed, and limited to two fish (minimum size, 37 inches total length) per angler per day.

Grouper (from the Portuguese *garoupa*) varieties are also known for their hard-fighting ways, luring anglers from Massachusetts to the waters off the coast of Brazil. Maybe it's due to the trauma of sex reversal, as the young start out predominantly female, transforming into males as they grow larger between the ages of 7 and 14 years or when they are 18 to 26 inches long. Groupers of all kinds love to ambush their prey (squid, small fish, shrimp, lobsters) and swallow them whole. Black grouper (*Mycteroperca bonaci*) may be olive, gray, or reddish brown to black with black, almost rectangular blotches and a squared-off tail. Red grouper (*Epinephelus morio*) is usually dark brownish red, especially around the mouth, and may have dark bars and blotches. Warsaw grouper (*Epinephelus nigritus*) weighs up to 300 pounds. It is sometimes sold as jewfish and its delicious firm flesh is perfect for grilling. The jewfish (*Epinephelus itajara*) is one of the largest of all the groupers. It can reach a length of 7 feet, weigh up to 700 pounds, and can live as long as 25 to 30 years. The all-tackle world record is a 436-pound, 12-ounce Florida fish. Groupers need structure for protection. That's why they cling to the rocky outcroppings or limestone ledges found in deep water. They also like to bite, then take the bait into those rocky ledges, making it even more difficult to reel them in.

GROUPER WITH DILLED CUCUMBER SAUCE

In this recipe, we make a basting brush of fresh dill; for other recipes, you can make basting brushes of tarragon, lemon balm, basil, or even fennel to lend a mild herbal flavor to the baste. (It also impresses your guests!)

MAKES 4 SERVINGS

1/4 cup (1/2 stick) unsalted
  butter
2 tablespoons fresh lemon
  juice
Four 6-ounce grouper fillets
Dilled Cucumber Sauce
  (page 316)
8 long sprigs fresh dill,
  wrapped together with
  florist wire to make a
  basting brush

1. Melt the butter in a small saucepan and add lemon juice. Set aside.

2. Prepare a hot fire.

3. When ready to grill, place the fish on an oiled grill rack. Grill until opaque and just beginning to flake when tested with a fork, 4 to 5 minutes per side, using the dill basting brush to apply the lemon–butter baste frequently.

4. Serve with the cucumber sauce.

Also good with: catfish, haddock, pompano, or walleye

GRILLED HADDOCK HOAGIES WITH COB-SMOKED CHEDDAR AND FRESH TOMATOES

When Judith and her family lived in Vermont, a twice-weekly seafood vendor would bring in caught-that-morning haddock and cod, kept on ice in his truck. This is one of the many delicious ways they enjoyed it, a sandwich with an added smoky flavor from Vermont cheddar, smoked over corn cobs. A good quality cheddar will also work well.

MAKES 4 SERVINGS

*Four 6- to 8-ounce
    haddock fillets*
1/4 cup extra virgin olive oil
*Sea salt and freshly ground
    pepper to taste*
*Basil Aioli by Hand (page
    311) or Spicy Chipotle
    Mayonnaise (page 309)*
*4 hoagie or kaiser rolls, cut
    in half lengthwise*
*1 cup grated cob-smoked or
    sharp cheddar*
*1 large, ripe tomato, cored
    and sliced*

1. Lay the fish on a plate and drizzle it with the olive oil and season with salt and pepper.

2. Prepare a hot fire.

3. When ready to grill, place the fish on the oiled grill rack and grill until opaque and just beginning to flake, 4 to 5 minutes per side, turning once.

4. To make the sandwiches, spread the aioli or mayonnaise on the bottom half of a hoagie and top with a grilled haddock fillet. Sprinkle the fillet with 1/4 cup of the cheddar, add sliced tomatoes, and top with the remaining half of the hoagie. Repeat with the remaining ingredients.

Also good with: catfish, char, mahimahi, salmon, or tilapia

NOT YOUR PLAIN OLD FISH SANDWICH

Fried fish on a bun with shredded lettuce and tartar sauce—the classic fish sandwich. But you can do more, much more. How about these delicious options, using freshly grilled or leftover grilled or smoked fish?

Lobster Burger: Decadent grilled lobster meat blended with mayonnaise and dolloped on half of a ciabattini, then run under the broiler until browned, then topped with the other half of the ciabattini.

Grilled Fish Wrap with Avocado and Four-Herb Chimichurri: On a flour tortilla laid flat, place a large and tender lettuce leaf, then pieces of grilled halibut or salmon, chunks of ripe avocado, then a drizzle of Four-Herb Chimichurri (page 324). Roll up and eat.

Smoked Whitefish on Rye with Dilled Mayonnaise: Blend 1 cup flaked smoked whitefish with 1/2 cup mayonnaise, 1 teaspoon dillweed, and 1 teaspoon fresh lemon juice. Spread this filling on good, crusty dark caraway rye. Add lettuce and tomato if you want.

Grilled Oyster Po' Boy: Grilled oysters, Sauce Rémoulade (page 308), and Napa Cabbage Slaw (page 60) on a split French roll.

Vietnamese Summer Rolls: Grilled shrimp/salmon/halibut/trout, fresh cilantro, Asian cellophane noodles, and Asian Slaw (page 350) rolled up in rice-paper wrappers. Serve with Vietnamese Dipping Sauce (page 329).

Focaccia with Grilled Tuna and Roasted Tomato–Olive Relish: Split a small focaccia in half horizontally, spread with Roasted Tomato–Olive Relish (page 337), then top with fresh baby greens, pieces of grilled tuna, and sliced provolone.

HADDOCK WITH HAZELNUT-LIME BUTTER

Brenda Burns is co-owner of Californos restaurant in Kansas City, Missouri, along with her husband, Terry. Her hallmark is simple recipes with the freshest of ingredients.

MAKES 4 SERVINGS

Four 6- to 8-ounce
    haddock fillets
1/4 cup extra virgin olive oil
Sea salt and freshly ground
    pepper to taste
Hazelnut-Lime Butter
    (page 299)

1. Drizzle the fish with the oil, coating it evenly, and season with salt and pepper.

2. Prepare a hot fire.

3. When ready to grill, place the fish on an oiled grill rack and grill the fish until opaque and just beginning to flake when tested with a fork, 4 to 5 minutes per side, turning once.

4. Serve with a dollop of the butter on top of each serving.

Also good with: catfish, grouper, halibut, or shell-fish (adjust the cooking time)

GRILLED HAKE WITH SPANISH SAUCE

We're amazed at all the delicious permutations that grilled fish, olive oil, onion, garlic, capers, and tomatoes can inspire.

MAKES 4 SERVINGS

2 tablespoons olive oil
1/2 cup chopped onions
1/2 cup seeded and chopped
    green bell pepper
2 cloves garlic, minced
2 pounds hake steaks
Spanish Sauce (page 326)
2 tablespoons chopped fresh
    Italian parsley for
    garnish

1. In a saucepan, heat the olive oil over medium heat, then add the onion, green pepper, and garlic and cook, stirring, until the onion is transparent, about 5 minutes. Remove from the heat and let cool to room temperature. Spread this vegetable paste on top of the hake, cover with plastic wrap, and let rest for 30 minutes in the refrigerator.

2. Prepare a hot fire.

3. When ready to grill, place the fish, vegetable paste side up, on the oiled grill rack and grill for 4 minutes, then turn and grill on the other side until the fish is opaque and just beginning to flake when tested with a fork, about another 4 minutes.

4. To serve, nap the fish with the warm sauce and sprinkle with the chopped parsley.

Also good with: sea bass, catfish, cod, haki, or walleye

TAPAS-STYLE GRILLED HAKE AND ZUCCHINI SKEWERS

Use only very small, fresh zucchini for this recipe, as the flavor is much better. And make sure you soak the wooden skewers in water at least 30 minutes before assembling the hake and zucchini. We've also done this in a stir-grill style, first marinating the hake and zucchini in the basting sauce, then stir-grilling it to serve with rice.

MAKES 4 MAIN-COURSE SERVINGS OR 8 APPETIZER SERVINGS

1/4 cup olive oil
1/4 cup finely chopped
   onion
2 cloves garlic, minced
1/4 teaspoon dried thyme
Salt and freshly ground
   black pepper to taste
4 small zucchini, ends
   trimmed and cut into
   1/2-inch-thick rounds
1 1/2 pounds hake fillets, cut
   into 1-inch pieces

1. Prepare a hot fire.

2. Meanwhile, in a small skillet, heat the olive oil over medium-high heat. Add the onion, garlic, and thyme and cook until the onion is translucent, about 5 minutes. Season with salt and pepper and set aside to cool for 5 minutes.

3. Assemble the skewers, starting with a piece of zucchini, then one of fish, beginning and ending with zucchini—2 pieces of fish and 3 zucchini coins on each wooden skewer. Allow room between the fish and vegetables, so everything will cook evenly.

4. When ready to grill, place the skewers on the oiled grill grates. Brush the skewers on all sides with the olive oil mixture. Grill until the fish is opaque and the zucchini has started to soften, 3 to 4 minutes per side, basting once more with the olive oil mixture. Serve hot or at room temperature.

Also good with: cod, haddock, halibut, mahimahi, or walleye

ROSEMARY-DIJON HALIBUT

The combination of rosemary and Dijon mustard that infuses this marinade gives it a gutsiness that stands up well to grilling. Before you grill the fish, make some Lemon Rice (page 380) to go alongside.

MAKES 4 SERVINGS

Four 6- to 8-ounce halibut fillets
3/4 cup olive oil
2 tablespoons Dijon mustard
2 teaspoons prepared horseradish
Juice of 1 lemon
1 teaspoon chopped fresh rosemary leaves or 3/4 teaspoon dried
Salt and freshly ground black pepper to taste
1/2 cup Persillade (page 282) for garnish

1. In a small bowl, combine marinade ingredients. Place the fish in a resealable plastic bag. Pour marinade into the bag, seal, and marinate fish in the refrigerator for about 1 hour.

2. Prepare a hot fire.

3. When ready to grill, remove the fish from the marinade and place on a plate. Pour the marinade into a small saucepan and boil for about 5 minutes to use as a baste. Place the fillets on the oiled grill racks and grill until the fish is opaque and just beginning to flake when tested with a fork, 4 to 5 minutes per side, turning once and basting frequently with the boiled marinade.

4. Serve garnished with the persillade.

Also good with: catfish, grouper, monkfish, or swordfish

STIR-GRILLED FISH TACOS

This lighter, fresher, leaner cousin of the traditional beef taco in a corn taco shell has made many converts, as we've prepared this in several cooking classes around the country. You can either stir-grill the halibut if you have bought halibut steaks to cut into pieces or you can grill a whole halibut fillet with the skin on and serve the whole fillet on a platter. Either way, it's fun for everyone to make up their own tacos. In place of halibut, you could also use any mild fish that will not flake apart too easily.

MAKES 4 SERVINGS

FISH:

1 1/2 pounds halibut steaks, cut into 2-inch pieces, or one 1 1/2-pound halibut fillet with skin on, left whole

2 to 3 tablespoons Fireworks Rub (page 279) or store-bought Cajun-style spice blend

NAPA CABBAGE SLAW:

2 cups cored and shredded Napa cabbage

1 cup shredded assorted baby greens, such as escarole, oak-leaf lettuce, baby spinach, mizuna, and Bibb or butter lettuce

1. Prepare a hot fire.

2. If using halibut pieces, coat the inside of a grill wok with nonstick cooking spray and set aside. Season the halibut with the rub and set aside.

3. Combine the cabbage and greens in a large bowl.

4. In a small bowl, combine the vinegar, sour cream, lemon juice, green onions, and salt to make a dressing. Pour the dressing over the cabbage mixture and toss to blend. Set aside.

5. When ready to grill, stir-grill the halibut in the wok, tossing the fish frequently with two wooden paddles until it is opaque, 8 to 10 minutes. Alternately, place the halibut fillet, flesh side down, on

¹/4 cup tarragon vinegar
¹/4 cup sour cream (may use lowfat)
Juice of 2 lemons
6 green onions, white part and some of the green, finely chopped
¹/2 teaspoon salt

8 flour tortillas
Lemon wedges and 1¹/2 cups salsa of your choice for garnish

the oiled grill rack and grill until opaque and just beginning to flake when tested with a fork, about 5 minutes per side, turning the fish once with a wide metal fish spatula and a grill spatula.

6. To make the tacos, place about ¹/3 cup of the cabbage slaw in the center of a flour tortilla. Top with 4 or 5 pieces of halibut and roll up. Garnish with lemon wedges and salsa.

Also good with: catfish, monkfish, orange roughy, shrimp, or swordfish

GRILLED HALIBUT WITH GOLDEN MOLE SAUCE, SALSA FRESCA, AND BLACK BEANS

It's not too far a journey from the icy waters off the Alaskan coastline to the dramatic peaks of Grand Teton National Park in Wyoming. There, at the Signal Mountain Lodge, Chef Todd Baron entices summer visitors with dishes like this one, which we have adapted for the grill. The Golden Mole Sauce is a taste revelation, and the vivid colors of this dish—yellow, red, and black—make a fabulous presentation. Make the mole sauce and salsa ahead of time, then grill the fish and assemble the dish right before serving.

MAKES 4 SERVINGS

GOLDEN MOLE SAUCE:

3 tablespoons corn oil

1/3 cup shelled, roasted, and salted sunflower seeds

3 cloves garlic, minced

3 large yellow bell peppers, seeded and chopped

1 large yellow onion, chopped

1 tablespoon ground cumin

1 teaspoon ground cinnamon

2 1/2 cups chicken broth

3/4 teaspoon salt

SALSA FRESCA:

Juice of 1 large lime

4 large, ripe Roma tomatoes, diced

1/4 cup finely diced red onion

1. Prepare a hot fire.

2. Meanwhile, to make the mole sauce, in a large saucepan over medium heat, heat the corn oil, then add the sunflower seeds, garlic, bell pepper, onion, cumin, and cinnamon and cook, stirring, until the onion is translucent, 5 to 7 minutes. Pour in the chicken broth, taste, and add salt if necessary. Cover and simmer over low heat for 20 minutes. Transfer sauce to a blender or food processor and process until smooth. Keep warm until needed.

3. Combine all the salsa ingredients in a large bowl and cover until needed. (You can refrigerate it up to 24 hours; let come to room temperature before serving.)

4. When ready to grill, brush the fish with olive oil and season with salt and pepper. Place the fish in an oiled hinged grill basket or on an oiled perforated grill rack. Grill until the fish is opaque and beginning to flake when tested with a fork, 4 to 5 minutes per side, turning once.

*¹/4 cup fresh cilantro leaves,
    finely chopped*
3 tablespoons olive oil
*Salt and freshly ground
    black pepper to taste*

FISH:

*Four 6- to 8-ounce halibut
    fillets*
Olive oil
*Salt and freshly ground
    black pepper to taste*

*Cooked black beans for
    garnish*

5. Serve the fish over the mole sauce topped with the salsa. Garnish with a spoonful of black beans.

Also good with: striped bass, John Dory, redfish, snapper, or whitefish

HALIBUT FILLET WITH
RED PEPPER BEURRE BLANC

Simply sublime! The creamy white, mild-flavored halibut paired with the slightly piquant Red Pepper Beurre Blanc is a visual and savory feast for the eyes and the palate. A crusty artisanal bread like Life-in-the-Fast-Lane Baguettes from *Prairie Home Breads* (Harvard Common Press, 2001), Judith's comprehensive bread-baking book, makes a perfect mop for the beurre blanc.

MAKES 6 SERVINGS

Six 6- to 8-ounce halibut fillets

2 tablespoons extra virgin olive oil

Red Pepper Beurre Blanc (page 306)

6 sprigs fresh basil for garnish

1. Brush the fillets with the olive oil.

2. Prepare a hot fire.

3. When ready to grill, place the halibut on the oiled grill racks and grill until opaque and just beginning to flake when tested with a fork, 4 to 5 minutes per side, turning once halfway through the grilling time.

4. Serve with the beurre blanc spooned over the fillets and garnished with a sprig of fresh basil.

Also good with: striped bass, John Dory, lingcod, or salmon

OKEYDOKEY HOKI WITH PESTO

Hoki is from Australian and New Zealand waters and is very similar to the delicate white-fleshed hake. It is primarily available in the U.S. as frozen or smoked fillets.

MAKES 4 SERVINGS

Juice of 1 lemon
Four 6-ounce hoki fillets
Freshly ground black
*   pepper to taste*
1 to 2 tablespoons olive
*   oil, as needed*
Pesto (page 325)
2 ripe tomatoes, sliced

1. Prepare a hot fire.
2. Meanwhile, drizzle the lemon juice over the fillets and season with pepper. Let stand for 15 minutes, then lightly drizzle with the olive oil. When ready to grill, place the fillets on an oiled grill rack and grill until the fish is opaque and just beginning to flake when tested with a fork, 4 to 5 minutes per side, turning once.
3. Serve each fillet topped with pesto and with sliced tomatoes on the side.

Also good with: catfish, hake, monkfish, or orange roughy

GRILLED SPICED JOHN DORY

Also known as St. Peter's fish, this is a most delicious fish, on par with Dover sole. It is tender, so you need to "grill" it in an aluminum pan, in a Nordicware fish boat, or wrapped in foil to avoid having it fall through the grill grates. Serve with Grilled Mediterranean Vegetables (page 375).

MAKES 4 SERVINGS

Four 6-ounce John Dory
  fillets
Vinaigrette Marinade
  (page 284)
Autumn Spice Herb Rub
  (page 275)

1. Place the fillets in a resealable plastic bag and add the marinade. Seal and let marinate for 1 hour, refrigerated.

2. Prepare a hot fire.

3. When ready to grill, remove the fillets from the marinade and sprinkle both sides with the spice rub. Place the fish fillets in a disposable aluminum pan. Grill until the fish is opaque and just beginning to flake when tested with a fork, about 10 minutes per inch of thickness. Do not turn.

Also good with: freshwater bass, catfish, fluke, sand dab, or turbot

GRILLED MACKEREL WITH ANCHOVY AND ROSEMARY

Holy mackerel! Maybe this saying comes from the fact that these are extremely resilient fish. Even though their wildlife management is not the best, they are abundant producers everywhere. Let's "pray" it stays that way. Mackerel are prime from spring to early summer, prior to spawning. With their high concentration of fish oils, mackerel spoil quickly and must be iced as soon as they are caught. If you can buy them in this freshest scenario, they are delicious grilled or smoked. Try them with Orange and Red Onion Salad (page 365).

MAKES 4 SERVINGS

Four 1-pound mackerel, dressed
1/4 cup (1/2 stick) unsalted butter, melted
8 anchovy fillets
1/2 teaspoon dried rosemary
Sprigs fresh Italian parsley for garnish
Lemon wedges for garnish

1. Prepare a hot fire.

2. Meanwhile, make 2 or 3 slashes on each side of the fish. Split each mackerel down the back and fold open. Brush both sides of the interior of the fish with the melted butter.

3. When ready to grill, place the fish skin side down on an oiled grill topper or perforated grill rack and set this above the fire. Arrange 2 anchovy fillets over the flesh of each mackerel and sprinkle each with 1/8 teaspoon of the rosemary. Grill until the flesh is opaque and just beginning to flake when tested with a fork, about 10 minutes. Do not turn. (Mackerel are so thin you don't have to turn them.)

4. Serve garnished with parsley sprigs and lemon wedges.

Also good with: amberjack, permit, tilapia, or yellowtail

ALMOND-BUTTERED MAHIMAHI

Also known as dorado and dolphinfish, mahimahi is a succulent, sweet, white-fleshed fish that is perfect for the grill. It also marries well with lots of different flavors. Try some of the other compound butters on pages 297–306 as a baste or finish to this fish, especially butters with nuts. Serve with Grilled Goat Cheese Tomatoes (page 374) on the side or on top of the fish.

MAKES 4 SERVINGS

Eight 4-ounce mahimahi
    fillets
1/4 cup extra virgin olive oil
Sea salt and freshly ground
    black pepper to taste
1/4 cup Almond Butter
    (page 300), softened

1. Prepare a hot fire.

2. When ready to grill, coat the fish with the olive oil and season with salt and pepper. Grill on an oiled grill rack until the fish is opaque and just beginning to flake when tested with a fork, about 5 minutes per side, turning once.

3. Serve 2 fillets per person topped with a pat of the almond butter.

Also good with: trout, walleye, or whitefish

MAHIMAHI WITH KIWI SAUCE

Fresh fruit purées make tasty, colorful sauces during warm-weather days. Experiment with pineapple, peaches, mangoes, and papayas—their tart flavors complement the sweetness of grilled fish.

Karen and her husband, Dick, have fished for dorado (mahimahi) while visiting their friends Don and Maureen Hasseltine in Cabo san Lucas. Their fresh-caught fish from the Sea of Cortez were nothing less than sublime when prepared on the grill.

MAKES 6 SERVINGS

KIWI SAUCE:

3 kiwis, peeled
1 teaspoon curry powder
1 teaspoon salt

Six 6- to 8-ounce
mahimahi fillets
1 to 2 tablespoons extra
virgin olive oil, as
needed
Sea salt and freshly ground
black pepper to taste
1 kiwi, peeled and sliced,
for garnish

1. To make the sauce, place the kiwis, curry powder, and salt in a food processor and process until smooth. Chill completely.

2. Prepare a hot fire.

3. When ready to grill, brush the fillets with the olive oil and season with salt and pepper. Grill on an oiled grill rack until the fish is opaque and just beginning to flake when tested with a fork, about 5 minutes per side, turning once.

4. Garnish with kiwi slices and serve with the sauce over the top.

Also good with: grouper, haddock, pompano, or sea scallops

TERIYAKI STIR-GRILLED MAHIMAHI

Marinated in an enhanced teriyaki sauce, grilled over fruitwood, and accompanied by fresh-tasting Island Salsa (page 331), this mahimahi has big flavor with very few calories.

MAKES 4 SERVINGS

1 1/2 pounds mahimahi
　　fillets or steaks, cubed
3/4 cup teriyaki sauce
1 tablespoon dry sherry
1 clove garlic, minced
1 cup wood chips or 1/3 cup
　　wood pellets

1. Place cubed fish in a resealable plastic bag and add the teriyaki sauce, sherry, and garlic. Seal the bag, shake to coat everything, and let marinate for at least 30 minutes in the refrigerator.

2. Place the wood chips in water to cover or the wood pellets in a heavy-duty aluminum foil packet with holes poked into it.

3. Prepare a hot fire.

4. When ready to grill, place the drained wood chips or foil packet on the fire. Set an oiled grill wok on the rack above the fire. Transfer the fish cubes to the wok using a slotted spoon to drain the excess marinade. Stir-grill until the fish is opaque, 12 to 15 minutes, using two long-handled wooden spoons to toss the mixture. Close the lid for an additional 2 to 3 minutes to heat thoroughly. Serve immediately.

Also good with: salmon, shrimp, or swordfish

Suggested wood smoke: apple, cherry, or pear

BALSAMIC-GLAZED MARLIN STEAKS

Dancing marlin are a sight to behold, their upright bodies twirling on their tails above the sea. They are mainly a sport fish and not easily found at seafood counters. If you are able to catch your own, try this simple recipe with a sweet-and-sour note. Serve with Grilled Garden Onions and Lemon Halves (page 362).

MAKES 4 SERVINGS

*Two 14- to 16-ounce
    marlin steaks
Sea salt and lemon pepper
    to taste
3 tablespoons unsalted
    butter
1/3 cup balsamic vinegar*

1. Prepare a hot fire.
2. Meanwhile, season the steaks with salt and lemon pepper. Let stand at room temperature for 10 to 15 minutes.
3. In a small saucepan, melt the butter and whisk in the balsamic vinegar to make a glaze. Set aside.
4. Grill the steaks on an oiled grill rack until they are opaque and just beginning to flake when tested with a fork, about 5 minutes per side, turning once and basting with the glaze.

Also good with: shark, shortbill spearfish, swordfish, or tuna

TAPAS-STYLE MONKFISH SKEWERS

Entertaining tapas-style with lots of little dishes full of fresh Mediterranean flavors works very well with grilled fish, which tastes great either hot off the grill or at room temperature. Make smaller skewers and serve them on a round platter in a sunburst pattern, with a bowl of sun-colored Cumin and Carrot Salad (page 352) in the middle.

MAKES 4 SERVINGS

1 pound monkfish fillets,
    cut into twelve 1¹/2-inch
    cubes total
2 slices thick-cut smoked
    bacon, cut into twelve
    1-inch squares
¹/2 large green bell pepper,
    seeded and cut into six
    1-inch squares
¹/2 large yellow or red bell
    pepper, seeded and cut
    into six 1-inch squares
Olive oil for brushing
Freshly ground black
    pepper and paprika
    to taste

1. Prepare a hot fire. Soak twelve 7- to 8-inch wooden skewers in water for at least 30 minutes before grilling.

2. Assemble the skewers starting with a piece of fish, then bacon, then pepper. Allow some space between the ingredients so that they will cook evenly.

3. When ready to grill, place the skewers on an oiled perforated grill rack and brush with olive oil. Grill, basting once more with olive oil, until the bacon has browned, the fish is opaque, and the pepper has softened, 3 to 4 minutes per side, turning once.

4. Sprinkle each skewer with pepper and paprika and serve hot or at room temperature.

Also good with: cod, halibut, shark, or shrimp

NEW DELHI–STYLE GRILLED MONKFISH

We can't think of a better hot-weather entrée than this one, sure to perk up anyone's flagging appetite. Whether you stir-grill this fish with wooden paddles in a grill wok or simply grill it on an oiled perforated grill rack, the flavor is fabulous. Serve with basmati rice.

MAKES 4 SERVINGS

1 1/2 pounds monkfish
    fillets, cut into 3/4-inch-
    wide strips
1 lemon, sliced, for garnish
1 large onion, sliced into
    rings, for garnish

GINGER-CILANTRO MARINADE:

4 garlic cloves, minced
1 teaspoon ground cumin
1 teaspoon salt
1 1/2 tablespoons finely
    chopped fresh cilantro
    leaves
One 1 1/2-inch piece fresh
    ginger, peeled and grated
Juice of 2 lemons
2 tablespoons olive oil

TOPPING:

Juice of 2 lemons
3 cloves garlic, minced
1/2 teaspoon salt
1 tablespoon olive oil

1. Pierce each fish strip 2 or 3 times with a fork, then place in a large resealable plastic bag.

2. To make the marinade, mash the salt and cumin into the minced garlic in a bowl. Add the cilantro, ginger, and lemon juice and stir well. Mix in the olive oil. Pour the marinade over the fish in the plastic bag, seal it, shake to coat everything, and refrigerate for 1 hour before grilling.

3. Prepare a hot fire.

4. Meanwhile, mix the topping ingredients together in a small bowl.

5. When ready to grill, remove the fish from the marinade; discard the marinade. Grill the fish on an oiled perforated grill rack until opaque and just beginning to flake when tested with a fork, turning once, 5 to 8 minutes total.

6. Remove the fish strips and brush them with the topping. Serve garnished with lemon and onion slices.

Also good with: sea bass, catfish, rockfish, or shrimp

MONKFISH SKEWERS WITH JALAPEÑO AND CILANTRO MARINADE

Use individual kabob baskets for an easy way to grill *en brochette* without having the extra step of sliding the food onto each skewer. If you're using kabob baskets, marinate the fish and vegetables first, then arrange them in the baskets.

MAKES 4 SERVINGS

1 1/2 pounds monkfish
    fillets
1 medium-size zucchini,
    ends trimmed and cut
    into 1/8-inch-thick
    rounds
8 button mushrooms
1 large red onion, quartered
    and separated into layers
Jalapeño and Cilantro
    Marinade (page 285)

1. Holding a knife at a slight angle, cut each monkfish fillet into diagonal slices so that you end up with 24 slices in total. Place the fish and vegetables in a glass dish and pour the marinade over them. Cover with plastic wrap and refrigerate for about 1 hour.

2. Prepare a hot fire.

3. When ready to grill, remove the fish and vegetables from the marinade. Alternate the fish and vegetables in the kabob baskets, allowing 2 kabob baskets per person. Grill until opaque, 8 to 10 minutes, turning every 2 minutes. Do not overcook or the fish will get tough.

4. Empty the baskets into a pretty serving bowl, loosely cover, and let stand in a warm place for 5 minutes before serving.

Also good with: shark, shrimp, or swordfish

LEMON-LIME MONKFISH

Monkfish is also known as poor man's lobster. Its meaty texture is very similar to that of lobster and shrimp.

MAKES 6 SERVINGS

*Lemon-Lime Marinade
    (page 288)
1 cup wood chips or 1/3 cup
    wood pellets
2 1/4 pounds monkfish
    fillets, cut into pieces
1 lemon, sliced
1 lime, sliced
3 cups cooked rice*

1. Pour 1 cup of the marinade into a resealable plastic bag, add the fish, seal, shake to coat everything, and refrigerate for 1 hour to marinate. Reserve the remaining marinade.

2. Place the wood chips in water to cover or the wood pellets in a heavy-duty aluminum foil packet with holes poked into it.

3. Prepare a hot fire.

4. When ready to grill, place the drained wood chips or foil packet on the fire. Set an oiled grill wok on the rack above the fire. Transfer the fish to the grill wok using a slotted spoon to drain the excess marinade. Stir-grill, tossing the fish and lemon and lime slices with two long-handled wooden spoons or grill spatulas until the fish is opaque, 3 to 5 minutes. Close the grill and cook for 3 to 4 minutes more.

5. Serve the fish and citrus slices over the rice and drizzle with the remaining marinade.

Also good with: catfish, sea bream, squid, or trout

Suggested wood smoke: mesquite, oak, or pecan

FRESH HERB–CRUSTED MULLET

One of our favorite cookbooks is *Cooking with the Seasons* (Henry Holt, 1997) by Monique Jamet Hooker, celebrating the foods she grew up with in Brittany. When she visited with our cookbook club on a beautiful summer evening at our friend Rose Kallas's home and we tasted her wonderful fresh-from-the-garden food, she inspired this dish. This fish recipe is prepared in the late summer with a medley of herbs that can still be gathered from the garden. Mullet are predominantly found in the South Atlantic and Gulf of Mexico and sold as either striped or silver mullet. It is a firm white fish with a mild nut-like flavor, perfect for the grill. Serve this with Grilled Red Potatoes, Capers, and Olives (page 368).

MAKES 6 SERVINGS

Six 4- to 5-ounce mullet
  fillets about 3/4 inch
  thick
1/2 cup chopped mixed fresh
  savory, oregano, and dill
1/4 cup finely ground blue
  corn chips
1/2 teaspoon sea salt
1/4 teaspoon freshly ground
  black pepper
1/4 teaspoon red pepper
  flakes
1 tablespoon olive oil in a
  spray bottle

1. Place the fish fillets on a large piece of plastic wrap.
2. In a small bowl, combine the herbs, corn chips, salt, and black and red peppers together. Sprinkle on both sides of the fish. Wrap the fish up tightly and refrigerate for 30 to 45 minutes.
3. Prepare a hot fire.
4. When ready to grill, remove the fillets from the refrigerator and lightly spray olive oil on both sides of the fish. Place the fish on an oiled grill rack and grill until opaque and just beginning to flake when tested with a fork, about 3 minutes on each side, turning only once. Serve immediately.

Also good with: freshwater bass, halibut, or salmon

GRILLED OCEAN PERCH

Fish names can be so confusing! Ocean perch is more popularly known as the red-fish. However, *Fish and Shellfish* (William Morrow, 1996) by James Peterson states that redfish is actually red drum. Another name for it is Norway haddock. In France these fish are known as *rascasse*. This is the fish that gained fame when it was first "blackened" in New Orleans. Try our Blackened Seasoning (page 280) and grill the fish directly over a very hot fire. Even better for a more authentic taste, place a cast-iron griddle or frying pan on the grill. Get it smoking hot and sear the fish directly on the hot cast-iron surface. This keeps the smoke outside instead of in your kitchen. Serve with Parmesan-Crusted Tomatoes (page 374).

MAKES 6 SERVINGS

1/2 cup (1 stick) unsalted
   butter
1/2 teaspoon dried
   marjoram
2 teaspoons fresh lemon
   juice
Six 6- to 8-ounce ocean
   perch fillets

1. Prepare a hot fire.

2. Meanwhile, in a small saucepan, melt the better and stir in the marjoram and lemon juice. Set aside.

3. When ready to grill, set an oiled perforated grill rack over the fire. Place the fillets on the rack and grill until the fish is opaque and just beginning to flake when tested with a fork, about 5 minutes per side, basting frequently with the herb butter.

Also good with: catfish, halibut, rockfish, salmon, or shrimp

Catch (or buy) a fish and have an outdoor party! The beautiful presentation of a whole salmon fillet is perfect for a buffet. We've included side dishes that keep well and a Fresh Blueberry Cheese Tart for dessert.

For an indoor party, think Aioli Platter. Grill Herb-Encrusted Salmon fillets (page 95) and place on platters. Offer other platters full of artfully arranged roasted fingerling potatoes, steamed baby carrots, marinated artichoke hearts, pitted Kalamata or niçoise olives, and a bowl of Aioli (page 311) in the center.

Barbecued Whole Salmon Fillets

MAKES 10 TO 12 SERVINGS

Two 2¹/₂-pound salmon fillets, with skin on
1 cup soy sauce
1 cup dry white wine
1 tablespoon firmly packed brown sugar
1 tablespoon toasted sesame oil
1 teaspoon peeled and minced fresh ginger
1 teaspoon freshly ground black pepper
2 cloves garlic, minced
¹/₂ cup hot barbecue sauce of your choice
12 sprigs fresh dill or fennel for garnish
4 lemons, thinly sliced, for garnish

1. Place the salmon fillets in a large glass casserole dish. In a small bowl, combine the soy sauce, wine, brown sugar, sesame oil, ginger, pepper, and garlic. Pour over the fillets and let marinate for 30 minutes in the refrigerator.

2. Prepare a hot fire. Place the fillets flesh side down and grill for about 5 minutes. Turn and grill another 5 minutes. Brush the flesh side with barbecue sauce, and cook for an additional 1 to 2 minutes to set and heat the sauce. (Grill the fillets for 10 minutes per inch of thickness measured from the thickest part of the whole fillet.)

3. Place the fillets on a fish platter. Garnish with a circle of lemon slices tucked under the fish and sprigs of dill or fennel tucked in here and there.

ASIAN NOODLES

NO! murky awful

This is one of the most popular dishes served at the Culinary Center of Kansas City, where we both teach cooking classes. Pair it with grilled fish or chicken for the most pleasing results.

MAKES 10 TO 12 SERVINGS

3/4 cup unsweetened coconut milk

3 tablespoons Thai red curry paste (available in Asian markets)

3/4 cup smooth or crunchy peanut butter

3/4 cup water

1/4 cup firmly packed brown sugar

Juice of 3 limes

2 tablespoons fish sauce (available in Asian markets)

1 teaspoon sea salt

1 1/2 pounds Asian egg noodles or thin spaghetti, cooked until al dente and drained

2 cups steamed broccoli florets for topping

2 cups chopped green onions for topping

1 cup chopped peanuts for topping

1 cup packed fresh cilantro leaves, chopped, for topping

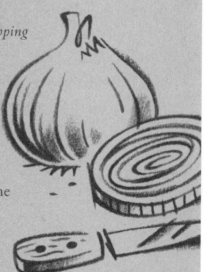

1. In a small saucepan, combine the coconut milk, red curry paste, peanut butter, water, brown sugar, lime juice, fish sauce, and salt. Bring gently to a boil, whisking until smooth. Remove from the heat and let cool to room temperature.

2. In a large bowl, combine the noodles with the sauce.

3. On a large platter, arrange the noodles and garnish with the broccoli, green onions, peanuts, and cilantro.

GRILLED ASPARAGUS WITH TAMARIND DIPPING SAUCE

For quicker grilling, blanch the asparagus in boiling water for a minute or two, then grill them for about 6 minutes over a hot fire.

MAKES 10 TO 12 SERVINGS

3 pounds fresh asparagus, bottoms trimmed
2 cups Spicy Tamarind Dipping Sauce (page 328)

1. Lay the asparagus spears in a deep glass casserole dish. Pour 1 cup of the dipping sauce over them.
2. Prepare a hot fire. Place the asparagus spears perpendicular to the grill grates so that they do not fall through the grates. Grill until crisp-tender and slightly charred, 8 to 10 minutes.
3. Drizzle some of the remaining sauce over the hot asparagus and serve. Or chill the asparagus and serve with sauce on the side.

TECHNICOLOR TOMATOES

This is a favorite recipe for the month of August, when home gardens and farmer's markets are bursting with ripe tomatoes.

MAKES 10 TO 12 SERVINGS

8 large, ripe tomatoes, preferably a mix of colors
1 pint grape, cherry, or yellow pear tomatoes
1 red onion, thinly sliced
2 cups chopped green onions
Sea salt and freshly ground black pepper to taste
1 1/2 cups Cider Marinade (page 288)
1/4 cup chopped fresh Italian parsley leaves
1/4 cup chopped fresh mint leaves

Slice the tomatoes and arrange, alternating colors, on a deep dish platter. Top with the cherry-sized tomatoes, onion slices, and chopped green onions. Season with salt and pepper. Drizzle with the marinade. Garnish with the parsley and mint and serve.

A PARTICULARLY GOOD LAYERED SALAD

Our first encounters with layered salads came in the early 1970s when we started attending and giving wedding showers. We needed to have luncheon dishes that required minimal expense and culinary skill. The layered salad fit the bill. Here is one adapted from many. It gets rave reviews. Prepare it in a glass bowl to show off the layers.

MAKES 8 TO 12 SERVINGS

3 cups chopped spinach
1 teaspoon sea salt
1/2 teaspoon freshly ground black pepper
2 teaspoons sugar
1 pound sliced bacon, fried until crisp, drained on paper towels, and crumbled
6 hard-boiled eggs, shelled and sliced
3 cups shredded curly green or red lettuce
1 cup thinly sliced celery
One 10-ounce package frozen peas
1/2 cup sliced green onions
1 package dry Caesar salad dressing mix
1 cup lowfat sour cream
1 cup mayonnaise
1 1/2 cups freshly grated Parmesan or Romano cheese

1. In a large 3-quart salad bowl, spread the chopped spinach. Sprinkle 1/2 teaspoon of the salt, 1/4 teaspoon of the pepper, and 1 teaspoon of the sugar over the spinach. Layer beginning with the crumbled bacon, sliced eggs, lettuce, celery, the remaining 1/2 teaspoon salt, 1/4 teaspoon pepper, 1 teaspoon sugar, the peas, and green onions.

2. In a small bowl, combine the salad dressing mix with the sour cream and mayonnaise. Spread over the top of the salad to seal. Sprinkle the cheese on last.

3. Refrigerate overnight covered tightly with plastic wrap. Toss just before serving.

FRESH BLUEBERRY CHEESE TART

This dessert gets ooh–la–las, from its crunchy sugar cookie crust to its cinnamon–laced whipped cream topping. The blueberry mixture is a great sauce to serve over toasted pound cake and homemade vanilla ice cream.

MAKES ONE 10-INCH TART; 10 TO 12 SERVINGS

1³/4 cups all-purpose flour
2/3 cup unsalted butter, melted
1¹/2 cups plus 1 tablespoon sugar
1 teaspoon ground ginger
Two 8-ounce packages cream cheese, softened
2 large eggs, beaten
2 teaspoons pure vanilla extract
6 cups fresh blueberries, picked over for stems
1/2 cup water
1 tablespoon chopped candied ginger
2 cups whipping cream
1 teaspoon ground cinnamon
10 to 12 sprigs fresh mint for garnish

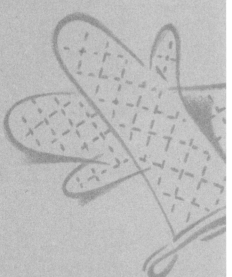

1. Preheat the oven to 350 degrees Fahrenheit.

2. In a large bowl, combine the flour, melted butter, and ¹/2 cup of the sugar. Pat the mixture evenly into the bottom and up the sides of a 10-inch spring-form pan. Bake until lightly browned, about 12 minutes. Set aside to cool. Increase the oven temperature to 400 degrees.

3. In a medium-size bowl, beat together cream cheese, ¹/2 cup of the sugar, the eggs, and vanilla. Pour the mixture into the crust. Bake for 20 to 25 minutes. Remove from the oven and let cool.

4. In a heavy saucepan, combine 3 cups of the blueberries with the water and 1/2 cup of the sugar in a medium-size heavy saucepan. Bring to a boil, stirring constantly. Reduce the heat to low and simmer, stirring, until the mixture thickens, about 15 minutes. Add the remaining 3 cups berries and the candied ginger. Spread the blueberries over the cream cheese tart filling. May be cooled and refrigerated for several hours, if desired.

5. When ready to serve, in a medium-size bowl, whip the cream with the cinnamon and the remaining 1 tablespoon sugar until stiff peaks form. Spoon the spiced whipped cream over each piece of tart and garnish with a sprig of fresh mint.

ORANGE ROUGHY IN ORANGE ZEST MARINADE

Orange roughy fillets are a perfect example of fillets that are tapered and thin at one end and considerably thicker at the other. To avoid overcooking the tapered end, simply fold the tip over to create an even thickness. For a double citrus kick, serve with Mandarin Orange Salad (page 366).

MAKES 4 SERVINGS

ORANGE ZEST MARINADE:

1/2 cup olive oil

1/4 cup dry white wine

1 clove garlic, finely chopped

1/2 teaspoon red pepper flakes

1/2 teaspoon chopped fresh Italian parsley leaves

1/4 teaspoon salt

1/4 teaspoon freshly ground black pepper

Grated zest of 1 orange

Juice of 1 orange

Four 6- to 8-ounce orange roughy fillets

1. Combine the marinade ingredients and pour into a resealable plastic bag. Add the fish, seal, shake to coat everything, and refrigerate for 1 hour.

2. Prepare a hot fire.

3. Remove the fish from the marinade. In a small saucepan, bring the marinade to a boil and cook for 5 minutes to use for basting.

4. When ready to grill, set an oiled perforated grill rack over the fire. Place the fish on the rack and grill until the fillets are opaque and just beginning to flake in the thickest part, but are still moist, 4 to 5 minutes per side, turning once and basting frequently with the marinade.

Also good with: catfish, cod, rockfish, scup, or walleye

ORANGE ROUGHY WITH SPICY
CANTALOUPE SLICES

Orange roughy is available year round as frozen fillets. Although roughy have been overfished, they are so well known that we decided to include recipes for them, but we also suggest more plentiful and delicious substitutes for this slowly replenishing fish.

MAKES 4 SERVINGS

Four 6- to 8-ounce orange
    roughy fillets
2 tablespoons olive oil
Sea salt and freshly ground
    black pepper to taste
8 to 12 thin wedges ripe
    cantaloupe, seeded and
    peeled
2 limes, halved
2 tablespoons chopped fresh
    mint leaves
1/2 teaspoon red pepper
    flakes
1 cup fresh blueberries,
    picked over for stems, or
    strawberries, hulled
    (optional)

1. Lightly oil the fish fillets and sprinkle with salt and pepper.

2. Prepare a hot fire.

3. When ready to grill, set an oiled perforated grill rack over the fire. Place the fish on the rack and grill until the fish is opaque and just beginning to flake when tested with a fork, 4 to 5 minutes per side, turning once.

4. Arrange the fillets on 4 serving plates. Fan 2 to 3 wedges of melon on each plate. Squeeze the juice of half a lime over the fish and melon. Sprinkle with the mint leaves, red pepper flakes, and blueberries or strawberries, if you are using them.

Also good with: catfish, hoki, oreo dory, or tilapia

GRILLED POMPANO WITH LIME AND OLIVE OIL

The Florida pompano is a culinary delicacy, with white, meaty flesh. Pompano is part of the jack family, which also includes amberjack and yellowtail. They are oily fish and similar to mackerel. Substitute any of them in this simple recipe.

MAKES 4 SERVINGS

Four 8-ounce pompano
fillets
1 tablespoon extra virgin
olive oil
Sea salt and freshly ground
black pepper to taste
2 limes, halved
2 tablespoons chopped fresh
Italian parsley leaves or
Persillade (page 282)

1. Rub the fillets with the olive oil and season with salt and pepper.
2. Prepare a hot fire.
3. When ready to grill, set an oiled perforated grill rack over the fire. Place the fillets on the rack and grill until the fish is opaque and just beginning to flake when tested with a fork, about 5 minutes per side.
4. Remove the fillets from the grill, squeeze 1/2 lime over each, sprinkle with the chopped parsley, and serve.

Also good with: amberjack, kingfish, permit, or yellowtail

SABLEFISH WITH SPICE ISLANDS RUB AND KERALA-STYLE YOGURT SAUCE

When Judith lived in London, where many Indian restaurants offer their regional cuisines, she and her family came to love the food of southern India, especially of Kerala on the southwest coast. This recipe is a version of fried fish originally calling for trout-size pomfret from the Malabar Coast, adapted for the grill and for the fish available here. Apart from feeling very exotic when we make this for our cooking classes, what we love about this dish is the unbeatable combination of high flavor and low fat.

MAKES 4 TO 6 SERVINGS

2 pounds sablefish (black cod) fillets, with skin on

SPICE ISLANDS RUB:

2 tablespoons finely grated onion
1 teaspoon minced garlic
1 teaspoon salt
1 tablespoon ground coriander
3/4 teaspoon cayenne pepper
1/2 teaspoon freshly ground black pepper

2 tablespoons vegetable oil
1 cup wood chips or 1/3 cup wood pellets

1. Lay the sablefish fillets skin side down in a shallow dish or pan. In a small bowl, combine the Spice Islands Rub ingredients with the vegetable oil to make a paste. Spread the paste over the top of the fish fillets, cover, and refrigerate for 1 hour.
2. Place the wood chips in water to soak or wood pellets in a heavy-duty aluminum foil packet with holes poked into it.
3. Prepare a hot fire.
4. Meanwhile, place the yogurt sauce ingredients in a food processor or blender and process until smooth.

(recipe continues next page)

KERALA-STYLE YOGURT SAUCE:

2 cups loosely packed fresh cilantro leaves

1 cup loosely packed fresh mint or lemon balm leaves

1 cup chopped onions

2 cloves garlic, minced

1 teaspoon peeled and grated fresh ginger

1 teaspoon ground cumin

2 tablespoons fresh lemon juice

1/2 cup lowfat plain yogurt

Salt to taste

5. When ready to grill, place the drained wood chips or foil packet on the fire. Place the fish, paste-covered side up, on an oiled perforated grill rack. Place the rack over the fire and grill until the fish is opaque and just beginning to flake when tested with a fork, 8 to 10 minutes. Do not turn.

6. Serve with the yogurt sauce on the side.

Also good with: cod, halibut, pomfret, or red snapper

Suggested wood smoke: oak or pecan

ASIAN-STYLE SALMON STEAKS

Asian-style marinades are a flavorful choice for almost all kinds of fish, especially salmon.

MAKES 4 SERVINGS

ASIAN MARINADE:

1/2 cup soy sauce

1/2 cup rice vinegar

2 to 3 cloves garlic, to your taste, minced

2 tablespoons honey

1 teaspoon ground ginger

2 teaspoons sesame seeds, toasted (page 372)

1/2 teaspoon lemon pepper

Six 6- to 8-ounce salmon steaks 1 inch thick

Asian Noodles (page 79)

1. In a small bowl, combine the marinade ingredients. Place the salmon in a large resealable plastic bag. Pour the marinade into the bag, seal, shake to coat everything, and marinate for up to 1 hour in the refrigerator.

2. Prepare a hot fire.

3. When ready to grill, remove the salmon from the marinade and grill directly on the grill grate until a milky juice appears on top of the thickest part of the salmon, about 5 minutes per side.

4. Plate the noodles and serve the salmon on top.

Also good with: catfish, monkfish, shrimp, swordfish, or tilapia

GRILLED SALMON STEAKS WITH MUSTARD-DILL SAUCE

With Blackened Green Beans (page 346) and boiled new potatoes, you have a great farm-fresh meal.

MAKES 4 SERVINGS

Four 6- to 8-ounce salmon steaks
1 tablespoon olive oil
4 teaspoons lemon pepper
Mustard-Dill Sauce (page 323)

1. Lightly brush the steaks with the olive oil and season with the lemon pepper.
2. Prepare a hot fire.
3. Grill the steaks on the grill grate until a milky juice appears on top of the thickest part of the salmon, about 5 minutes per side.
4. Serve with the sauce on top or on the side.

Also good with: drum, mahimahi, marlin, shark, or tilapia

GRILLED HERBED SALMON

Serve this with Warm Red Lentils (page 348). The beautiful rose-gold colors in the salmon and its side dish are lovely to serve with a green vegetable or salad.

MAKES 4 SERVINGS

PEPPER-HERB MARINADE:

3 tablespoons olive oil

1 tablespoon chopped fresh thyme leaves

1 tablespoon chopped fresh marjoram leaves

1/4 teaspoon red pepper flakes

1/4 cup dry white wine

1 tablespoon fresh lemon juice

2 tablespoons chopped fresh Italian parsley leaves

Sea salt and freshly ground black pepper to taste

Four 6- to 8-ounce salmon fillets, with skin on

1. In a small bowl, combine the marinade ingredients. Place the salmon in a resealable plastic bag, add the marinade, seal, shake to coat everything, and marinate in the refrigerator for 30 minutes.

2. Prepare a hot fire.

3. When ready to grill, remove the salmon from the marinade and set on a plate. Pour the marinade into a small saucepan, bring to a boil, and let boil for 5 minutes. Place the salmon flesh side down on the grill rack and grill, basting with the cooked marinade, until a white milky juice appears on top of the thickest part of the salmon and it just begins to flake with a fork, about 5 to 6 minutes per side. Turn the salmon once during grilling.

Also good with: catfish, halibut, sea trout, or trout

STIR-GRILLED SALMON WITH SUGAR SNAP PEAS

This is our favorite grill-wok recipe, and we have made it countless times. It combines texture, color, and taste at its best! Variations abound. For a spicier version, add red pepper flakes. If you like bell peppers, add yellow, red, and green. Want some crunch? Add water chestnuts, celery, or jicama. Whatever you add, just think colorful.

MAKES 4 SERVINGS

*Soy-Ginger Marinade
   (page 289)
1 pound salmon steak or
   fillets, cubed
1/2 pound sugar snap peas
   or snow peas, strings
   removed
12 cherry tomatoes
1/2 red onion, cut into small
   wedges
3 cups cooked basmati rice*

1. Place the marinade in a resealable plastic bag. Add the salmon, snap peas, tomatoes, and onion wedges, seal, shake to coat everything, and marinate for 30 to 45 minutes in the refrigerator.
2. Prepare a hot fire.
3. When ready to grill, set an oiled grill wok on the rack above the fire. Transfer the ingredients to the grill wok using a slotted spoon to drain the excess marinade. Stir-grill until the salmon is opaque, 6 to 8 minutes, using two long-handled wooden spoons to toss the mixture. Move the wok to the indirect-heat side of the grill. Close the lid on the grill and cook for another 4 to 5 minutes.
4. Serve ladled over the rice.

Also good with: catfish, John Dory, monkfish, or shrimp

BARBECUED SALMON WRAPPED IN FOIL

Using aluminum foil on the grill makes for very easy cleanup. There are foil packet products that are handy, too. This would also be a great way to cook on the grill for an outdoor picnic in a park.

MAKES 4 SERVINGS

Four 8-ounce skinless
   salmon fillets
1 cup finely chopped carrots
1 cup seeded and finely
   chopped red bell peppers
1 cup finely chopped mushrooms
1 cup fresh corn kernels, cut
   off the cob
1 teaspoon chopped fresh
   rosemary leaves
1/4 cup dry white wine
Sea salt and freshly ground
   black pepper to taste

1. Prepare a hot fire.

2. When ready to grill, oil 4 pieces of aluminum foil or a foil pouch and place 1 salmon fillet on each. Distribute the chopped vegetables evenly over the fillets, splash each with 1 tablespoon of the wine, and sprinkle 1/4 teaspoon of the rosemary across the tops. Tightly wrap each fillet in foil. Grill the foil packets for about 15 minutes (do not turn).

3. Place a packet on each of 4 dinner plates and serve with sea salt and pepper for seasoning. Diners should be cautioned to open their packets carefully, as there will be a burst of hot steam.

Also good with: freshwater bass, butterfish, cod, or pink or red snapper

SALMON WITH TUNISIAN SPICED VEGETABLES

This succulent fish and medium-heat vegetable dish is delicious with saffron rice or rice pilaf. The citrus wedges help to cool the heat of the vegetables for those with a milder palate. For a variation, the vegetables can be grilled separately in a grill wok for more direct heat and charred flavor.

MAKES 8 SERVINGS

TUNISIAN SPICED VEGETABLES:

1/2 cup fresh lemon juice

2 large, ripe tomatoes, diced

1 large white onion, diced

1 green bell pepper, seeded
 and diced

1 red bell pepper, seeded
 and diced

2 poblano chiles, seeded
 and diced

3 cloves garlic, minced

1 tablespoon cumin seeds

1 tablespoon extra virgin
 olive oil

1/2 teaspoon sea salt

1/2 teaspoon freshly ground
 black pepper

Olive oil for spraying

Eight 6-ounce salmon fillets

2 lemons, cut into 8
 wedges, for garnish

2 oranges, cut into 8
 wedges, for garnish

1 cup fresh Italian parsley
 leaves, chopped, for
 garnish

1. Prepare a hot fire.

2. Meanwhile, in a large bowl, combine all of the Tunisian vegetable ingredients.

3. When ready to grill, cut eight 8 x 10-inch pieces of aluminum foil, spray with olive oil, and place a salmon fillet on each. Top the salmon fillets evenly with the spiced vegetables. Wrap the foil tightly around the fish and vegetables. Grill the foil packets for 10 minutes (do not turn).

4. Place a packet on each plate, garnish with lemon and orange wedges, and sprinkle with the parsley. Caution your guests to take care opening the packets, as there will be a burst of hot steam.

Also good with: orange roughy, tilefish, turbot, or walleye

HERB-ENCRUSTED SALMON WITH SUN-DRIED TOMATO VINAIGRETTE

An herb-and-mustard crumb crust keeps the salmon moist and flavorful while it is grilled. The Sun-Dried Tomato Vinaigrette adds a final sunny taste of summer to the finished dish.

MAKES 6 SERVINGS

SUN-DRIED TOMATO VINAIGRETTE:

2 cloves garlic, peeled

1/2 teaspoon sea salt

2 tablespoons chopped oil-packed sun-dried tomatoes

1 tablespoon fresh lemon juice

3 tablespoons extra virgin olive oil

Freshly ground black pepper to taste

2 tablespoons Dijon mustard

1 tablespoon finely chopped fresh tarragon leaves

1 tablespoon finely chopped fresh thyme leaves

1 tablespoon finely chopped fresh basil leaves

2 pounds salmon fillets

2 cups dry bread crumbs

1. To make the vinaigrette, finely crush the garlic and salt together in a mortar with a pestle until the garlic makes a paste. Blend in the tomatoes, lemon juice, and olive oil until smooth. Taste for seasoning and set aside.

2. In a small bowl, combine the mustard and herbs. Coat the salmon with the mustard-herb mixture, then dredge in the bread crumbs to coat evenly. Cover and refrigerate for 30 minutes.

3. Prepare a hot fire.

4. When ready to grill, place the fish on an oiled perforated grill rack over the fire. Grill until the salmon flakes with a fork but is still moist inside, 12 to 15 minutes, turning once about halfway through the grilling.

5. Serve drizzled with the vinaigrette.

Also good with: catfish, char, moonfish, sturgeon, or swordfish

PACIFIC RIM SALMON

Salmon from the northeastern rim of the Pacific (Alaska and Washington) meets up with a marinade from the western rim of the Pacific (China, Japan, and Hong Kong). Grilled fish cooks about 10 minutes per inch of thickness, so measure your fillet at the thickest part before grilling and adapt your timing accordingly. You could also use halibut in place of the salmon.

MAKES 4 SERVINGS

HOISIN-SOY MARINADE:

1/2 cup soy sauce

1/2 cup rice vinegar

2 to 3 cloves garlic, to your taste, minced

2 tablespoons firmly packed brown sugar

2 tablespoons hoisin sauce

1 teaspoon ground ginger

2 teaspoons sesame seeds, toasted (page 372)

1/2 teaspoon lemon pepper

1 salmon fillet (about 2 1/2 pounds), with skin on

2 teaspoons black sesame seeds, toasted (page 372), for garnish

1. Combine the marinade ingredients and pour over the salmon in a shallow glass dish. Cover and let marinate for 1 hour in the refrigerator.

2. Prepare a hot fire.

3. Grill the salmon, flesh side down first, directly on the grill grate, for about 5 minutes. Using both a wide metal fish spatula and a grill spatula, carefully turn the fillet over onto the skin side and grill for another 5 minutes, until a milky juice appears on top of the thickest part of the fillet.

4. Serve immediately, sprinkled with the black sesame seeds.

Also good with: halibut, shrimp, or snapper

SALMON CHARMOULA

Charmoula, a traditional Moroccan herb and spice mixture, lends a delicious flavor to grilled fish, as well as chicken.

One 3- to 3 1/2-pound
    salmon fillet, with skin
    on, or 6 salmon steaks

CHARMOULA:

1 large clove garlic, peeled
2 tablespoons chopped fresh
    Italian parsley leaves
2 tablespoons chopped fresh
    cilantro leaves
1 teaspoon salt
1 tablespoon ground cumin
1 tablespoon paprika
1/2 teaspoon cayenne
    pepper
1/4 cup fresh lemon juice,
    plus more for the sauce
1/4 cup olive oil

Sprigs fresh Italian parsley
    and cilantro for garnish

1. Arrange the salmon in a large shallow dish. To make the charmoula, combine the garlic, parsley, cilantro, salt, cumin, paprika, and cayenne in a food processor and process until smooth or simply chop everything together finely by hand. Add the lemon juice and olive oil and process or mix into a smooth paste. Spread half the charmoula mixture over the flesh of the fish, cover, and refrigerate for at least 1 hour and up to 12 hours. Cover and refrigerate the remaining charmoula mixture until ready to serve.
2. Prepare a hot fire.
3. Grill the fillet skin side down directly on the grill grate until a milky, opaque juice appears on top of the thickest part of the fillet and it just begins to flake when tested with a fork, about 10 minutes per inch of thickness at the thickest part of the fillet. Do not turn.
4. To serve, whisk the remaining charmoula mixture with lemon juice to taste. Pass the sauce at the table.

Also good with: halibut, mahimahi, monkfish, orange roughy, or walleye

GRILLED SALMON IN CORN HUSKS

Salmon can be cooked in many ways, but here's a novel technique that you may never have heard of: salmon baked in corn husks. It's a bit time-consuming, but your efforts will be well rewarded. Make the job a little easier by doing the prep work in the morning before guests arrive.

MAKES 4 SERVINGS

4 ears of corn, with husks on
Four 6-ounce skinless
*   salmon fillets*
4 green onions, chopped
1/4 cup seeded and chopped
*   red bell pepper*
4 teaspoons capers, drained
1/4 cup (1/2 stick) unsalted
*   butter, cut into tablespoons*
4 sprigs fresh thyme
Sea salt and freshly ground
*   black pepper to taste*

1. Peel back the corn husk and remove the silk on all 4 ears of corn. Break off the corn cob at the base, leaving the husk attached. With a sharp knife, slice the kernels off the cobs of 2 of the ears. Put aside the other 2 ears for another use.

2. Prepare a hot fire.

3. Fold back a few of the leaves of each corn husk and place a salmon fillet in each. Top each fillet with one quarter of the corn kernels, green onions, bell pepper, capers, and butter and top with a sprig of thyme. Season with salt and pepper to taste. Tie the husk together with strips of the corn husk or kitchen twine. (This can be done earlier in the day and kept refrigerated until ready to grill.)

4. When ready to grill, place the salmon in corn husks on the grill directly over the fire and grill for 5 minutes. Then move to the indirect side of the grill and continue to cook for another 6 to 7 minutes with the grill lid closed.

5. Serve the corn husk packets by folding back the top of the corn husk to display the salmon inside.

Also good with: catfish, cod, haddock, or halibut

GRAPE LEAF–WRAPPED SARDINES

Sardines are extremely perishable and are mainly found in coastal markets. Grilling them wrapped in grape leaves is an easy way to keep them moist; this technique has great eye appeal, too.

MAKES 4 SERVINGS

*2 pounds very fresh
   sardines*
*24 large grape leaves, or
   more, depending on size
   of fish*
*1 bunch water-soaked dried
   grape vines*
*1 cup Citrus Herb Garnish
   (page 283)*

1. Wrap each sardine in 1 or 2 grape leaves.
2. Prepare a hot fire.
3. When ready to grill, add the grape vines to the fire. Place the grape leaf–wrapped sardines on the grill and grill for about 4 minutes per side, turning them once.
4. Remove the sardines from the grill. Peel off the grape leaves, which will remove the skin at the same time. Sprinkle with the garnish and serve.

Also good with: anchovies, smelts, or trout

BALSAMIC GRILLED SHARK

Contrary to the rule of grilling fish 10 minutes per inch of thickness, shark needs only 7 to 8 inches per inch of thickness. Overcooking makes shark tough.

MAKES 4 SERVINGS

BALSAMIC MARINADE:

1/2 cup extra virgin olive oil
1/4 cup balsamic vinegar
1 1/2 tablespoons sugar
1 tablespoon Worcestershire
* sauce*
2 medium-size green
* onions, minced*
1 teaspoon dry mustard
1 clove garlic, minced
Tabasco sauce to taste
Sea salt and freshly ground
* black pepper to taste*

Four 6- to 8-ounce shark
* steaks*

1. Combine the marinade ingredients and pour into a resealable plastic bag. Add the shark steaks, seal, and shake to coat them. Refrigerate for about 1 hour.

2. Prepare a hot fire.

3. When ready to grill, remove the shark to a plate. In a small saucepan, boil the marinade for about 5 minutes to use for basting. Grill the steaks until opaque, about 4 minutes per side, turning once and basting occasionally with the marinade. Do not overcook.

Also good with: monkfish or swordfish

MAKO SHARK WITH CILANTRO-LIME BUTTER

This is a delicious way to "grill" fish, keeping it moist and flavorful.

1 tablespoon unsalted
   butter
Six 8-ounce mako shark
   steaks
2 large, ripe tomatoes,
   chopped
1 bunch green onions,
   chopped
3 tablespoons Cilantro-
   Lime Butter (page 298)

1. Prepare a hot fire.

2. Meanwhile, grease 6 sheets of aluminum foil with the butter and top each with a shark steak, one sixth of the chopped tomatoes and green onions, and a pat of the butter. Fold and seal the foil into a packet and poke several holes in the top. (Or butter a disposable aluminum pan or fish boat and place the vegetables in the pan and place the steaks on top. Cover with aluminum foil and poke several holes in the foil.)

3. When ready to grill, place the foil packets or aluminum pan over the fire and cook for 8 to 10 minutes (do not turn).

4. Place a packet on each serving plate. Caution your guests to be careful when opening the packet, as there will be a burst of hot steam.

Also good with: monkfish, swordfish, or tuna

SKATE WITH BROWN BUTTER

Skate is delicious and this is the classic way to serve it. It has a tendency to get sticky, so make sure that the grill grates are well oiled before you start the fire. Accompany the skate with fluffy rice.

MAKES 4 SERVINGS

Four 8-ounce skate wings,
   cleaned and skinned
1/4 cup olive oil
Sea salt and freshly ground
   black pepper
2 tablespoons capers in
   vinegar, drained and
   chopped if large
2 tablespoons chopped fresh
   Italian parsley leaves
2/3 cup unsalted butter

1. Place the skate wings on a large platter and coat with the olive oil.

2. Prepare a hot fire.

3. Grill the skate wings until they just begin to flake when tested with a fork, 4 to 5 minutes on each side.

4. Transfer the skate to a warmed serving dish, season with salt and pepper, and sprinkle on the capers and parsley. Keep hot.

5. In a small saucepan, heat the butter over medium heat until it foams and turns a rich nutty brown. Drizzle it over the skate and serve immediately.

Also good with: catfish, flounder, hake, halibut, John Dory, or sole

RED SNAPPER YUCATÁN-STYLE

This classic Yucatán dish is traditionally served beach side with fresh-caught fish wrapped in banana leaves and cooked over a driftwood fire. Since we don't live by a beach, our style includes preparing it while sipping on margaritas or Cuba libres and accompanying it with Avocado Relish (page 319).

MAKES 6 TO 8 SERVINGS

1/2 cup fresh orange juice
1/4 cup fresh lime juice
1/2 teaspoon sea salt
1/2 teaspoon cracked black
* peppercorns*
1/4 cup olive oil
Six to eight 4- to 6-ounce
* red snapper fillets*

OLIVE AND RED PEPPER SAUCE:

1/4 cup olive oil
1/2 cup diced white onion
2/3 cup quartered pimiento-
* stuffed olives*
1/4 cup red bell pepper strips
2 tablespoons chopped fresh
* cilantro leaves*
2 teaspoons minced garlic
1/2 cup fresh lime juice
2 1/2 tablespoons Sauce
* Rémoulade (page 308)*
2 tablespoons red vermouth
Salt and freshly ground
* black pepper to taste*

2 limes, cut into wedges

1. In a small bowl, blend the juices, salt, pepper, and olive oil.

2. Place red snapper fillets in a resealable plastic bag and add the marinade. Seal and shake to coat. Let marinate in the refrigerator for 2 to 4 hours.

3. Prepare a hot fire.

4. Meanwhile, make the pepper sauce. Heat the olive oil in a medium-size skillet, add the onion and cook over medium heat, stirring, until translucent, about 5 minutes. Add the olives, red pepper, cilantro, and garlic and simmer until tender, about 5 minutes. Add the lime juice, rémoulade, and vermouth. Season with salt and pepper. Simmer, uncovered, until most of the liquid has evaporated, about 10 minutes. (Note: Sauce may be prepared up to 3 days in advance and stored in the refrigerator. Bring it back to room temperature before using.)

5. When ready to grill, remove the fish from the marinade and grill until opaque and just beginning to flake when tested with a fork, about 4 minutes on each side.

6. Serve with the pepper sauce spooned on top and with a wedge of lime on the side.

Also good with: striped bass, catfish, porgy, or other snappers

THAI-STYLE STIR-GRILLED SNAPPER IN LEMONGRASS MARINADE

For this recipe, choose firm-fleshed warm-water fish. Serve this with Texas pecan or the more fragrant jasmine rice.

1 pound red snapper fillets, cut into 1-inch pieces

1/2 cup green onions cut into 1-inch lengths on the bias

1 cup chopped Napa cabbage

LEMONGRASS MARINADE:

1 tablespoon thinly sliced fresh lemongrass (peel tough outer leaves away and slice tender core; available at Asian markets)

1 garlic clove, minced

1 tablespoon peeled and grated fresh ginger

1 teaspoon fish sauce (available at Asian markets)

1 teaspoon rice vinegar

2 teaspoons cornstarch

1. Place the snapper, green onions, and cabbage in a resealable plastic bag. In a medium-size bowl, mix together the marinade ingredients and pour over the snapper mixture. Seal, then shake to coat the fish and vegetables with the marinade. Let marinate in the refrigerator for 30 minutes.

2. Prepare a hot fire.

3. When ready to grill, coat the inside of a grill wok with nonstick cooking spray. Transfer the marinated fish and vegetables into the wok, using a slotted spoon to drain the excess marinade. Place the wok

1 tablespoon peanut or
  other vegetable oil
½ cup chicken or vegetable
  broth
1 teaspoon soy sauce
1 teaspoon toasted sesame
  oil
Salt and freshly ground
  white pepper

Sesame seeds, toasted (page
  372), for garnish

on the grill. Using two long-handled wooden spoons
or grill spatulas, turn and toss the fish and vegetables
until the fish is opaque and the vegetables have lightly
browned, about 15 minutes.

4. Serve over rice, garnished with toasted sesame
seeds.

Also good with: cobia, mullet, porgy, or redfish

WHOLE SNAPPER WITH TARRAGON BUTTER AND WILTED SPINACH

There are more than 250 species of snapper in the world. They include red snapper, pink snapper (also known as opakapaka in Hawaii), mutton snapper, vermilion snapper, silk snapper with its yellow tail, not to be confused with yellowtail snapper, not to be confused with Pacific yellowtail, which is an entirely different species altogether. (Are you confused yet?) Snappers have been endangered for quite some time, so if you'd like to be "green," substitute another fish.

MAKES 4 SERVINGS

1 cup wood chips or 1/3 cup wood pellets
Two 20- to 24-ounce whole red snapper, dressed
2 leafy sprigs fresh dill
1/4 cup extra virgin olive oil
Tarragon Butter (page 298)
Wilted Spinach (page 107)

1. Place the wood chips in water to soak or wood pellets in a heavy-duty aluminum foil packet with holes poked into it.

2. Prepare a medium-hot fire.

3. Meanwhile, place a frond of dill in the cavity of each fish. Cut 2 diagonal slashes in the side of each fish. (This keeps the whole fish from curling.) Brush the fish with the olive oil.

4. When ready to grill, place the drained wood chips or foil packet on the fire. Place the fish directly above the fire. Grill until opaque and just beginning to flake when tested with a fork, turning once or twice, for a total grilling time of 20 to 25 minutes.

5. Fillet the fish and serve 1 fillet per person topped with a pat of the tarragon butter and wilted spinach alongside.

Also good with: sea bass, John Dory, mullet, or trout

Suggested wood smoke: oak or pecan

WILTED SPINACH

Simply sublime!

MAKES 4 SERVINGS

1/4 cup Tarragon Butter
(page 298), plus more
for serving

1 1/2 pounds spinach,
washed well and heavy
stems removed

1. In a large skillet over medium heat, melt the tarragon butter.

2. Add the spinach and cook until wilted, 5 to 7 minutes. Serve warm with a drizzle more of the butter.

DON'T BE A NEANDERTHAL—EAT FISH!

Did eating fish give Cro Magnons a crucial edge over Neanderthals, who became extinct? New research suggests just that.

Erik Trinkhaus of Washington University in St. Louis, along with other colleagues, analyzed 20,000 to 28,000 year-old human bones found in Britain, Russia, and the Czech Republic. The analysis revealed that these bones were from people who had diets rich in fish and seafood. Neanderthal bones from the same areas, which had been previously analyzed, show their diet consisted mainly of red meat.

"The apparently broader dietary spectrum of the early human economy may have rendered humans more resilient to natural pressures and the increasingly packed social environments of Late Pleistocene Europe," Trinkhaus and fellow researchers concluded in a study that appeared in "Proceedings of the National Academy of Sciences."

SNAPPER STIR-GRILL

We both caught on to the grill wok in the late 1980s. It's one of our favorite grill gadgets and we've taught thousands of people how to use it. Always coat the wok with nonstick spray inside and out before putting it on the grill. Use a medley of colors for this recipe. Serve over rice or pasta for an easy one-dish meal.

MAKES 4 SERVINGS

1 pound red snapper fillets

2 cups sliced mushrooms

1 green bell pepper, seeded and cut into 1/4-inch-wide strips

1 red bell pepper, seeded and cut into 1/4-inch-wide strips

1 small onion, cut into 1/4-inch-wide strips

CURRY MARINADE:

1 tablespoon curry powder

1/2 teaspoon ground coriander

1/4 teaspoon ground cumin

1 clove garlic, minced

1 tablespoon olive oil

1 tablespoon toasted sesame oil

Juice of 1 lemon

Crusty bread

1/2 cup Herb Butter (page 297)

1. Cut the fish fillets into 1-inch cubes or strips. Place the fish and vegetables in a large bowl.

2. In a small bowl, combine the marinade ingredients, pour over the fish and vegetables, cover, and refrigerate for 30 minutes.

3. Prepare a hot fire.

4. When ready to grill, set an oiled grill wok on the rack above the fire. Transfer the ingredients to the grill wok using a slotted spoon to drain the excess marinade. Stir-grill for 6 to 8 minutes, using two long-handled wooden spoons for tossing. Close the lid on the grill and cook for 4 to 5 minutes more.

5. Serve hot with crusty bread spread with Herb Butter.

Also good with: sea bass, catfish, dory, halibut, or shrimp.

PACIFIC SNAPPER WITH CHERVIL BUTTER

Here we go again with more confusing fish facts. It's likely that the Pacific snapper you buy is really rockfish or Pacific rockfish. This unusual fish species, according to the National Audubon Society, comes in all sizes and shapes. Some swim in schools, while others are loners. Some live in the depths of the ocean, while others live close to shore. Some lay eggs, while others reproduce live young. It's thought that much of the species is endangered, but the Pacific snapper is the most abundant.

MAKES 4 SERVINGS

Four 6- to 8-ounce Pacific snapper fillets
Juice of 1 lemon
Sea salt and freshly ground black pepper to taste
¼ cup olive oil
Chervil Butter (page 298)
Sprigs fresh chervil for garnish
Thin lemon slices for garnish

1. Prepare a hot fire.

2. Meanwhile, sprinkle the lemon juice over each fillet, then season with salt and pepper. Let sit for 10 to 15 minutes.

3. Grill the fish fillets until opaque and just beginning to flake when tested with a fork, about 4 minutes per side, turning once and basting with the olive oil.

4. Serve each fillet with a pat of the chervil butter and garnished with a sprig of chervil atop a lemon slice.

Also good with: catfish, John Dory, or tilapia

BASIL-MARINATED STURGEON AND GRILLED PORTOBELLO SALAD

Prehistoric-looking sturgeon has a sharklike body equipped with bony plates called scutes. This tough customer swims the bottoms of lakes and rivers across the upper United States—from the Pacific Northwest (white sturgeon) to the Midwest (green sturgeon) to the East Coast (Atlantic sturgeon). Yet it has still been a victim of overfishing because of its prized roe, which is processed into caviar.

Today, white sturgeon is farmed in California and is justly popular for grilling and smoking, with a taste and texture similar to that of turkey. Because its meaty texture can turn dry if cooked over high heat, we recommend marinating sturgeon first, searing it over hot coals, then finishing it over an indirect fire. The mushrooms will grill over direct heat.

MAKES 4 SERVINGS

BASIL MARINADE:

1 cup olive oil

8 cloves garlic, minced

1/2 cup fresh basil leaves, chopped

2 teaspoons salt

2 teaspoons freshly ground black pepper

1/2 cup balsamic vinegar

1. In a medium-size bowl, mix together the marinade ingredients. Lay the sturgeon fillets in a shallow dish and drizzle with 1/2 cup of the marinade; reserve the remaining marinade. Cover and let marinate in the refrigerator for 1 hour.

2. Place the wood chips in water to soak or wood pellets in a heavy-duty aluminum foil packet with holes poked into it.

3. Prepare an indirect fire.

4. When ready to grill, place the drained wood chips or foil packet on the fire. Remove the sturgeon from the marinade and sear over direct heat for 1 minute on each side. Transfer to indirect heat and cook until the fish is opaque and just beginning to flake when tested with a fork, 10 to 15 minutes, turning once halfway through the grilling time.

1 1/2 pounds sturgeon fillets
1 cup wood chips or 1/3 cup
wood pellets
1 1/2 pounds portobello
mushroom caps
4 cups mixed salad greens
Fresh basil leaves for
garnish

5. While the sturgeon is grilling, place the portobellos on a plate. Drizzle them with 1/2 cup of the reserved marinade and grill over direct heat until they soften and brown, 8 to 10 minutes, turning 3 or 4 times. Slice the mushrooms and keep warm.

6. To serve, place a cup of salad greens on each plate and top with a sturgeon fillet and the sliced mushrooms. Drizzle each salad with some of the remaining marinade and garnish with fresh basil leaves.

Also good with: catfish, shark, spearfish, or tilapia

Suggested wood smoke: alder, hickory, mesquite, or oak

SWORDFISH STEAKS WITH PINEAPPLE SALSA

This giant of a fish grows to be 16 feet long! Readily available all year long, its mild-flavored, dense flesh is perfect for the grill.

MAKES 6 SERVINGS

PINEAPPLE SALSA:

1 fresh, ripe pineapple, cored, peeled, and quartered

1/2 cup seeded and diced red bell pepper

1/2 cup seeded and diced green bell pepper

1/4 cup finely chopped red onion

2 tablespoons olive oil

2 tablespoons finely chopped fresh cilantro leaves

1 tablespoon fresh lime juice

1 tablespoon snipped fresh chives

1 tablespoon finely chopped fresh Italian parsley leaves

2 teaspoons seeded and minced serrano chile

1/2 teaspoon sea salt

1/2 teaspoon freshly ground black pepper

Six 7- to 8-ounce swordfish steaks

3 lemons, quartered

Sea salt and freshly ground white pepper to taste

3 tablespoons olive oil

1. To prepare the salsa, arrange the pineapple on a baking sheet and place under a preheated broiler until it just begins to brown, about 5 minutes per side. Cut into 1/4-inch cubes and place in a large glass bowl. Add the rest of the ingredients and toss to blend. Cover and refrigerate for 2 hours.

2. Prepare a hot fire.

3. Meanwhile, lay the steaks in a glass casserole and squeeze 1 lemon wedge over each. Lightly season each steak with salt and white pepper, then drizzle them with the olive oil.

4. Grill the swordfish until opaque, about 4 minutes per side. Do not overcook; swordfish dries out quickly.

5. To serve, place each steak on a bed of the salsa and garnish with the remaining lemon wedges.

Also good with: marlin, salmon, shark, tilapia, or wahoo

STIR-GRILLED SWORDFISH

Swordfish holds together well in stir-grilling. This medley of fish and vegetables can be served as is or try serving it on a bed of cooked soba noodles or basmati rice.

Four 6-ounce swordfish
    steaks
1/2 pound shiitake
    mushrooms, stems
    removed
1/4 pound snow peas,
    strings removed
1 red bell pepper, seeded
    and cut into 1/4-inch-
    wide strips
One 14-ounce can
    artichoke hearts, drained
1/2 cup soy sauce
1/2 cup dry sherry
1 tablespoon fresh lemon
    juice
1/4 cup vegetable oil
2 cloves garlic, minced

1. Remove the skin and cut the steaks into 1-inch cubes. Place the cubes and vegetables in a large bowl.

2. In a small bowl, combine the remaining ingredients. Pour over the fish and vegetables. Toss to coat everything, cover with plastic wrap, and refrigerate for about 1 hour to marinate.

3. Prepare a hot fire.

4. When ready to grill, set an oiled grill wok on the rack above the fire. Transfer the fish and vegetables to the grill wok using a slotted spoon to drain the excess marinade. Stir-grill until the fish is opaque, 12 to 15 minutes, using two long-handled wooden spoons to toss the mixture. Close the cover of the grill to heat through for the last 5 minutes of cooking. Serve immediately.

Also good with: monkfish, sea scallops, shrimp, or sturgeon

SWORDFISH KABOBS

Swordfish meat is so firm that it cuts into perfect square pieces for skewering. For this recipe, grill whole steaks if you'd rather. Either way, it's a homey meal that's perfect for friends and family.

MAKES 6 TO 8 SERVINGS

TERIYAKI BARBECUE SAUCE:

1 cup water
1 cup prepared chili sauce
1/2 cup vegetable oil
1/4 cup fresh lemon juice
1/4 cup teriyaki sauce
1/4 cup steak sauce
2 tablespoons cider vinegar
1/4 cup chopped onion
1/4 cup seeded and minced
    green bell pepper
1 jalapeño, seeded and
    minced
2 cloves garlic, chopped
2 teaspoons sugar
2 teaspoons paprika
1 teaspoon salt
1 teaspoon dry mustard
1 teaspoon ground ginger
1/2 teaspoon cayenne
    pepper, or to taste

3 pounds swordfish steaks

1. In a large saucepan, combine all of the sauce ingredients and bring to a boil. Reduce the heat to low and simmer for 1 hour. Let cool. (Extra sauce will keep in refrigerator for up to 2 weeks.)

2. Prepare a hot fire.

3. Meanwhile, cube the fish and thread onto metal skewers. Grill until opaque, 8 to 10 minutes, basting with the sauce and turning the skewers often.

4. Serve with additional sauce on the side.

Also good with: mahimahi, salmon, or yellowtail

SWORDFISH WITH TARRAGON BEURRE BLANC, TOMATOES, AND BLACK OLIVES

If you like, serve this grilled swordfish with fettuccine tossed with olive oil, a little lemon juice, and Italian parsley so you can mop up the sauce with the pasta. Swordfish can dry out quickly if overcooked; that's why we suggest a thick 1-inch cut.

MAKES 4 SERVINGS

1 cup wood chips or 1/3 cup wood pellets

Four 1-inch-thick sword-fish steaks

Olive oil

Salt and freshly ground black pepper to taste

Tarragon Beurre Blanc (page 303)

1 large, ripe tomato, peeled, seeded, and chopped

2 tablespoons capers, drained

1 cup Kalamata or niçoise olives, drained and pitted

Sprigs fresh tarragon for garnish

1. Place the wood chips in water to soak or wood pellets in a heavy-duty aluminum foil packet with holes poked into it.

2. Prepare a hot fire.

3. Meanwhile, brush the swordfish steaks with olive oil, and season with salt and pepper.

4. When ready to grill, place the drained wood chips or foil packet on the fire. Grill until the fish is opaque and just beginning to flake when tested with a fork, about 5 minutes per side.

5. To serve, spoon the beurre blanc over the swordfish and scatter the chopped tomato, capers, and olives around the perimeter of the plate. Place a tarragon sprig on the top of each swordfish steak and serve hot.

Also good with: sea bass, halibut, John Dory, or salmon

Suggested wood smoke: apple or oak

ROSEMARY AND GARLIC GRILLED SWORDFISH

Rosemary and garlic flavor this grilled fish, making for an aromatic and savory meal. Pair with the likewise perfumed Fried Potatoes (page 368) and a fresh green salad simply dressed.

MAKES 4 SERVINGS

*Four 1-inch-thick sword-
  fish steaks*

ROSEMARY MARINADE:

*6 tablespoons olive oil
1 teaspoon dried rosemary
1 clove garlic, minced
1/2 teaspoon paprika
Salt and freshly ground
  black pepper to taste*

1. Place the swordfish steaks in a resealable plastic bag. In a small bowl, mix the marinade ingredients together and pour over the swordfish. Secure the bag and turn several times to coat the fish with the marinade. Refrigerate and let marinate for several hours.
2. Prepare a hot fire.
3. When ready to grill, remove the swordfish from the marinade and discard the marinade. Grill until the steaks are firm to the touch, about 5 minutes per side. Serve hot.

Also good with: amberjack, char, halibut, or salmon

VIETNAMESE-STYLE GRILLED TILAPIA

A savory paste gently flavors the fish 30 minutes before grilling. Serve this fragrant fish with steamed rice and cucumbers in a rice wine, red pepper flake, and sesame oil marinade. This is also good served with Spicy Tamarind Dipping Sauce (page 328).

MAKES 4 SERVINGS

2 pounds tilapia fillets, with skin on

FLAVORING PASTE:

3 tablespoons chopped shallots

3 tablespoons chopped garlic

2 tablespoons firmly packed dark brown sugar

2 teaspoons five-spice powder (available at Asian markets)

2 tablespoons mirin or dry sherry

1 tablespoon rice vinegar

2 tablespoons fish sauce (available at Asian markets)

1 teaspoon toasted sesame oil

1/2 teaspoon freshly ground black pepper

1. Lay the tilapia fillets out on a flat surface. In a medium-size bowl, mix together the flavoring paste ingredients. With a rubber spatula or your hands, coat both sides of each fillet with the paste. Cover with plastic wrap and refrigerate for 30 minutes.

2. Prepare a hot fire.

3. When ready to grill, place the tilapia fillets flesh side down on the grill. Grill until the fish is opaque and just beginning to flake when tested with a fork, 4 to 5 minutes per side, turning only once.

Also good with: amberjack, catfish, grouper, or monkfish

THAI GRILLED TILAPIA

We prepared this on a summer night for our cooking class students—to rave reviews. The tender, sweet tilapia and the fragrant Thai paste make a delicious combination. Grill the tilapia on one side only, so that the Thai paste/marinade remains intact.

MAKES 4 SERVINGS

SPICY THAI PASTE:

12 cloves garlic, minced
1/2 cup fresh cilantro leaves
1/4 cup fresh lime juice
1/4 cup vegetable oil
2 tablespoons fish sauce (available at Asian markets)
2 teaspoons ground coriander
2 teaspoons freshly ground white pepper
2 teaspoons sugar
1 teaspoon sea salt

Four 6-ounce tilapia fillets

1. Place the paste ingredients in a food processor or blender and process into a paste. (More lime juice, oil, and fish sauce may be added if you wish to make a marinade.) Spoon the paste over the top of the fillets and let marinate in a glass dish in the refrigerator for about 30 minutes.

2. Prepare a hot fire.

3. When ready to grill, place the tilapia fillets, paste side up, on an oiled perforated grill rack and grill until opaque and just beginning to flake when tested with a fork, 8 to 20 minutes; do not turn the fillets over.

4. Serve the fish hot.

Also good with: sea bass, pompano, red snapper, or rock cod

CHIPOTLE GRILLED TILAPIA

The *Southwestern Grill* (Harvard Common Press, 2000) author Michael McLaughlin is the inspiration for this recipe, especially since it's his Chipotle Vinaigrette recipe, which always receives rave reviews. Serve Jicama Sticks (page 360) for a crisp side dish and whip up a batch of margaritas or serve Mexican beer with lime wedges for a border bash.

MAKES 4 SERVINGS

Four 6- to 8-ounce tilapia fillets
1 cup Chipotle Vinaigrette (page 294)
1 cup wood chips or 1/3 cup wood pellets

1. Place the fillets in a glass dish. Pour 1/2 cup of the vinaigrette over the fish. Reserve 1/4 cup for basting and 1/4 cup for the jicama, if making Jicama Sticks. Cover and let the fish marinate for 30 minutes in the refrigerator.

2. Place the wood chips in water to soak or wood pellets in a heavy-duty aluminum foil packet with holes poked into it.

3. Prepare a hot fire.

4. When ready to grill, place the drained wood chips or foil packet on the fire. Remove the fish from the marinade, discarding the used marinade. Grill the fish until opaque and just beginning to flake when tested with a fork, 4 to 5 minutes per side, turning once and basting with the reserved marinade.

Also good with: catfish, mahimahi, shrimp, or tuna

Suggested wood smoke: mesquite

GRILLED TILAPIA WITH GARLIC-ANCHOVY BUTTER AND BLACK OLIVES

In the French port of Marseilles, seafood is often grilled and served in this simple manner—with a touch of fennel and a flavored butter.

MAKES 4 SERVINGS

Four 6- to 7-ounce tilapia
    fillets
Olive oil
1 teaspoon fennel seeds
    (optional)
Salt and freshly ground
    black pepper to taste
Garlic Anchovy Butter
    (page 300)
1 cup dry-cured niçoise
    olives, pitted and
    chopped

1. Prepare a hot fire.

2. Brush the fish with olive oil and sprinkle with the fennel seeds, if using.

3. Grill until the tilapia is opaque and just beginning to flake when tested with a fork, 3 to 4 minutes per side, turning once. Season with salt and pepper.

4. Place a pat of the garlic butter on each fillet and garnish with the chopped olives.

Also good with: amberjack, cobia, or mackerel

GRILLED TILEFISH SALAD WITH DILLED SOUR CREAM DRESSING

It's nice to grill or smoke extra fish for dinner one night, then serve the cooked fish the next day for a delicious cold summer salad. Tilefish is an excellent choice, with its delectable, sweet flavor and firm texture. It's a relatively "new" fish, first discovered in 1879. You can find it fresh along the upper Atlantic seaboard.

MAKES 4 SERVINGS

Four 6- to 8-ounce tilefish
  fillets
Seasoned pepper blend,
  such as lemon pepper,
  three-pepper, or spicy
  pepper
1 head Boston lettuce
1 head red-leaf lettuce
1 cucumber, peeled, seeded,
  and sliced
1 small red onion, thinly
  sliced into rings
2 lemons, cut into wedges,
  for garnish
Dilled Sour Cream
  Dressing (page 315)

1. Place the fish in a glass dish and sprinkle liberally with seasoned pepper.

2. Prepare a hot fire.

3. Grill the fish until opaque and just beginning to flake when tested with a fork, 4 to 5 minutes per side, turning once. Remove skin if any and set aside. (At this point, the fish may be chilled and served the next day.)

4. Wash the lettuce and arrange the leaves on 4 plates. Place a fish fillet on top of the lettuce. Garnish with cucumber slices, red onion slices, and lemon wedges. Serve with the dressing on the side.

Also good with: catfish, monkfish, salmon, shrimp, or trout

ZESTY LEMON-BASTED TROUT

The first time Karen and her husband, Dick, grilled trout was many years ago in Colorado. They had been pond fishing and caught two beautiful rainbows. Dick went to a convenience store in search of lemons. He returned with a box of lemon pudding and a bottle of lemon extract (there were no fresh lemons). Karen remedied the situation by making a baste from orange juice, butter, and some of the lemon extract. It was the best grilled trout they ever had!

MAKES 6 TO 8 SERVINGS

Four 12- to 16-ounce
   rainbow trout, dressed
2 lemons, thinly sliced
1 small onion, thinly sliced
8 sprigs fresh Italian
   parsley
Sea salt and freshly ground
   black pepper to taste
Zesty Lemon Baste (page
   294)

1. Prepare a medium-hot fire.
2. Meanwhile, place 2 or 3 lemon slices, 2 onion slices, and a sprig of parsley in the cavity of each fish and season with salt and pepper.
3. Grill until the meat is opaque and just beginning to flake when tested with a fork, 8 to 10 minutes per side, turning once and brushing frequently with the lemon baste.
4. Serve garnished with the remaining lemon slices and parsley.

Also good with: catfish, char, or whitefish

Fish Tales: What Trout Eat

In the process of researching this book, and after reading several extensively detailed articles on the behavior of trout, we came to the conclusion that if men paid as much attention to the behavior of women as they do trout (or quarterbacks, or performance cars, or elk, etc.), the world would be a better place.

However, we're not entirely sure we could stand that much single-minded attention. Maybe it's better that these anglers train their radar-beam attention on the habits of fish—all for the purpose of reeling them in. Then we all get to enjoy their efforts.

One such expert is angler Norm Crisp, who grew up in New Hampshire. His job after school was "catching dinner," he laughs. "I learned pretty quickly that the sooner I caught some trout, the sooner I could go play baseball with my friends. So I got pretty good at it." The secret was in understanding the feeding behavior of trout. "Trout live in the edges, the sedges, and the foam by the rocks, but not too far from the current. Their food supply is carried down by the current, and the easiest way for them to feed is to be close enough to grab whatever they want that comes by. The foam carried by the current is their buffet line. The secret to catching them is to know where they're likely to be and cast your line right there," he says.

The other secret is to know what they eat. That foamy, floating buffet line carries all kinds of things to grab a trout's attention: bits of decaying vegetation, small twigs, and insects of all kinds. Trout, which have surprisingly refined taste buds, prefer gourmet bugs, if they can get them: March brown nymphs, caddis fly pupae, black stonefly nymphs, and winged flies (known as duns). Given a choice, the trout will go for the larger, recognizable insects. Trout are also not afraid to try something new; they'll just spit it right out if it doesn't meet the taste test.

That's why making specialized "flies" to attach to a hook is such an art. It's not easy making something that looks like a preteen insect with all its tiny parts. A fly fisherman's tackle box is filled with tiny bodies, feathers, eyes, wings, and other parts in the hope that the angler can create a fly that a trout just can't resist.

CILANTRO-BUTTERED TROUT
WITH TOMATO SALSA

A grilled fish dish with the taste of summer; it's great for an outdoor campfire or a backyard barbecue.

MAKES 6 TO 8 SERVINGS

*1/2 cup (1 stick) unsalted
    butter*
*2 tablespoons fresh lemon
    juice*
*1 tablespoon chopped fresh
    cilantro, plus 4 sprigs*
2 lemons, thinly sliced
*Four 12- to 16-ounce
    rainbow trout, dressed*
*Sea salt and freshly ground
    black pepper to taste*
Tomato Salsa (page 333)
3 cups cooked brown rice

1. Prepare a medium-hot fire.
2. In a small saucepan over medium heat, melt the butter, then add the lemon juice and chopped cilantro.
3. When ready to grill, place 2 or 3 slices of lemon and 1 sprig of cilantro in the cavity of each fish. Season with salt and pepper. Grill the trout until the meat is opaque and just beginning to flake when tested with a fork, 8 to 10 minutes per side, turning once and basting occasionally with the cilantro-butter mixture.
4. Serve over the brown rice with the salsa.

Also good with: catfish, char, or whitefish

HEARTH-GRILLED TROUT WITH LEMON AND ROSEMARY

In a fireplace in a rustic cabin at a fishing lodge, indoors in your family room hearth, in an outdoor fireplace on your patio, or outside over a campfire—grilled trout so hot from the coals it makes your fingers burn is the just reward of the angler (or the shopper). Again, measure your fish at the thickest part so you can gauge your cooking time—12 to 15 minutes per inch of thickness for whole fish.

MAKES 4 SERVINGS

Four 12-ounce trout, dressed
1/4 cup olive oil, plus more for brushing
Twenty-four 1/8-inch-thick lemon slices
8 sprigs fresh rosemary
Salt and freshly ground black pepper to taste

1. Prepare a wood fire in an indoor or outdoor fireplace, using seasoned hardwoods such as oak or hickory. Do not use pine, as it lends a resinlike taste and causes flare-ups.

2. Place each trout skin side down on a flat surface. Drizzle 1 tablespoon of the olive oil in each cavity, then place 6 lemon slices and 2 branches of rosemary in the cavity. Brush each trout with more olive oil.

3. Place the fish in two oiled hinged grill baskets. When the coals have turned gray and you have a medium-hot fire, grill the fish for 5 minutes on one side, then turn the baskets over and cook the fish on the other side. Keep turning until the fish is opaque and just beginning to flake when tested with a fork, 24 to 30 minutes total.

Also good with: catfish, char, or whitefish

OAK-GRILLED GRAPE LEAF–WRAPPED TROUT

Opening a leaf-wrapped fish is akin to unwrapping a special gift. For a delicious departure from standard brunch fare, serve this grilled trout with Savory Leek and Herb Custard (page 361). With hot biscuits, a fruit compote, and rich, dark coffee, it's worth waking up for.

MAKES 6 SERVINGS

1 cup wood chips or ⅓ cup
  wood pellets
Six 14- to 16-ounce trout,
  cleaned
6 tablespoons olive oil
Twenty-four ⅛-inch-thick
  lemon slices
12 sprigs fresh thyme
Salt and freshly ground
  black pepper to taste
24 grape, romaine, or
  Savoy cabbage leaves

1. Place the wood chips in water to soak or wood pellets in a heavy-duty aluminum foil packet with holes poked into it.

2. Prepare an indirect fire.

3. Meanwhile, bring a large pot of water to a boil. Place each trout skin side down on a flat surface. Drizzle 1 tablespoon of the olive oil in each cavity, then place 6 lemon slices and 2 sprigs thyme in the cavity. Set aside.

4. Blanch the grape leaves for 1 minute to wilt them, then transfer the leaves to paper towels and pat dry. Wrap each trout up in 4 leaves. Secure the leaves to the fish by running two wooden skewers through the fish on the diagonal, starting at the back and coming out of the cavity.

5. When ready to grill, place the drained wood chips or foil packet on the fire. Grill the fish 3 to 4 minutes on each side over high heat to char the skin, then transfer the fish and finish the cooking over indirect heat, until the fish is just beginning to flake when tested with a fork, 20 to 25 minutes, turning occasionally.

6. Set the trout on each dinner plate for each diner to open the leaves themselves and find the succulent fish.

Also good with: salmon or sea trout

Suggested wood smoke: oak or pecan

PEPPERED AHI TUNA

One spring, Karen and Dick Adler and their friends, the Youngbloods, fished for yellowfin tuna in the Sea of Cortez off Baja, California. The May day was clear, the ocean smooth, and the catch plentiful—8- to 12-pounders and the fish were fighters. The ocean sights for the day included a huge Portuguese man-of-war, gray whales, a shark fin above the water, and a dancing marlin or sailfish. Their fresh catch was grilled that night—simplicity itself—a straightforward taste of fresh fish. Try this recipe substituting swordfish, if you have finicky "we-don't-like-to-eat-fish" eaters at your table. They'll think they're having a peppered steak dinner.

MAKES 4 SERVINGS

Four 6- to 8-ounce tuna steaks
2 tablespoons olive oil
1/4 cup pink peppercorns
1/4 cup green peppercorns
2 lemons, halved

1. Prepare a hot fire.

2. Meanwhile, crush the pink and green peppercorns together by hand with a mortar and pestle or in a clean electric coffee or spice grinder, then coat the surface of each fish steak and the lemon halves with them.

3. Grill the tuna for about 3 minutes per side. (Notice the short cooking time; tuna will toughen if overcooked.) Put the lemons on to grill, cut side down, when you turn the tuna.

4. Serve the tuna and lemon halves together, squeezing the peppered lemons over the tuna.

Also good with: escolar, marlin, sailfish, swordfish, or triggerfish

GRILLED TUNA WITH
FRESH PEACH AND ONION RELISH

Serve this peppery tuna and refreshing peach relish with roasted ears of sweet corn.

MAKES 4 SERVINGS

*Four 8-ounce tuna steaks
    1 inch thick
1/4 cup extra virgin olive oil
1 teaspoon sea salt
4 teaspoons freshly ground
    black pepper
Fresh Peach and Onion
    Relish (page 339)*

1. Prepare a hot fire.

2. When ready to grill, lightly rub the tuna steaks with the olive oil and season generously with the salt and pepper. Grill the tuna for about 3 minutes per side (do not overcook).

3. To serve, spoon the relish with its juices onto each plate. Top with the tuna and serve immediately.

Also good with: sea bass, mahimahi, marlin, shark, or swordfish

GRILL WOK–SEARED TUNA OVER BABY LETTUCES WITH LIME-GINGER VINAIGRETTE

Lively and full of flavor, this dish is inspired by one served at the late Barbara Tropp's China Moon Café in San Francisco. We love the flavored oils she has created in *The China Moon Cookbook* (Workman, 1992), and have made them ourselves. Feel free to substitute the same amount of a Chinese-flavored oil for the toasted sesame oil in the marinade. The addition of a slightly smoky flavor elevates this dish to another dimension.

MAKES 4 SERVINGS

1½ pounds ahi or yellowfin tuna, ½ inch thick, cut into 3-inch triangular steaks
2/3 cup soy sauce
1/4 cup rice vinegar or dry sherry
2 tablespoons toasted sesame oil
1 tablespoon sugar
4 green onions, cut into 1-inch pieces on the diagonal
1 tablespoon peeled and grated fresh ginger
4 cups mixed baby lettuces (such as mizuna, radicchio, mâche, curly cress, and bok choy)
Lime-Ginger Vinaigrette (page 291)

1. Prepare a hot fire.

2. Meanwhile, place the tuna in a shallow dish or pan in a single layer. In a small bowl, whisk together the soy sauce, vinegar, sesame oil, sugar, green onions, and ginger. Pour over the tuna, coating evenly, and let marinate for 15 minutes at room temperature. (Do not overmarinate, as the tuna will turn white.)

3. When ready to grill, with tongs transfer the tuna to the grill. Discard the marinade. Sear the tuna on both sides, about 5 minutes total. The tuna should still be rare, but browned and charred on the edges.

4. To serve, arrange 1 cup of baby lettuces on each plate. Place the seared tuna over the lettuces and drizzle with the vinaigrette.

Also good with: cobia, mahimahi, shark, spearfish, or yellowtail

PROVENÇAL GRILLED TUNA
WITH SAUCE RÉMOULADE

A very aromatic marinade infuses the tuna with the essence of the south of France. With an authentic sauce rémoulade, a platter of summer tomatoes, good crusty bread, and a chilled dry rosé to accompany this dish, you'll want to sit outside at a long table on a gravel terrace and while away the evening.

MAKES 4 SERVINGS

Four 6-ounce tuna steaks
1 1/4 inches thick
1/4 cup olive oil
1 bay leaf
2 tablespoons tarragon
vinegar
Sauce Rémoulade (page
308)

1. Place the tuna in a resealable plastic bag. In a small bowl, mix together the olive oil, bay leaf, and tarragon vinegar. Pour over the tuna. Secure the bag and turn to coat the fish. Let marinate in the refrigerator for 1 to 2 hours.
2. Prepare a hot fire.
3. When ready to grill, remove the tuna from the marinade and grill for 4 to 5 minutes on each side for medium. (If you like your tuna medium-rare, reduce the grilling time to 3 to 4 minutes per side.)
4. Serve with the rémoulade on the side.

Also good with: catfish, halibut, shark, or swordfish

GRILL-SEARED AHI TUNA WITH TAHINI-WASABI VINAIGRETTE

A light and refreshing entrée, full of flavor. Serve with Asian Slaw (page 350). Both pickled ginger and pickled cabbage are available in Asian markets.

MAKES 4 SERVINGS

1 pound ahi tuna or other good-quality tuna
8 ounces pickled Chinese cabbage
Tahini-Wasabi Vinaigrette (page 291)
2 ounces pickled ginger for garnish

1. Prepare a hot fire.
2. When ready to grill, place the tuna on the oiled grill grates and sear for 1 minute on each side for rare. (Grill longer if you do not care for rare tuna or perhaps try another recipe.)
3. To serve, arrange pickled cabbage on each plate. Slice the seared ahi into thin slices, arrange on top of the pickled cabbage, and drizzle with the vinaigrette. Garnish with the pickled ginger and serve immediately.

Also good with: other high-grade tunas available at upscale fish markets

GRILLED WALLEYE

When the weather gets hot, anglers know that early-morning fishing for walleye in the shallows of Midwestern lakes is a must if they want to catch anything. The heat of midday drives the fish to the cooler depths and out of reach, so the early angler gets the fish. Serve the grilled fillets with Herbed Creamed Corn (page 357) and buttermilk mashed potatoes.

MAKES 4 SERVINGS

Four 6- to 8-ounce walleye
fillets
Olive oil
Salt and freshly ground
black pepper to taste

1. Prepare a hot fire.

2. Brush the fillets with olive oil and season with salt and pepper.

3. When ready to grill, place the fillets in an oiled, hinged grill basket or on an oiled perforated grilling rack. Grill until opaque and just beginning to flake when tested with a fork, 4 to 5 minutes per side.

Also good with: catfish, cod, lake perch, or tilapia

AMARETTO-BASTED WALLEYE

Walleye is one of the prize catches of our northern states and Canada. It has a delicate flavor and an excellent moderately firm texture.

MAKES 4 SERVINGS

*Sea salt and freshly ground
    black pepper to taste*
*Four 6- to 8-ounce walleye
    fillets*
*1/2 cup Amaretto Baste
    (page 295)*

1. Prepare a hot fire.
2. Lightly salt and pepper fish fillets.
3. When ready to grill, set an oiled perforated grill rack above the fire. Place the fillets on the rack and grill until opaque and just beginning to flake when tested with a fork, 4 to 5 minutes per side, turning once and basting frequently with the baste.
4. To serve, place the fillets on plates and spoon the remaining amaretto baste over each.

Also good with: catfish, monkfish, orange roughy, or trout

GREEK-STYLE WHITEFISH

Refreshing and light, both in taste and in fat, this entrée is perfect for a summer meal outside. You can almost feel the sea breeze off the Aegean Sea. Serve with Tzatziki (page 317), warm pita bread that has been lightly brushed with olive oil and grilled on both sides, and sliced fresh tomatoes from the garden.

MAKES 4 SERVINGS

2 pounds whitefish fillets
1 teaspoon dried marjoram
Juice of 2 lemons
2 tablespoons olive oil
1/2 cup dry white wine
4 green onions, cut into
   2-inch lengths

1. Place the whitefish fillets in a shallow pan or glass dish. In a small bowl, whisk together the marjoram, lemon juice, wine, and green onions. Pour over the fish evenly to coat, cover, and let marinate in the refrigerator for at least 30 minutes.

2. Prepare a hot fire.

3. When ready to grill, coat a perforated grill rack with nonstick cooking spray on both sides. Pour the marinade off the fish, reserving the green onions. Place the fish and onions on the prepared rack and grill until the fish is opaque and just beginning to flake when tested with a fork, 3 to 4 minutes per side, turning once.

Also good with: cod, flounder, hake, sand dab, or turbot

WHITEFISH AND THREE-PEPPER STIR-GRILL

Although the Door County Fish Boil—in which a kettle of fish, potatoes, and onions is boiled to overflowing over an outdoor fire—is certainly one of the big summer attractions in this part of Wisconsin, we think that whitefish served this way looks just as dramatic—without the danger of scalding!

MAKES 4 SERVINGS

Four 6- to 8-ounce white-
  fish fillets
1 red bell pepper, seeded
  and cut into thin strips
1 green bell pepper, seeded
  and cut into thin strips
1 yellow bell pepper, seeded
  and cut into thin strips
1 ripe tomato, seeded and
  cut into very thin wedges
1/2 onion, cut into thin
  strips
Garlic-Herb Marinade
  (page 286)

1. Place the fish fillets in a resealable plastic bag. Place the vegetables in a separate resealable plastic bag. Pour 1/4 cup of the marinade into the fish bag. Pour the remaining marinade into the vegetable bag. Seal both, shake them to coat evenly, and let marinate in the refrigerator for 30 minutes.

2. Prepare a hot fire.

3. When ready to grill, set an oiled grill wok on the grill rack above the fire. Transfer the vegetables to the wok using a slotted spoon to drain the excess marinade. Reserve the marinade. Stir-grill the vegetables until crisp-tender, 12 to 15 minutes, using two long-handled wooden spoons to toss the mixture. Close the lid of the grill to heat through for last 5 minutes of cooking.

4. At the same time, remove the fish fillets from the marinade and place on the grill beside the wok. Grill until opaque and just beginning to flake when tested with a fork, 4 to 5 minutes per side, turning once and basting with the reserved vegetable marinade.

5. Serve the fillets on a bed of vegetables.

Also good with: striped bass, catfish, porgy, or snapper

GRILLED WHITEFISH WITH STRAWBERRY SALSA

A delicious freshwater fish found in North American lakes and streams, whitefish is most commonly found smoked, although it is also delicious grilled whole, filleted, or in steak form. The mustard butter adds a tart, piquant flavor to the fish, which contrasts and complements the sweet strawberry salsa.

MAKES 4 SERVINGS

MUSTARD BUTTER:

6 tablespoons (3/4 stick) unsalted butter
2 teaspoons Dijon mustard

Four 6- to 8-ounce white-fish fillets or steaks
Strawberry Salsa (page 332)

1. In a small saucepan over medium heat, melt the butter and whisk in the mustard.
2. Prepare a hot fire.
3. When ready to grill, place an oiled grill rack over the fire. Lightly baste each side of the fish with the mustard butter and place on the rack. Grill until opaque and just beginning to flake when tested with a fork, 4 to 5 minutes per side, turning once and basting frequently with the mustard butter.
4. Serve with the salsa on the side.

Also good with: catfish, cod, mahmahi, tilapia, or walleye

GRILLED YELLOWTAIL WITH MANDARIN ORANGE AND WATER CHESTNUT RELISH

Chris Schlesinger, coauthor of *The Thrill of the Grill* (William Morrow, 1990) and *License to Grill* (William Morrow, 1997), holds a Ph.B. from the Kansas City Barbeque Society Greasehouse University—that's Doctor of Barbecue Philosophy! Chris says, "Yellowtail is a mild-tasting, large-flaked fish with a firm texture that makes it a natural for grilling." It's not to be confused with the darker fleshed yellowfin tuna.

MAKES 4 SERVINGS

*Four 8- to 10-ounce yellow-
   tail fillets, with skin on*
*3 tablespoons extra virgin
   olive oil*
*Sea salt and cracked black
   peppercorns to taste*
*Mandarin Orange and
   Water Chestnut Relish
   (page 338)*

1. Rub the fillets with the olive oil. Season with salt and pepper.
2. Prepare a hot fire.
3. When ready to grill, place the fish flesh side down and grill to form a light golden crust, about 5 minutes. Flip to skin side down and grill until opaque and just beginning to flake when tested with a fork, about 5 minutes more.
4. Serve accompanied by the relish.

Also good with: sea bass, mahimahi, or swordfish

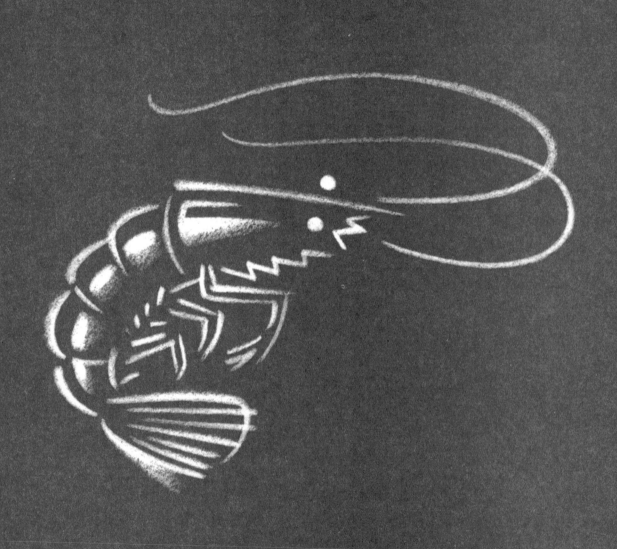

SHELLFISH ON THE GRILL

SOFT-SHELL CRABS WITH TANGY SEAFOOD SAUCE

In mid-May, blue crabs molt or shed their hard outer shells. And suddenly there is a feeding frenzy. Unlike the false urgency created by savvy marketers (think Beaujolais Nouveau), harvesting a soft-shell crab is a matter of delicate timing. Once molted, the blue crab's shell stays soft for only a few hours, so it must be caught right away. Out of the water, the blue crab's shell will not harden, but the blue crab itself will survive for only a few days. So grill your soft-shell crabs right away! In the Midwest, our soft-shell crabs are available already cleaned. If yours are not, ask your fishmonger to do so.

MAKES 4 SERVINGS

8 soft-shell crabs, cleaned

1/4 cup (1/2 stick) unsalted butter, melted

1/4 cup fresh lemon juice

Sea salt and freshly ground black pepper to taste

Tangy Seafood Sauce (page 318)

1 lemon, cut into 8 wedges, for garnish

1. Prepare a hot fire.

2. Meanwhile, in a small bowl, combine the melted butter and lemon juice and season with salt and pepper.

3. When ready to grill, brush the crabs on both sides with the lemon butter and place upside down on the grill. Grill for 4 to 5 minutes, baste, and turn. Grill for another 4 to 5 minutes, basting frequently.

4. Serve warm with the seafood sauce and lemon wedges.

PERNOD-BUTTERED LOBSTER TAILS

Before lobsters were heavily fished, they grew to tremendous sizes in comparison to today's catch of around 2 to 3 pounds. A 1930s report cites a lobster 3 feet long and 45 pounds heavy off the coast of Virginia (according to *The Seafood Lover's Almanac*, National Audubon Society, 2000). Gourmands know, however, that smaller lobsters (like smaller zucchini) are more delicious than the giants. Serve this with Sautéed Corn and Wilted Lettuce Salad (page 356).

MAKES 4 SERVINGS

Four 8-ounce rock lobster
    tails
1/4 cup (1/2 stick) unsalted
    butter, melted

PERNOD BUTTER:

1/2 cup (1 stick) unsalted
    butter
2 tablespoons Pernod or
    other anise-flavored
    liqueur
3 tablespoons chopped fresh
    tarragon leaves

1. Prepare a hot fire.

2. Meanwhile, cut the top membrane from the lobster tails and discard. Loosen the meat from the shell and brush with the melted butter.

3. Prepare the Pernod butter. In a small saucepan over medium heat, melt the butter, then add the Pernod and tarragon. Keep warm.

4. When ready to grill, place the lobster tails on the grill cut side down and grill for 2 to 3 minutes. Turn the tails and grill until done, 7 to 9 minutes. The shell may char, but the meat should be an opaque white.

5. Serve with the Pernod butter on the side for dipping.

GRILLED LOBSTER-PAPAYA QUESADILLAS WITH PINEAPPLE CREAM

You may want to double this delicious and refreshing recipe. If papayas aren't available, try substituting mango or pineapple. Papayas are ripe when you can smell their fragrance and the flesh gives slightly. They ripen quickly at room temperature in a brown paper bag. A fresh tropical relish goes nicely with this.

MAKES 4 SERVINGS

PINEAPPLE CREAM:

3/4 cup sour cream
1/4 cup crushed pineapple, drained
1 teaspoon fresh lemon juice

2 ounces fresh goat cheese, crumbled
2 ounces feta cheese, crumbled
1/2 poblano chile, roasted (page 314), peeled, seeded, and diced
1/2 red bell pepper, roasted (page 314), peeled, seeded, and diced
1/4 cup chopped green onions
1 clove garlic, minced
2 teaspoons chopped fresh cilantro leaves
2 teaspoons fresh lime juice
1/4 teaspoon sea salt
4 ounces grilled lobster meat (page 241)
1 ripe papaya, peeled, seeded, and chopped
Four 6-inch flour tortillas, at room temperature
2 tablespoons olive oil

1. Prepare a hot fire.

2. Meanwhile, combine the pineapple cream ingredients in a small bowl and put in the refrigerator to chill.

3. In a large bowl, combine the cheeses, peppers, green onions, garlic, cilantro, lime juice, and salt.

4. Chop the lobster meat. Fold the lobster and papaya into the cheese mixture.

5. Brush one side of each tortilla with olive oil and place oil side down on a grill rack. Spread some lobster mixture over half of each tortilla and fold over. Grill the quesadillas for 3 to 4 minutes on each side until cheese melts.

6. Cut each quesadilla into 3 triangles and serve with the pineapple cream.

To Market, To Market

Tamashiro Fish Market, Hawaii: Since 1954, the bright pink building in the middle of a multi-ethnic community has been a culinary landmark. Tamashiro's stocks not only Hawaiian freshwater and ocean fish, but also Maine lobsters, Atlantic and Pacific salmon, Dungeness crab, oysters, and clams. They also offer fresh fish prepared in the Hawaiian poke (pronounced po'kay) manner: cubes of raw fish tossed with a marinade of chopped seaweed, sliced onion, soy sauce, sesame oil, and crushed red pepper.

Pike Place Market, Oregon: Established in 1907 at the corner of Pike Street and First Avenue in Seattle, Pike Place Market is a great place to buy everything for a grilled or smoked fish dinner. Besides oysters, salmon, rockfish, and lobsters, you can buy free-range lamb, Bavarian sausages, Estonian piroshky, organic vegetables, and Cashmere peaches.

Mercado de Mariscos (Ensenada Fish Market), Baja California: Located on the waterfront, the mercado was established in 1958. Today, you can get fresh jumbo shrimp, octopus, fresh or smoked tuna, squid, albacore, lobster, and clams, as well as delicious *tacos de pescado* (fish tacos) served in warm flour tortillas and accompanied by large radishes.

Lexington Market, Maryland: Tourists visiting Baltimore will be dazzled by the number of choices and wide variety of all types of foods, including fresh seafood from the Chesapeake and outstanding Maryland lump crab cakes available from 140 individual stalls. Since 1782, Lexington Market has purveyed the best the area produces, from soft-shell crabs in late spring to oysters in the fall. When Ralph Waldo Emerson visited the market in the mid-nineteenth century, he proclaimed Baltimore the "gastronomic capital of the world." During the height of immigration before World War I, a Greek-Italian peanut war cut prices 3 cents a quart and prompted a stall sign proclaiming: "Remember, We Do Not Sell Common Peanuts Here."

Long before dawn, lobstermen in the tiny harbors along the flinty coast of northeastern Maine leave their warm beds to trek down sandy pathways, past clutches of scrub pine near each wind-scoured frame house, leading to the wharf. With steaming cups of coffee in their work-roughened hands, they contemplate another day's pursuit of *Homarus americanus*—the American lobster.

Once so plentiful that the Pilgrims regarded it as poor man's food, according to legend, it took the influence of the Rockefellers to change lobster's image—and price. In 1910, when the Rockefellers were visiting their summer home in Mount Desert Island, Maine, the scion of the family was mistakenly served a bowl of lobster stew meant for the servants. John D. was so impressed that he championed the cause of lobster stew in particular, and Maine lobster in general, back in New York.

Although the American lobster's habitat ranges along 1,500 miles of Atlantic coastline, from Newfoundland to the Carolinas, it is Maine lobster that has the recognition, not New Jersey lobster or Delaware lobster.

So, before the sun rises, Maine lobstermen head down to their boats, which hold anywhere from 300 to 1,000 traps. Although some fishermen still use the old wood lathe traps, the more modern traps of wire on a metal frame are less picturesque, but last longer. The bait inside lures the lobster through the front chamber to be caught in the inner chamber. Although it is difficult for lobsters to escape the trap, lobstermen find that if they don't check on traps within 48 hours, the traps are empty. Most check and reset their traps in the early morning because they believe that's when lobsters are most active.

Lobstermen who stick close to home throw their traps overboard to settle on the ocean floor at depths anywhere from 10 to 250 feet. Offshore lobstermen many miles away from the coastline can set their traps as deep as 1,500 feet. These offshore boats stay out for days, and must also have facilities to keep the caught lobsters moist, cool, and alive.

Old-timers used to haul up the traps the hard way, but today a hydraulic winch does much of the work. When the lobsters are released from the traps, they must be measured to make sure they're of legal size, usually 3¹/4 to 5 inches from the eye socket to the carapace, or main part of the body. Deft fingers place rubber bands on the claws of the lobsters that make the grade; the others go back into the sea. More bait is placed inside the trap, then the trap is thrown overboard again. All of this takes just seconds.

At the dock, lobstermen get around $9 per pound. A small lobster weighs about 1$\frac{1}{8}$ pounds; medium, 1$\frac{1}{4}$ pounds; large, 1$\frac{1}{2}$ pounds. If you order lobster at a restaurant or from a live-lobster shipper, you'll pay about $25 to $40 for the same lobster.

Although the standard cooking method is boiling a live lobster quickly, we like the Venetian method of boiling, then grilling lobster. The lobster goes into a pot of boiling water as the grill is heating up to hot. The lobster is cooked until it turns red, usually in a few minutes. The head and claws are removed and the tail of the lobster is split in half, horizontally. The claws and split lobster tail are brushed with olive oil and briefly grilled over a wood fire—just enough to slightly caramelize the sweet lobster meat and lend a hint of wood smoke to the flavor. Then the lobster is served with a brush of more olive oil, a drizzle of lemon juice, and a sprinkling of Italian parsley. When you take a bite, you could be transported to a little trattoria in Venice, but grilled over a driftwood fire on a chilly Maine beach or on a charcoal grill in a sun-blasted Midwestern patio, this lobster is certain to give you a glimpse of paradise wherever you are.

GRILLED LOBSTER PARFAIT WITH BRANDIED TOMATO CREAM

As a chilled appetizer or summer salad, grilled lobster meat is layered with crisp, shredded lettuce, fresh orange segments, and a brandied tomato cream. Garnish each parfait with a dollop of sour cream and insert a green onion stem as a "straw."

MAKES 4 SERVINGS

BRANDIED TOMATO CREAM:

1 1/2 tablespoons tomato
    purée
1 clove garlic, minced
1 tablespoon fresh lemon
    juice
1 tablespoon brandy
2 tablespoons finely
    chopped onion
1/4 cup dry white wine
1 cup mayonnaise
1 tablespoon sour cream
1 teaspoon paprika
1/2 teaspoon garlic salt
1/2 teaspoon Maggi
    seasoning or Worcester-
    shire sauce

2 pounds grilled lobster
    meat (page 241)
1 cup shredded iceberg
    lettuce
1 cup fresh orange segments
Sour cream and 4 green
    onions, green part only,
    end trimmed, for garnish

1. Place the tomato purée, garlic, lemon juice, brandy, onion, and wine in a blender or food processor and process until smooth. Transfer the mixture to a small saucepan and bring to a boil over medium-high heat. Let boil for 2 to 3 minutes to let the mixture reduce, then remove from the heat, cover, and chill.

2. In a medium-size bowl, blend the chilled mixture with the mayonnaise, sour cream, paprika, garlic salt, and Maggi.

3. Place 1 tablespoon of the tomato cream in the bottom of each of 4 parfait glasses. Alternate layers of the lobster, lettuce, orange, and sauce, ending with the sauce on top. Garnish each parfait with a dollop of sour cream and a green onion "straw." Serve chilled.

BLACK FETTUCCINE WITH GRILLED MUSSELS, GARLIC, AND PARSLEY

Black fettuccine is colored with squid ink and makes a dramatic presentation with grilled mussels. However, even if you use regular fettuccine, the delicate flavors of grilled mussels and dry white wine make this a singular pasta dish to serve your guests. For a slightly smoky dish, add mesquite wood chips or pellets to your fire.

MAKES 4 SERVINGS

3 pounds fresh mussels in their shells
3 tablespoons olive oil
1 clove garlic, minced
1/4 cup dry white wine
1 pound black or regular fettuccine, cooked al dente, drained (reserving 1/4 cup of the pasta cooking water), and kept warm
2 tablespoons chopped fresh Italian parsley leaves
Salt and freshly ground black pepper to taste

1. Prepare a hot fire.

2. Meanwhile, scrub the mussels clean, pulling off their stringy beards. Discard any mussels with shells that are not tightly closed. Place the mussels in a grill wok, close the lid, and grill until all the shells have opened, 4 to 5 minutes. Set aside to cool slightly. Discard any mussels that haven't opened.

3. Heat the olive oil in a medium-size saucepan over medium heat and cook, stirring, the garlic until golden, 2 to 3 minutes. Pour in the wine and the reserved pasta water and bring to a boil. Reduce the heat to low and stir in the parsley.

4. When the mussels are cool enough to handle, remove them from their shells, using a paring knife. Add the mussels to the olive oil-and-wine sauce and stir to blend.

5. Transfer the fettuccine to a large serving bowl. Pour the mussels and their sauce over the hot pasta, season with salt and pepper to taste, and toss. Serve hot.

GRILLED BABY OCTOPUS

Serve as an appetizer or pair it with one of our potato dishes on the side for a meal.

*2 pounds baby octopus,
    cleaned (page 179)*
1/2 cup red wine
*3 tablespoons balsamic
    vinegar*
3 tablespoons soy sauce
3 tablespoons hoisin sauce
*1 1/2 tablespoons fresh
    lemon juice*
1 clove garlic, minced
*1/2 teaspoon red pepper
    flakes*

1. Place the octopus in a large bowl. Add the remaining ingredients and stir to blend and coat the octopus completely. Cover the bowl and refrigerate several hours or overnight.

2. Prepare a hot fire.

3. When ready to grill, drain the octopus, transfer the marinade to a small saucepan, and boil for about 5 minutes. Place the octopus on a hot, lightly oiled grill rack (or in a hot oiled cast-iron skillet on the grill). Grill until the octopus flesh turns white, 3 to 5 minutes, basting with the reserved marinade while cooking. Serve warm or cold.

Also good with: cuttlefish, scallops, shrimp, or squid

CUTTLEFISH?

Cuttlefish, though not widely available in the United States, is part of the cephalopod family, which includes octopus and squid.

GRILLED OCTOPUS WITH ROASTED TOMATO–OLIVE RELISH

When Karen traveled in Spain, she loved stopping at various tapas bars to sample all the little dishes that the owners did best, like this one. When she got home, she re-created this dish from her taste memory. Make sure you let the octopus marinate for at least 3 to 4 hours, as this improves the flavor and the texture, which still will be slightly rubbery. The chopped grilled octopus and the relish are delicious served alone, on good crusty bread, or tossed with hot pasta, all accompanied by a glass of dry white wine or chilled very dry sherry, in the Spanish manner. Whole baby squid is also delicious prepared this way. Both squid and octopus are usually sold already cleaned, or ask your fishmonger to clean them. Rinse them again before marinating.

MAKES 4 SERVINGS

PEPPERED SHERRY MARINADE:

1/4 cup olive oil
1/4 cup dry sherry
6 garlic cloves, minced
1 tablespoon dried oregano
1 teaspoon red pepper flakes
1 teaspoon paprika
1/2 teaspoon salt

One 1 1/2-pound octopus, cleaned (page 179)
Finely chopped fresh Italian parsley for garnish
Roasted Tomato–Olive Relish (page 337)

1. Mix the marinade ingredients together in a small bowl. Place the octopus in a resealable plastic bag and pour the marinade over the octopus. Secure the bag and shake it several times. Let the octopus marinate in the refrigerator for 3 to 4 hours.

2. Prepare a hot fire.

3. When ready to grill, remove the octopus from the marinade and place on an oiled perforated grill rack. Discard the marinade. Grill until the octopus is opaque lavender-white and firm in the thickest part, 2 to 3 minutes on each side.

4. Transfer to a cutting board. Using a chef's knife, chop the octopus into small pieces, place in a serving bowl, garnish with the parsley, and serve with the relish on the side.

GRILLED OYSTERS IN PESTO

Now that we're not limited to months with an *R* in them to eat oysters, you can grill your favorite oyster and top it with pesto made from fresh summer basil. Enjoy these oysters as an appetizer, or removed from their shells and tossed with hot pasta for a fragrantly delicious main course. The flavor combination of the briny-sweet oyster, wood smoke, and basil is one of our favorites. This recipe makes more pesto than you really need for the oysters, unless you want to toss them with pasta, but we believe you can never have too much pesto! Cover and refrigerate any that's leftover.

MAKES 4 SERVINGS

*3 dozen oysters on the half
  shell*
Pesto (page 325)
*Chopped fresh Roma
  tomatoes and black
  olives for garnish*

1. Prepare a hot fire. For extra smoke flavor, place water-soaked wood chips or chunks on top of the coals, if you wish.

2. When ready to grill, arrange the oysters in a single layer on an oiled perforated grill rack. Spoon about 1 teaspoon of the pesto over each oyster. Place the oysters on the grill, cover, and grill until the pesto is bubbling and the edges of the oysters have begun to curl, 3 to 5 minutes.

3. Serve immediately with the chopped tomatoes and olives sprinkled on top for garnish.

NORTH AMERICAN OYSTER VARIETIES

North American oysters descend from four different species (*Crassostrea frons* or small oysters along the Carolina coast; *C. gigas* or the rough-surfaced Pacific oyster; *C. sikamea* or the small Kumamota oyster; and *C. virginica* or the oyster common to the Atlantic and Gulf areas) and most are named after the area in which they're found or raised.

The taste of an oyster "will be a concentration of its last habitat," writes Joan Reardon in her wonderful cookbook *Oysters: A Culinary Celebration* (The Lyons Press, 2000). Restaurants such as McCormick & Schmick's Seafood Restaurant now offer tasting menus of a variety of oysters, with flavor descriptions such as buttery, sweet, clean, briny, clear, coppery, or tinny.

When you grill or smoke North American oysters, you add another flavor note—wood smoke. The traditional oyster "roast" in New England was really grilling oysters over a hot fire. With our shellfish smoking technique, you grill the oysters first for several minutes until they open, then transfer them to indirect heat to slow smoke. Whether you grill or smoke oysters, there are many different North American varieties to try:

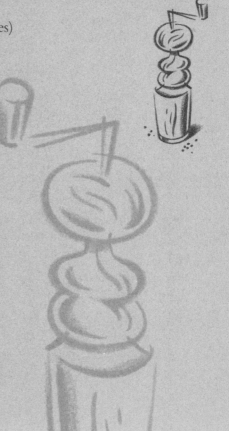

- Apalachicola (Florida)
- Blue Point (Northeastern United States)
- Bras d'Or (Nova Scotia)
- Caraquet (New Brunswick)
- Chincoteague (Maryland, Virginia)
- Cotuit (Massachusetts)
- Cuttyhunk (Massachusetts)
- Dungeness (Washington)
- Galveston Bay (Texas)
- Hammersley (Washington)
- Kumamoto (California)
- Malpeque (Prince Edward Island)
- Olympia (Washington)
- Pearl Point (Oregon)
- Plaquemimes Parrish (Louisiana)
- Prudence Island (Rhode Island)
- Quilcene (Washington)
- Royal Miyagi (British Columbia)
- Sunset Beach (Washington)
- Tomales Bay (Washington)
- Wellfleet (Massachusetts)

STIR-GRILLED SCALLOPS AND MUSHROOMS CAPRI

A classic sauce of flamed cognac, tomatoes, and cream gently bathes plump and juicy grilled scallops and mushrooms over tender pasta. Who could resist? Not us! Before you try flambéing, please read How to Flambé—Safely on page 25.

MAKES 4 SERVINGS

1 1/2 pounds sea scallops

1 pound button mushroom caps

2 to 3 tablespoons extra virgin olive oil, as needed

Sea salt to taste

2 tablespoons unsalted butter

1/3 cup chopped shallots

3 tablespoons cognac

3 tablespoons dry vermouth

2 cups peeled, seeded, and chopped fresh plum tomatoes

1 cup heavy cream

1 large egg yolk

Juice of 1 lemon

1 pound spinach pasta, cooked al dente, drained, and kept warm

1/2 cup Persillade (optional; page 282)

1. Place the scallops and mushrooms in a large bowl. Drizzle with the olive oil and sprinkle with salt. Toss to coat well. Keep in the refrigerator until ready to grill.

2. Prepare a hot fire.

3. Meanwhile, in a large skillet over medium heat, melt the butter. Add the shallots and cook, stirring, until softened, 2 or 3 minutes. Add the cognac and carefully flame. When the flames completely subside, add the vermouth, bring to a boil, and reduce by half. Add the tomatoes and cream and cook over medium heat for about 5 minutes.

4. In a small bowl, place the egg yolk and add a little of the hot cream sauce to gently heat the egg. Return everything to the skillet and stir in the lemon juice. Keep warm.

5. When ready to grill, set an oiled grill wok on the rack above the fire. Transfer the scallops and mushrooms to the grill wok and stir-grill until the scallops are opaque, 10 to 12 minutes, using two long-handled wooden spoons to gently toss the mixture.

6. Place the pasta on each serving plate. Top with scallops and mushrooms. Spoon the hot tomato sauce over each plate and garnish with persillade, if you wish.

GRILLED SEA SCALLOPS WITH PANCETTA AND BASIL AIOLI

We love the texture of scallops on the grill, and we love them wrapped with pancetta, the tender, unsmoked Italian bacon. Serve with aioli, grilled fresh asparagus, and sautéed new potatoes for a combination that can't be beat.

MAKES 4 SERVINGS

1/2 cup extra virgin olive oil
2 cloves garlic, minced
1 tablespoon cracked black peppercorns
1 tablespoon fresh lemon juice
1 1/2 pounds sea scallops
1 cup Basil Aioli by Hand (page 311)
4 thin slices pancetta (available at Italian markets)

1. A day in advance, combine the olive oil, garlic, peppercorns, and lemon juice in a resealable plastic bag. Add the scallops, seal, turn a few times to coat everything, and let marinate in the refrigerator overnight.

2. Make the aioli a day ahead. Keep refrigerated until ready to use.

3. Prepare a hot fire.

4. Meanwhile, place the pancetta in a medium-size skillet and cook over medium-high heat until crisp. Remove to paper towels to drain, then crumble.

5. When ready to grill, remove the scallops from their marinade and place directly on the grill or a heated grill rack and grill for about 3 minutes before turning. If the scallops stick, cook them a little longer, until they turn easily. After turning, cook long enough to heat through, 1 to 2 minutes.

6. Spoon 1/4 cup of the aioli onto each of 4 serving plates and spread around. Arrange scallops on top of the sauce and garnish with the crumbled pancetta.

GRILLED SCALLOPS WITH RASPBERRY-THYME BEURRE BLANC

When Judith's wild raspberries ripened in early July, we knew we had to try this dish. Adapted from a recipe by Michael McLaughlin of *The Southwestern Grill* (Harvard Common Press, 2000) fame, the combination of the sweet yet smoky scallops and tart but luscious raspberry sauce had us swooning. We hope you will be too.

MAKES 4 SERVINGS

1 cup wood chips or ¹/3 cup wood pellets
2 pounds large sea scallops
2 tablespoons unsalted butter, melted
Raspberry-Thyme Beurre Blanc (page 302)
Sprigs fresh thyme and fresh raspberries for garnish

1. Place the wood chips in water to soak or wood pellets in a heavy-duty aluminum foil packet with holes poked into it.

2. Prepare a hot fire.

3. When ready to grill, place the drained wood chips or foil packet on the fire. Brush the sea scallops with the melted butter and place on an oiled perforated grill rack. Grill about 3 minutes before turning. If the scallops stick, cook them a little longer, until they turn easily. After turning, grill long enough to heat through, 1 to 2 minutes.

4. To serve, divide the beurre blanc among 4 warm dinner plates. Place the grilled scallops on top of the sauce and garnish with sprigs of thyme and raspberries.

Suggested wood smoke: fruitwoods or oak

OAK-GRILLED SCALLOPS WITH BABY BOK CHOY AND SOY-GINGER BEURRE BLANC

This dish is almost too beautiful to eat, but not quite! The mild, toasty oak flavor of the scallops is well matched with the sassy, buttery sauce. For ginger lovers, this beurre blanc could become one of your favorites. Serve with lots of good, crusty bread to mop up the sauce.

MAKES 6 SERVINGS

1 cup wood chips or ⅓ cup wood pellets
24 sea scallops (4 per person)
3 small heads baby bok choy, bottoms intact and cut in half lengthwise
Olive oil
Salt and freshly ground black pepper to taste
Soy-Ginger Beurre Blanc (page 303)
Seeded and finely chopped red bell pepper for garnish

1. Place the wood chips in water to soak or wood pellets in a heavy-duty aluminum foil packet with holes poked into it.
2. Prepare a hot fire.
3. When ready to grill, place the drained wood chips or foil packet on the fire. Place the scallops and bok choy on an oiled perforated grill rack. Brush the scallops and bok choy with the olive oil and season with salt and pepper. Grill the bok choy about 1 minute per side, just enough to wilt and slightly char the leaves. Transfer the bok choy to a platter to keep warm. Grill the scallops 2 to 3 minutes per side, until firm and opaque and still juicy, not dry.
4. To serve, place a portion of the beurre blanc on each plate. Place a half head of bok choy leaves on the sauce, then place 4 scallops on the leaves. Scatter the red bell pepper over all and serve immediately.

Suggested wood smoke: mesquite, oak, or pecan

STIR-GRILLED PRAWN SATAY

What is a prawn? Beats us! No, really there are three different definitions of what a prawn is in Sharon Tyler Herbst's *Food Lover's Companion* (Barron's, 1990): 1. A prawn is a species of the lobster genus that includes varieties called the Dublin Bay prawn, Danish lobster, Italian scampi, *langoustine* (French), and *langostino* (Spanish); 2. The freshwater prawn distinguishes itself from the saltwater shrimp, but, in fact, the prawn migrates from salt water to freshwater to spawn; 3. The term "prawn" is loosely used to describe jumbo shrimp. So, if you have difficulty finding prawns labeled as such, substituting jumbo shrimp will also work.

MAKES 6 TO 8 SERVINGS

SATAY SAUCE:

2 cups unsweetened coconut milk

1/4 cup soy sauce

One 1-inch piece fresh ginger, peeled and chopped

3 cloves garlic, minced

3 tablespoons fresh lime juice

1 tablespoon firmly packed brown sugar

1 tablespoon chili powder

Sea salt and freshly ground black pepper to taste

3 pounds freshwater prawns, shelled and deveined

3 cups Peppery Couscous (page 378)

1. In a large bowl, combine the satay sauce ingredients. Place the prawns in a large glass dish and cover with the sauce. Cover and marinate for at least 30 minutes in the refrigerator.

2. Prepare a hot fire.

3. When ready to grill, set an oiled grill wok on the rack above the fire. Transfer the shrimp to the wok using a slotted spoon to drain the excess sauce; discard the sauce. Stir-grill until the prawns become firm and opaque, 12 to 15 minutes, using two long-handled wooden spoons to toss the mixture.

4. Serve immediately with the couscous on the side.

GRILLED PRAWNS IN GARLIC AND CHILE OIL

A simple yet sophisticated appetizer. Serve with plenty of good crusty bread to mop up the delicious oil, and a slightly chilled young red wine, such as a Beaujolais or Cabernet.

MAKES 4 SERVINGS

1 cup wood chips or 1/3 cup
   wood pellets

**GARLIC AND
CHILE OIL:**

3/4 cup olive oil
1 teaspoon red pepper
   flakes
4 cloves garlic, minced

24 jumbo prawns, shelled
   and deveined

1. Place the wood chips in water to soak or wood pellets in a heavy-duty aluminum foil packet with holes poked into it.

2. Prepare a hot fire.

3. Meanwhile, heat the olive oil, red pepper flakes, and garlic in a medium-size saucepan over medium heat. Cook, stirring, until the garlic starts to turn golden, about 5 minutes.

4. When ready to grill, place the drained wood chips or foil packet on the fire. Drizzle the prawns with 1/4 cup of the flavored oil and place them in a fish basket or an oiled grill wok. Grill until the prawns turn opaque, 3 to 4 minutes per side.

5. Place 6 grilled prawns in each of 4 shallow dishes or bowls and drizzle with the remaining warm oil. Serve warm with good bread.

Suggested wood smoke: apple, cherry, mesquite, or oak

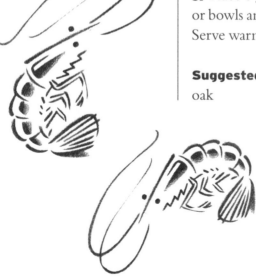

GRILLED CARIBBEAN PRAWNS ON TROPICAL FRUIT PLANKS

This colorful and refreshing appetizer can be served with hot shrimp on cool fruit or with everything at room temperature. Skewer the prawns and papaya, pineapple, or honeydew together right before serving, not hours before; both pineapple and papaya contain a tenderizing enzyme that can turn the prawns mushy if left together for several hours.

MAKES 6 TO 8 SERVINGS

1 1/2 pounds large prawns,
   peeled and deveined

CARIBBEAN MARINADE:

1/2 cup dark rum
1/2 cup fresh lime juice
1/2 cup soy sauce
1/2 cup extra virgin olive oil
1/4 cup peeled and grated
   fresh ginger
1/2 cup firmly packed brown
   sugar
2 teaspoons freshly grated
   nutmeg
1 teaspoon ground allspice
1 teaspoon ground
   cinnamon

1 cup peeled and cored
   pineapple chunks
1 cup peeled and seeded
   papaya chunks
1 cup peeled and seeded
   honeydew melon chunks

1. Place the prawns in a resealable plastic bag. In a large bowl, whisk the marinade ingredients together. Pour half of the marinade over the prawns. Reserve the remaining marinade in the bowl. Secure the bag and toss to blend. Let the prawns marinate in the refrigerator for at least 2 hours.

2. Prepare a hot fire.

3. When ready to grill, remove the prawns from the marinade, discarding the used marinade. Place the prawns in an oiled grill wok, hinged brochette grill basket, or on a perforated metal grill rack. Grill, turning frequently, until the seam along the back of the prawn has just turned from opaque to white, 4 to 5 minutes.

4. Pour the reserved unused marinade into individual ramekins to use as a dipping sauce for the prawns. To serve, toothpick each prawn to a piece of pineapple, papaya, or honeydew and dip in the sauce. Serve hot or at room temperature.

LOWFAT GRILLED FISH AND SHELLFISH

Many types of fish and seafood are very low in fat. Cod, mahimahi, haddock, lobster, and scallops have less than 9 percent of their calories from fat. Flounder, grouper, tuna, walleye, snapper, sole, and shrimp have between 9 and 15 percent of their calories from fat. For fish higher in oils such as monkfish, rockfish, ocean perch, mackerel, herring, salmon, trout, and orange roughy, it's still only about 15 percent calories from fat.

When you pair grilled fish with a lowfat side dish, you get a meal with a high flavor, but a lowfat celebration of taste. Try Teriyaki Catfish with Wasabi Cucumber Salad (page 39), Tandoori Stir-Grilled Cod (page 45), Stir-Grilled Fish Tacos (made with low-fat sour cream, page 60), Teriyaki Stir-Grilled Mahimahi (page 70) with Island Salsa (page 331), Tapas-Style Monkfish Skewers (page 72) with Cumin and Carrot Salad (page 352), Orange Roughy with Spicy Cantaloupe Slices (page 85), Sablefish with Spice Islands Rub and Kerala-Style Yogurt Sauce (page 87), Stir-Grilled Salmon with Sugar Snap Peas (page 92), Salmon Charmoula (page 97) with Mediterranean Orzo Salad (page 379), Grilled Sea Bass with Black Bean Sauce (page 26) and Chinese Grilled Asparagus (page 346), Tequila-Lime Grilled Shrimp (page 167), Grilled Tuna with Fresh Peach and Onion Relish (page 128), Grilled Whitefish with Strawberry Salsa (page 136), Greek-Style Whitefish (page 134) with Tzatziki (page 317), or Grilled Yellowtail with Mandarin Orange and Water Chestnut Relish (page 137) to see all the high-flavor, lowfat combinations that great grilled fish can inspire.

HONEY-GLAZED SHRIMP WITH
CARROT-GINGER SAUCE

Use colossal-sized whole (head-on) shrimp, if you can find them, for this recipe, adapted from one served at Aquagrill in the SoHo district of New York City.

MAKES 4 SERVINGS

HONEY GLAZE:

3/4 cup honey
1/2 teaspoon ground coriander
1/2 piece star anise (available at Asian markets)
1/4 teaspoon ground cloves
1/2 stick cinnamon
1 tablespoon fresh lemon juice
1 1/2 teaspoons peeled and grated fresh ginger
1/2 teaspoon minced garlic
1 1/2 tablespoons packed chopped fresh cilantro leaves
2 tablespoons rice vinegar
2 tablespoons ketchup
1 tablespoon soy sauce

1. In a small saucepan, combine the honey glaze ingredients and bring to a boil, then reduce the heat to low and simmer until the glaze is syrupy, 20 to 25 minutes. Remove from the heat and set aside.

2. To make the sauce, combine the carrot juice, ginger, cilantro, and lemon juice in a medium-size saucepan and bring to a boil. Reduce the heat to medium-low and simmer until only about 1/2 cup is left. Remove from the heat and set aside.

3. Place the wood chips in water to soak or wood pellets in a heavy-duty aluminum foil packet with holes poked into it.

4. Prepare an indirect fire.

5. When ready to grill, place the drained wood chips or foil packet on the fire. Brush the shrimp with olive oil and season with salt and pepper. Place the shrimp over direct heat and sear until pink, 1 to 2 minutes per side. Transfer the shrimp to the indirect side and brush with the honey glaze. Grill over indirect heat for 5 minutes, turning once.

CARROT-GINGER SAUCE:

2 cups fresh carrot juice
(available at health food
markets)

1 tablespoon peeled and
grated fresh ginger

1 1/2 tablespoons packed
chopped fresh cilantro
leaves

1 tablespoon fresh lemon
juice

1 cup wood chips or 1/3 cup
wood pellets

8 colossal-size shrimp,
shelled and deveined

Olive oil for brushing

Salt and freshly ground
black pepper to taste

1 tablespoon vegetable oil

1/2 cup cooked cranberry or
black beans, drained

1/2 cup chopped bok choy
leaves, blanched in
boiling water for 1 to 2
minutes and drained

1/2 cup peeled and diced
jicama

2 tablespoons fresh lemon
juice

6. Heat the vegetable oil over medium-high heat in a medium-size skillet. Add the beans, bok choy, and jicama and stir-fry until hot. Drizzle with the lemon juice and portion out the mixture onto the center of 4 plates.

7. To serve, artfully place two grilled shrimp on top of the vegetable mixture. Drizzle or spoon the sauce around the edge of the plate and serve immediately.

Suggested wood smoke: preferably pecan, also fruitwood or oak

LEMON-BASIL BASTED SHRIMP

Shrimply delicious!

24 jumbo shrimp (about
  1 1/4 pounds), shelled
  and deveined
2 teaspoons finely chopped
  garlic
2 teaspoons finely chopped
  shallots
1 1/2 teaspoons Dijon
  mustard
1/3 cup dry white wine
1/3 cup fresh lemon juice
1/4 teaspoon freshly ground
  black pepper
1/2 cup extra virgin olive oil
1/3 cup finely chopped fresh
  basil leaves

1. In a large nonreactive bowl, combine all the ingredients. Toss until the shrimp are thoroughly coated. Cover and let marinate for 20 to 30 minutes in the refrigerator.

2. Prepare a hot fire.

3. When ready to grill, remove the shrimp from the refrigerator and transfer them to a plate using a slotted spoon. Pour the marinade into a saucepan and boil for about 5 minutes. Place the shrimp on an oiled perforated grill rack, keeping them flat. Grill until the shrimp can be lifted from the grill without sticking, about 3 minutes. Turn and grill for 2 minutes more.

4. Arrange the shrimp on a platter and spoon the cooked marinade over all. Serve immediately.

GRILLED BLACK TIGER SHRIMP

These are the giants of the shrimp world, growing to over a foot long. They are very handsome in their gray-black striped shells. Tigers are a successfully farm-raised species of shrimp, although some can be slightly mushy in texture. Ask your fishmonger for the best ones. Serve this with Sesame Seed Spinach Salad (page 372).

MAKES 4 SERVINGS

1 cup (2 sticks) unsalted butter
4 green onions, finely minced
2 cloves garlic, finely minced
1 tablespoon finely chopped fresh Italian parsley leaves
1 cup dry white wine
2 tablespoons fresh lemon juice
2 pounds Black Tiger shrimp
Sea salt and freshly ground pepper to taste

1. In a medium-size skillet, melt the butter. Add the green onions, garlic, and parsley and cook, stirring, for 2 or 3 minutes. Add the wine and lemon juice.

2. Place the shrimp in a large glass bowl. Pour the marinade over the shrimp, cover, and let marinate in the refrigerator for 2 hours.

3. Prepare a hot fire.

4. When ready to grill, drain the shrimp, transfer the marinade to a small saucepan, and boil the marinade for about 5 minutes. Season the shrimp with salt and pepper and place on an oiled perforated grill rack. Grill for 2 to 3 minutes per side, basting frequently with the boiled marinade. Serve immediately.

Although we love crisp and light Pinot Grigios with white fish, oaky chardonnays with smoked fish, a young Cabernet or Pinot Noir with salmon, and beer with mussels, we also like these mixed drinks, which can make a grilled fish or seafood dinner a celebration. Make your own pineapple vodka as the basis for the Island Getaway or a tropical version of vodka and tonic. The refreshing Mojito tastes best if you let the sugar, lime juice, and mint leaves infuse together for at least 30 minutes before adding the rum.

ISLAND GETAWAY

MAKES 1 DRINK

2 ounces pineapple vodka (see below)
Juice of 1 lime
Club soda as needed

Pour the pineapple vodka over crushed ice in a tall glass. Stir in the lime juice, then add club soda to taste.

PINEAPPLE VODKA

MAKES 1 LITER

1 ripe pineapple, peeled, cored, and sliced into rings
One 1-liter bottle good-quality vodka

Place the pineapple rings in a large wide-mouth jar or a large glass container with a spigot. Pour in the vodka so that it completely covers the pineapple rings. Cover the jar and let the pineapple infuse the vodka for at least 10 days, refrigerated, before using. Refill the jar with vodka to keep the pineapple covered for a second "brew."

Mojito

MAKES 1 DRINK

1 teaspoon sugar
1 tablespoon fresh lime juice
8 to 10 fresh mint leaves
1 ounce good-quality white rum
2 ounces club soda
Sprig fresh mint for garnish

1. In the bottom of each tall glass, mash
the sugar, lime juice, and mint leaves
together with a wooden spoon. (This step can
be done up to 30 minutes ahead of time if you are serving
numerous glasses. The longer it sits, the better the flavor.)
2. Add crushed ice to each glass, then pour in the rum and club soda. Stir well
and garnish each drink with a sprig of mint.

SHRIMP ON A STICK WITH SHERRIED MUSTARD SAUCE

Make life simple with this easy-to-prepare meal. Steam some broccoli or asparagus to serve on the side. Either vegetable marries well with the sauce. Finish the meal with crusty sourdough bread that you warm on the grill.

MAKES 4 SERVINGS

1/2 cup (1 stick) unsalted butter, melted
Grated zest and juice of 2 lemons
2 pounds large shrimp, shelled and deveined
Sherried Mustard Sauce (page 322)

1. Prepare a hot fire.

2. If using wooden skewers, soak them in water for at least 30 minutes.

3. Meanwhile, in a small saucepan over medium heat, melt the butter with the lemon zest and juice; set aside for basting.

4. When ready to grill, thread the shrimp onto the skewers. Grill for 5 to 6 minutes, turning often and basting with the lemon butter.

5. Serve with a bowl of the sauce for dipping.

TEQUILA-LIME GRILLED SHRIMP

For a marvelous combination of colors and flavors, serve this with Cold Green Beans and Crumbled Queso Fresco (page 347).

MAKES 4 SERVINGS

2 pounds large shrimp, shelled, deveined, and butterflied
Tequila-Lime Marinade (page 290)
6 tablespoons (3/4 stick) unsalted butter, chilled and cut into pieces

1. In a large bowl, place the shrimp and pour half the marinade over the shrimp. Reserve the other half of the marinade in a glass jar with a lid in the refrigerator. Cover the bowl of shrimp and refrigerate overnight, turning occasionally to coat all of the shrimp well.

2. Prepare a hot fire.

3. Meanwhile, place the remaining marinade in a small saucepan over high heat. Bring to a boil and let continue to boil until reduced by half. Remove from the heat and whisk in the chilled butter until the sauce thickens. Keep warm, but do not return to a boil.

4. When ready to grill, place the shrimp on an oiled perforated grill rack and grill 5 to 6 minutes, turning once. Do not overcook.

5. Serve the shrimp warm with the butter sauce.

FISH TALES: WHO YOU CALLIN' SHRIMP?

When is a shrimp a shrimp and not a prawn, a small lobster, or even a giant shrimp (a seeming oxymoron)? Americans eat close to 1 billion shrimp a year. In fact, we eat more shrimp than any other fresh or frozen seafood.

With shrimp, it's size that counts. The larger the shrimp, the more expensive. Whether shrimp are weighed headless, or with head on, the count per pound is how the industry sizes them. So don't worry about looking for a particular kind of shrimp. Buy shrimp for freshness and size.

Head-on shrimp weigh more, and thus are more expensive (besides being a little more fiddly to eat), but we think the flavor is worth it. Chefs at Aquagrill, Esca, and Molyvos in New York City agree—they are serving grilled head-on giant shrimp. "The flavor is great," says Jeremy Marshall, chef and co-owner of Aquagrill. "You can take the head off and suck it like a crayfish, and you get all that juicy, creamy flavor."

- *Giant shrimp*, also known as Maya shrimp, are caught wild off the coast of Guatemala and are usually sold with the head on, numbering 5 to 10 to the pound.
- *Giant prawns*, caught in the Mediterranean, number anywhere from 6 to 10 per pound.
- *Super Colossals* are fewer than 12 to the pound.
- *Colossals* are 15 to the pound.
- *Dublin Bay prawns*, which look like small lobsters, are cold-water shrimp that are harvested in northern waters. Also known as langoustines and Danish lobsters, they number anywhere from 15 to 20 per pound.
- *Jumbos* number from 16 to 25 shrimp per pound.
- *Large shrimp* number from 26 to 35 per pound.
- *Medium shrimp* number from 36 to 40 per pound.
- *Salad or bay shrimp*, usually available precooked and frozen, can number from 40 to 100 per pound.

PROVENÇAL GRILLED SHRIMP AND PASTA GRATIN

The ultimate macaroni and cheese in under 30 minutes. While the pasta is cooking, grill the shrimp, assemble the dish, and pop it into a hot oven. With a garlicky green salad and a glass of chilled dry rosé, you've got a simple meal with big, bold flavors. When fresh tomatoes are out of season, use canned Italian plum tomatoes, preferably those from San Marzano.

MAKES 4 TO 6 SERVINGS

1 cup wood chips or 1/3 cup wood pellets

1 pound medium-size shrimp, shelled and deveined

1/3 cup olive oil

8 ounces (about 3 cups) tubular pasta

1 1/2 cups brine-cured niçoise or Kalamata olives, drained, pitted, and chopped

5 medium-size ripe tomatoes, peeled, seeded, and chopped (about 2 cups)

2 teaspoons chopped fresh thyme leaves

1/2 teaspoon salt

1/2 teaspoon freshly ground black pepper

2/3 cup freshly grated Parmesan or Asiago cheese

1. Place the wood chips in water to soak or wood pellets in a heavy-duty aluminum foil packet with holes poked into it.

2. Prepare a hot fire.

3. Preheat the oven to 400 degrees Fahrenheit. Coat the inside of a 1-quart casserole with nonstick cooking spray and set aside. Bring a large pot of water to a boil.

4. When ready to grill, place the drained wood chips or foil packet on the fire. Brush the shrimp with about 2 tablespoons of the olive oil and place in an oiled grill wok or on an oiled perforated grill rack. Grill the shrimp, turning them with tongs, until opaque, about 2 minutes per side.

5. Cook the pasta in the boiling water until *al dente*. Drain the pasta and place in a large bowl. Stir in the grilled shrimp, the remaining olive oil, the olives, tomatoes, thyme, salt, and pepper and blend well. Spoon this mixture into the prepared casserole and sprinkle the top with the cheese. Bake until the cheese has browned on top, about 10 minutes. Serve warm.

Suggested wood smoke: mesquite

GRILLED SHRIMP, FETA, SPINACH, AND ARTICHOKE SALAD

She starts with a pastel plate, like a blank canvas. Then Jody Adams adds caught-that-morning seafood, pristine lettuces, and other impeccable ingredients to create salads that are culinary works of art. Most recently at the Rialto Restaurant in the Charles Hotel in Cambridge, Massachusetts, Chef Adams says, "I like a salad to have clear, clean flavors, texture, and color." We agree wholeheartedly, as we offer our version of a Jody Adams creation. Serve with lots of crusty bread, such as Ciabatta or Rustic French Bread from Judith's book *Prairie Home Breads* (Harvard Common Press, 2001).

MAKES 4 SERVINGS

2 cups extra virgin olive oil
1 tablespoon coriander seeds
1 tablespoon fennel seeds
1 teaspoon red pepper flakes
1 teaspoon dried oregano
4 cloves garlic, minced
Grated zest of 1 lemon
1 teaspoon salt
One 10-ounce package frozen artichoke hearts
Juice of 1/2 lemon
12 large shrimp, shelled and deveined
1 pound baby spinach leaves
2 tablespoons chopped fresh mint leaves
2 tablespoons chopped fresh oregano leaves
4 ounces feta cheese, crumbled

1. Place the olive oil, coriander, fennel, red pepper flakes, dried oregano, garlic, lemon zest, and salt in a medium-size saucepan over medium-low heat. Bring to a simmer, reduce the heat to low, and let simmer for 10 minutes. Add the artichoke pieces to the flavored oil and simmer until the artichokes are tender, about 25 minutes. Remove the artichokes to a bowl, using a slotted spoon, and drizzle with the lemon juice.

2. Prepare a hot fire.

3. Meanwhile, place the shrimp and 1 cup of the flavored oil in a bowl and let marinate until the grill is ready, about 30 minutes.

4. In a large skillet over medium-high heat, heat 2 tablespoons of the flavored oil, add the spinach and cook, stirring, until it has wilted and turned a brilliant green. Set aside.

5. When ready to grill, remove the shrimp from the marinade and grill on an oiled grill rack or in a grill basket until they turn opaque, 2 to 3 minutes per side.

6. To assemble the salad, arrange the wilted spinach, artichokes, and shrimp on 4 salad plates. Drizzle each salad with 1 teaspoon of the flavored oil. Sprinkle with the mint, fresh oregano, and feta cheese and serve.

GRILLED SHRIMP AND CRISPY NOODLE SALAD WITH ANCHO-LIME VINAIGRETTE

A refreshing summer salad with big flavor and lots of color, based on one served at Cascabel in San Antonio, Texas. We've added the marinated and grilled shrimp (whole shrimp with the heads on, if you can get them) and tweaked the vinaigrette for a main-dish salad that will knock your cowboy hat off—and maybe your boots, too.

MAKES 4 TO 6 SERVINGS

1 pound jumbo shrimp,
  shelled and deveined
Ancho-Lime Vinaigrette
  (page 000)
3 cups vegetable oil
1/2 package wonton skins,
  cut into 1/4-inch-wide
  strips
Three quarters of an
  8-ounce package
  rice sticks (available at
  Asian markets)
4 cups fresh baby spinach
  leaves, shredded
1 yellow bell pepper, seeded
  and slivered
1/2 cup sliced almonds,
  toasted in a 350°F oven
  until light brown
1/4 cup fresh basil leaves,
  cut into thin strips

1. Place the shrimp in a resealable plastic bag and add half the vinaigrette. Seal and toss to coat the shrimp. Let the shrimp marinate for at least an hour in the refrigerator. Cover and reserve the remaining vinaigrette in the refrigerator until ready to serve.

2. Prepare a hot fire.

3. Meanwhile, heat the vegetable oil in a large pot over medium-high heat and fry the wonton strips in batches until brown and crispy, about 2 minutes. Remove with a slotted spoon and drain on paper towels. Then fry the rice sticks until they puff up, immediately remove from the oil with a slotted spoon, and drain on paper towels; set aside.

4. Place the spinach, bell pepper, toasted almonds, and basil leaves in a large bowl and set aside.

5. When ready to grill, remove the shrimp from the marinade using a slotted spoon and place in an oiled grill wok or on an oiled perforated grill rack. Grill until the shrimp are opaque, 2 to 3 minutes per side.

6. Toss the salad ingredients in the bowl with the hot shrimp, won tons, and rice sticks. Pour the reserved vinaigrette on top and toss to blend. Serve immediately.

GRILLED SHRIMP SCAMPI

All you need to serve with this simple grilled shrimp entrée is Panzanella Salad (page 373)—it's a perfect combination for a summer party (see Party sidebar, page 78).

MAKES 8 TO 10 SERVINGS

5 pounds Black Tiger
  shrimp, shelled and
  deveined
12 cloves garlic, minced
3/4 cup extra virgin olive oil
3/4 cup fresh orange juice
1/4 cup chopped fresh
  Italian parsley leaves
2 tablespoons torn fresh
  basil leaves
Sea salt and freshly ground
  white pepper to taste

1. Place the shrimp in a large bowl. Combine the rest of the ingredients and pour over the shrimp. Cover and let marinate in the refrigerator for 1 hour.

2. Prepare a hot fire.

3. When ready to grill, remove the shrimp from the marinade, reserving the marinade, and place half the shrimp in a large, oiled perforated grill wok. Stir-grill the shrimp for 12 to 15 minutes using two long-handled wooden spoons to toss the mixture several times. Close the lid on the grill the last 5 minutes to heat through. Remove from the wok and repeat with the remaining shrimp.

4. Meanwhile, pour the marinade into a small saucepan and heat to a boil for use as a serving sauce.

5. Place the cooked shrimp in a large serving bowl, pour the hot marinade over the top, and serve.

CITRUS SEAFOOD SKEWERS

Skewers can be a fun way to serve a dish like this for an appetizer, too. Just cut back on the amount skewered so that it's bite-sized. If you're using wooden skewers, remember to soak them for about 30 minutes in water before threading on the fish. Place the entire skewer with fish in a container with a tight-fitting lid so that the wood stays moist.

MAKES 4 SERVINGS

1 pound sea scallops
1 pound jumbo shrimp,
    shelled and deveined
Grated zest and juice of 2
    lemons
Juice of 1/2 orange
1/4 cup orange-flavored
    liqueur
1 cucumber, peeled, seeded,
    and thinly sliced, for
    garnish
2 or 3 oranges, thinly
    sliced, for garnish

1. In a large bowl, combine all of the ingredients, except the garnishes. Cover and marinate for 1 to 2 hours in the refrigerator.

2. Prepare a hot fire.

3. When ready to grill, drain the marinade into a small saucepan and boil for about 5 minutes to use for basting. Thread the scallops and shrimp alternately onto 8 skewers. Place the skewers on the grill and baste frequently with the boiled marinade until just cooked through, 6 to 8 minutes. Turn the skewers 3 or 4 times during grilling.

4. For a colorful presentation, serve the skewers on a bed of thinly sliced cucumbers and oranges.

GRILLED SEAFOOD PAELLA

A luscious and lavish way to entertain your guests. Grilling the seafood instead of cooking it in the oven adds a slight smoky dimension to this classic Spanish dish. Any firm-fleshed fish such as monkfish or sea bass or lobster or can be substituted for the halibut.

MAKES 8 SERVINGS

1/2 cup olive oil

1 large onion, chopped

1 large green pepper, seeded and diced

6 cloves garlic, minced

2 cups medium-grain rice, like Valencia

1 teaspoon saffron threads

2 cups peeled and chopped fresh tomatoes

4 cups chicken stock

1 teaspoon garlic salt

1 teaspoon Maggi seasoning or Worcestershire sauce

1/2 teaspoon Tabasco sauce

1 cup canned artichoke hearts, drained

1 cup frozen baby peas, defrosted

1 cup cooked green beans, cut into 1 1/2-inch lengths

1/2 cup diced pimentos

Salt and freshly ground black pepper to taste

1. Prepare a hot fire.

2. Meanwhile, heat the olive oil in a large saucepan over medium heat, add the onion, green pepper, and garlic and cook, stirring, for 5 minutes. Stir in the rice to coat it with the onion mixture, then add the saffron, tomatoes, and chicken stock. Bring to a boil, reduce the heat to medium-low, and simmer until most of the liquid has been absorbed, 20 to 25 minutes.

3. While the rice is cooking, grill the halibut until opaque and just beginning to flake when tested with a fork, 4 to 5 minutes per side. Grill the shrimp in an oiled grill wok, tossing with two long-handled wooden spoons until opaque, about 4 minutes. Remove the halibut and shrimp to a platter. Place the mussels and clams in the grill wok, close the grill for 3 to 4 minutes, then remove the mussels and clams that have opened to the platter. Keep grilling for 2 to 3 minutes more until the remaining mussels and clams have opened. Transfer those to the platter and bring indoors. Any that have not opened should be discarded.

2 pounds large shrimp,
   shelled and deveined
1 pound halibut steak
2 dozen mussels, rinsed
   and beards removed
   (page 247)
2 dozen clams, cleaned
1/2 cup chopped fresh
   Italian parsley leaves for
   garnish
Steamed crisp-tender thin
   spears asparagus for
   garnish
Pimento strips for garnish

4. Stir the artichoke hearts, peas, green beans, and pimento into the rice mixture and cook for 5 minutes. Stir in the halibut and shrimp and turn the mixture out onto a large serving platter. Arrange the mussels and clams on top, then garnish with the asparagus and pimentos. Sprinkle with the parsley and serve immediately.

SPIEDINI DE PESCE

Three different kinds of seafood—shrimp, monkfish, and salmon—are skewered with pancetta, then marinated for several hours and grilled to perfection. Served with crisp Italian Fennel Salad (page 360), this is summer eating at its best. (If you are using wooden skewers, remember to soak them in water for 30 minutes before assembling the spiedini.)

MAKES 4 SERVINGS

6 ounces large shrimp
 (about 12), shelled and
 deveined
One 1/2-pound monkfish
 fillet, cut into 1 1/2-inch
 cubes
One 1/2-pound salmon
 fillet, cut into 1 1/2-inch
 cubes
Four 1/2-inch-thick slices
 pancetta, each slice cut
 into 4 pieces

MARINADE:

1 clove garlic, minced
1/4 cup snipped fresh chives
1 tablespoon chopped fresh
 Italian parsley leaves
3 tablespoons olive oil
Juice of 1 large lemon
Salt and freshly ground
 black pepper to taste
1 teaspoon paprika

1. Thread pieces of shrimp and fish, alternating with the pancetta, onto each skewer. Place the skewers in a shallow glass dish or pan and set aside.

2. In a small bowl, whisk the marinade ingredients together. Pour the marinade over the skewers, turning to coat the shrimp and fish. Cover and refrigerate for several hours.

3. Prepare a hot fire.

4. When ready to grill, remove the skewers from the marinade and grill until the shrimp and fish have turned opaque, 3 to 4 minutes per side. Serve hot.

GRILLED BABY SQUID

After enjoying a wonderfully garlicky meal at a small tapas bar in Chicago, we knew we had to recreate it for this book. Serve this with Tapas-Style Potato Salad (page 370) for a true garlic-lover's experience. A platter of fresh sliced tomatoes or a simply dressed green salad with a bowl of charmoula (page 97) plus lots of crusty bread are the perfect accompaniments.

MAKES 4 SERVINGS

16 baby squid, not more
    than 3 inches long,
    cleaned (page 179)
1/4 cup extra virgin olive oil
2 cloves garlic, minced
1 teaspoon paprika
Sea salt
Chopped fresh Italian pars-
    ley leaves for garnish

1. Prepare a hot fire.

2. When ready to grill, place the squid on an oiled perforated grill rack. In a small bowl, mix the olive oil, garlic, and paprika together. Pour half the olive oil mixture into a condiment dish and set aside. Brush the baby squid all over with the olive oil mixture in the bowl and sprinkle with sea salt. Grill until the squid turns opaque and has a slightly rubbery texture, 2 to 3 minutes per side. Do not overcook or the squid will become tough.

3. To serve, place 4 squid on each plate, drizzle with the olive oil mixture in the condiment dish, and garnish with parsley.

LATIN LOVER'S GRILLED BABY SQUID

Baby squid are unusual and delicate sea creatures. They are a snap to grill. The biggest mistake in grilling them is overcooking. To avoid this, grill quickly over a very hot fire, as hot and brief as the romantic attention span of a Latin lover or millionaire playboy (although we don't know any, sad to say). To add the romance, the achiote sauce has a lightly musky flavor. Keep the meal simple. Serve sliced fresh tomatoes, corn, or new potatoes. A fruit salsa is also a refreshing addition to this meal.

MAKES 6 SERVINGS

2 pounds baby squid, cleaned (page 179)

1/4 cup achiote paste (found in Latin grocery stores)

1/4 cup fresh lime juice

1/4 cup fresh orange juice

2 tablespoons fresh lemon juice

Sea salt and freshly ground black pepper to taste

1. Prepare a very hot fire.

2. Meanwhile, set the squid in a large glass bowl. In a small bowl, combine the achiote paste and fruit juices. Pour 1/2 cup of the marinade over the squid and let marinate for about 5 minutes. Reserve the remaining marinade for basting.

3. When ready to grill, place the squid on an oiled perforated grill rack over the fire. Grill for about 4 minutes, turning once and basting with the marinade. The squid should be brown and crusty. Serve immediately.

FISH TALES: IN SEARCH OF THE GIANT CEPHALOPODS

What weighs 500 pounds, has 8 arms that are 6 feet long, two eyes that are each the size of a dinner plate, a beak, and a 6-foot mantle? (No, it's not a dinner table and chairs sitting in a room with a fireplace!) It also has 32-foot-long tentacles. Yes, it's the giant squid.

This creature is the stuff of nightmares. It is surely where the phrase "denizens of the deep" comes from. The largest known of the cephalopods comes from the waters off New Zealand. The mature size of a giant squid from head to tentacle is 35 to 40 feet long or the size of a bus.

CLEANING SQUID AND OCTOPUS

To clean squid, rinse thoroughly under cold running water. Hold the body firmly in one hand. Grasp the tentacles at the base of the body and firmly pull the head off the body. The soft yellowish entrails will come out; discard them. Use a sharp knife to cut the tentacles from the head of the squid. Discard the hard beak in the center of the tentacles. Discard the head. Pull the skin off the body and the quill out of the body; discard both. Keep the body and the tentacles whole for easier grilling. Or ask your fishmonger to clean the squid for you.

To clean octopus, rinse thoroughly under cold running water. Use a small sharp knife to slit open the head; remove the gut. Grasp the body firmly and push the beak out with your finger. Remove and discard the beak and eyes. If the octopus is large, cut the tentacles in half. Or ask your fishmonger to clean the octopus for you.

GRILLED SQUID WITH FRESH HERB STUFFING

The mildly savory stuffing keeps the squid moist and tender during the quick grilling process.

1 cup wood chips or ⅓ cup
    wood pellets
8 squid, 6 to 8 inches long,
    cleaned (page 179)
½ cup chopped mixed fresh
    herbs, such as tarragon,
    Italian parsley, chives,
    and/or basil
½ cup fine dry bread
    crumbs
2 cloves garlic, minced
½ cup ricotta cheese, at
    room temperature
¼ cup freshly grated
    Parmesan cheese
Salt and freshly ground
    black pepper to taste
¼ cup olive oil

1. Place the wood chips in water to soak or the wood pellets in a heavy-duty aluminum foil packet with holes poked into it.

2. Prepare a hot fire.

3. Meanwhile, place the squid on a flat surface and open the body cavity. In a medium-size bowl, mix together the herbs, bread crumbs, garlic, ricotta, Parmesan, salt, and pepper. Stuff the cavity of each squid with the herbed stuffing. Pin the cavity closed with toothpicks. Brush the squid all over with the olive oil and place on an oiled perforated grill rack or in hinged grill baskets.

4. When ready to grill, place the drained wood chips or foil packet on the fire. Grill the squid until the exterior is slightly charry, the squid is opaque, and the stuffing has warmed through, 2 to 3 minutes per side. Serve hot.

Suggested wood smoke: hickory, mesquite, or the woody stalks of rosemary or lavender

PART 2

SMOKING FISH & SHELLFISH

There are basically two kinds of smoking for fish and shellfish: cold smoking and hot smoking.

Cold smoking involves curing or brining the fish or shellfish for several hours, washing some of the brine or cure off, and letting the rest dry on the surface of the fish to form a sort of burnished glaze, what's called the pellicle. Then the fish or shellfish is smoked over low, indirect heat, under 200 degrees Fahrenheit. Cold smoking requires specialized equipment, as the food must be held far away from the heat source. Smoked at this low temperature, the fish or shellfish is preserved, but doesn't really cook. This is the process that yields the translucent, moist, thin fillets of smoked salmon that are available in flat packages.

Hot smoking involves first marinating or seasoning the fish or shellfish, which may also be lightly brined ahead of time. Then the fish or shellfish is smoked over indirect heat (not directly over the fire as in grilling), at a temperature between 200 and 250 degrees Fahrenheit on most charcoal and electric smokers. The Big Green Egg smoker uses higher temperatures, closer to 300 degrees, and stovetop or oven smoker bags require a temperature of 500 degrees. With the hot smoking process, the fish is cooked, not preserved, although it will last several days in the refrigerator and for months in the freezer. The end result is a moist, tender, opaque fish with a smoky flavor.

The smoked fish and shellfish recipes in this book are all prepared using the hot smoking method, as hot smoking equipment— kettle grills, Kamados, electric and charcoal bullet smokers, and gas grills—is readily available to backyard enthusiasts and home cooks.

The Difference Between Grilling and Smoking

For most people, outdoor cooking or barbecuing means grilling directly over a medium to hot fire for a short period of time. Grilling fish takes approximately 10 minutes per inch of thickness for a one-inch fish fillet. Shellfish out of the shell take even less time. This method is quick, easy, and familiar. It is as simple to grill directly over a charcoal fire as it is to cook directly over a gas-grill flame.

There is a mystery to smoke cooking mainly because it is not as familiar to most people. It also takes a little longer. But we encourage you to slow down and savor the wonderful scent of wood smoke! It makes your backyard smell great and your fish and shellfish taste sublime.

For Just a Kiss of Smoke

For just a kiss of smoke, throw a handful of water-soaked wood chips onto your charcoal fire. If using a gas grill, the water-soaked wood chips need to be loosely wrapped in foil or placed in a metal wood smoker box. The chips should then be placed directly over the flame. The fish or shellfish is cooked over the direct flame. Because the cooking time is short, the wood smoke flavor from grilling will be very mild. There will be more smoke aroma in the air than infused into your fish or shellfish. But if you like doing this, then we ask you to take the next step and try slow smoke cooking.

Slow Smoking

The main ingredients of wood smoking are a grill or smoker with a lid that closes. Wood product is necessary for smoking. We prefer wood chunks or flavored compressed wood pellets. A low temperature is necessary for smoking, usually around 250 degrees Fahrenheit. Gas and electric smokers heat at a set temperature or have controls that you may use to set the temperature of the fire. If smoking over a charcoal fire, we suggest using an oven thermometer placed inside the grill or smoker to gauge the temperature of your fire. We also like to use a water pan when we smoke.

Preparing an Indirect Fire

To slow smoke food, you need to prepare an indirect fire so you can cook the food away from the direct heat of the fire. The way you do this depends on the type of equipment you have.

Smokers. Most smokers are set up to make indirect cooking a snap. For example, in a bullet-shaped water smoker the heating unit is at the base of the smoker. The heat source is where the water-soaked wood chunks are placed. The next tier (above the fire or heat) is where the water pan is placed so that the heat source becomes indirect. The next tier is the cooking rack. The fish, shellfish, or side dishes are placed on the cooking rack and separated from the heat source with the water pan. The lid is then closed. In a large horizontal smoker, the fire is usually in a fire box off to the side, with dampers that can be opened or closed to regulate how much heat goes through the cooking chamber. The wood is placed in this fire box. The temperature needs to be controlled to about 250 degrees Fahrenheit.

Charcoal grill. Any kind of grill that has a lid may be set up for indirect cooking. On a charcoal grill, set up the charcoal fire on one side of the bottom of the grill. Add the water-soaked wood chunks or foil packet of wood pellets to the fire. Place a water pan on the rack above the fire. Place the fish or shellfish that you wish to smoke on the opposite side of the grill. This is the indirect heat side of the grill.

Gas grill. First, make sure you have the kind of gas grill with two separate burners. Follow the manufacturer's instructions to turn the grill on High. Let it heat for about 10 to 15 minutes. Then turn one side of the burners off. Turn the remaining gas burner to low or medium-low. Try to regulate the internal heat of the grill to about 250 degrees Fahrenheit with the lid closed. Place a foil packet or metal wood box of water-soaked wood chips or a foil packet of dry wood pellets above the side with direct heat. Place the fish, shellfish, or side dishes on the opposite side of the grill over low heat. This is the indirect heat side of the grill. Now you're smoking!

The Importance of Fresh Fish and Shellfish

The best smoked fish and shellfish start with the freshest product available. Your fishmonger also can suggest similar-type fish when you need to substitute, or use the Fish and Shellfish Substitution Guide for the Grill on pages 12 and 13. Choose fish with bright, clear eyes, make sure the flesh is fresh and moist, and beware of an overpowering fishy or ammonia odor. Choose scallops and shrimp that are firm and clean smelling; select clams, oysters, and mussels with intact, tightly closed shells. Rely on your fishmonger to help you select the best among wild and farm-raised fish and shellfish.

Healthy Smoking

Hot smoking is a very healthy way to impart more flavor to food without adding calories or fat grams. There are no flare-ups and no carcinogens to worry about with smoking and no added chemicals. Fish in the smoker is usually basted with or smoked in a flavored liquid such as cider, vermouth, or beer—all of which contain no fat, as opposed to the oil that is often brushed on or is part of a marinade used with fish before grilling. Sometimes we spray the fish with a little olive oil for a very simple smoked fish.

Preparing Fish and Shellfish for the Smoker

Preparing fish for the smoker or indirect cooking is the same as for grilling. Always rinse fish in cold water to remove any bacteria and pat it dry before marinating, seasoning, or cooking it. Fish that is to be smoked needs a liquid as a baste or cooking medium; the longer smoking process can dry out fish that is not properly moistened.

Rinse scallops and shrimp in cold water and pat dry before marinating, seasoning, or cooking. Clean clam, oyster, and mussel shells under cold running water. Trim or cut away any fibrous beard and discard shellfish with cracked or open shells.

Preparing the Smoker, Smoking Equipment, and Utensils

The grill or smoker should be clean and the grill rack(s) lightly oiled (use a long-handled brush and any vegetable oil, taking care to avoid dripping oil). Oil the inside of all grill equipment and utensils that will directly touch the fish or seafood: disposable aluminum pans, fish spatula, or fish boat. This will keep the fish from adhering to the grill or smoker equipment. Have all of your equipment handy and your smoking experience will be relaxing and enjoyable.

THE UTENSILS

Several basic tools make smoking fish easier. A local restaurant supply store or a barbecue and grill shop is a good source for finding the items listed, and professional utensils are superior in quality and durability.

- A stiff wire brush with a scraper makes cleaning the grill or smoker a simple job (tackle this while the grill or smoker is still warm).

- Use a natural-bristled basting brush to baste the fish during smoking.
- Disposable aluminum pans are the easiest utensils to use on a grill or smoker and are available at the grocery store. Always oil the pans before using so fish won't stick.
- Heat-resistant oven or grill mitts offer the best hand protection.
- Long-handled, spring-loaded tongs are easier to use than the scissors type. They are great for turning shrimp, scallops, sliced vegetables, and skewers.
- A long, wooden-handled offset spatula with a 5- to 6-inch blade is essential for turning fish fillets. Oil it well to avoid sticking.
- A grill thermometer, available at hardware and home-improvement stores as well as barbecue and grill shops, helps you monitor the temperature if you are using a charcoal kettle grill, a big smoking rig, or a gas grill.

For the novice fish smoker, whole fish (trout, char, or catfish) or thick fillets will be the easiest to smoke. Just place the fish in the disposable aluminum pan, add the appropriate cooking liquid, cover, and smoke. No turning, but maybe a little basting. Smoking, especially with an electric bullet smoker, is very easy—like a slow cooker outside!

Shellfish takes the least time and effort to smoke. Just place the shellfish in a disposable aluminum pan and drizzle with the appropriate cooking liquid.

SMOKING AN EEL

Neither one of us is prissy, picky, or prudish. We try many different things in our kitchens. Both of us have pets who bring various critters—squirrels, birds, rabbits—into the house that we have to rescue and return to the wild—or bury. Both of us have baited the hook, reeled in the catch, and cleaned and scaled our fresh-caught fish.

But eel did us in.

We considered having a smoked eel recipe in this book, but we couldn't get past how you had to prepare it. First of all, you have to buy a live eel. In Kansas City, that means going to the Vietnamese or Chinese market downtown, a 30-minute drive from our houses. That means 30 minutes with a live eel squirming in a plastic bag next to the driver. But the fun has only just begun.

Once you get home, you have to kill the eel. And you kill it by holding the base of its head with an old towel and thwacking its head on the kitchen counter. Some chefs also recommend that you hit the eel on the head with a hammer to finish the job, so the eel won't surprise you by wrapping itself around your arm like a cliché from a suspense movie . . . just when you thought it was dead. . . .

When you're sure the eel is dead, you make a small cut at the base of its neck and use needle-nose pliers to start removing the skin. Once the skin is off, you gut the eel by making a shallow cut on the underside of the eel, from head to toe, so to speak. Cookbook author Jim Peterson says that even then, the eel will still be "wiggling around," and he pours himself a glass of wine.

If you really like eel and want to prepare and smoke it, here's how:

1. Cut the skinned, dressed eel into 6-inch pieces and place them in a disposable aluminum pan. Drizzle with olive oil and a little lemon juice, then season with salt and pepper.

2. Prepare an indirect fire.

3. When ready to smoke, place 3 drained, water-soaked mesquite chunks on the fire in a kettle grill or charcoal smoker; in an electric smoker, place the chunks around the heating element. Fill the water pan and place in the smoker.

4. Place the pan with the eel on the smoker rack, cover, and smoke until it begins to flake when tested with a fork, $1^1/2$ to 2 hours.

Setting Up the Smoker and Starting the Fire

Smoking is defined as the art of cooking indirectly over a low-temperature wood fire—s-l-o-w-l-y. With most types of grill or smoker, you can slow smoke fish and seafood for a wonderful taste treat.

CHARCOAL KETTLE GRILL

The most basic kind of smoking can be done with a charcoal kettle grill. Use hardwood charcoal to start a fire. When the coals have ashed over, use a long grill spatula to push them over to one side of the grill. Place a metal or disposable aluminum pan of water on the bottom of the grill next to the coals. Place the grill rack over the top. The side with the coals is direct heat; the side with the pan of water is indirect heat. Use a grill thermometer to monitor the temperature. Ideally, smoking is done at a temperature (measured on the indirect side) of 200 to 250 degrees. (Karen has this type of grill.)

CHARCOAL BULLET SMOKER

Three vertical chambers—for charcoal, the water pan, and the grill racks—create the "bullet" shape of this smoker. We recommend using real hardwood charcoal, not chemically treated and compressed charcoal. Hardwood charcoal gives a better flavor and is better for the environment. We also discourage the use of charcoal lighter fluid, as it can infuse the fish with an unpleasant chemical flavor. Start your fire and charcoal in a metal charcoal chimney, available at hardware, discount, and home-improvement stores. Place the coals in the bottom third of the bullet smoker. Previously soaked wood chunks or wood chips or aluminum foil packets of wood pellets can be placed on the coals for more smoke flavor. Fill the water pan with water and place in the second part of the smoker. The smoker racks take up the top third of the charcoal smoker. A charcoal bullet smoker provides only indirect heat (so it is not used for planking).

GAS OR ELECTRIC GRILL

Follow your manufacturer's directions for starting your gas or electric grill. To prepare an indirect fire on a gas or electric grill, you need the type of grill that has two separate burners. Turn one burner on, and leave the other one off. The side with the burner on is direct heat; the side with the burner off is indirect heat. You can place a water pan in the back of the grill on the indirect side, or just place your fish in a cooking liquid and baste. A gas or electric grill is very easy to use, but will not impart the flavor that hardwood charcoal or wood pellet smoking does. To get more wood smoke flavor, moisten wood chips or place wood pellets in a packet made from heavy-duty aluminum foil. Poke holes in the packet and place directly over the lava rock. The wood chips or wood pellets will smolder rather than burn and give an added wood smoke flavor. Some gas or electric grills also have a smoker box, to which you can add moistened wood chips or dry wood pellets. Do not put these directly on the lava rock, as the residue could block the holes in the burners. Both Karen and Judith have this type of grill; Judith's is an older gas grill and doesn't have separately operating burners (so no smoking on her gas grill!).

WOOD PELLET GRILL

This new type of grill—used for grilling and smoking—uses an electric starter along with compressed wood pellets for fuel and flavor. Most wood pellet grills have two separate burners, so you can prepare an indirect fire or use the smoker setting. The wood pellets are available in many different types of wood so you can get the appropriate flavor in your food. (Judith has this type of grill.)

ELECTRIC BULLET SMOKER

We both have electric bullet smokers and love to use them because they are as easy as having a slow cooker outdoors! Like charcoal smokers, the electric smokers are built in three sections. The bottom section is a bed of lava rock in which an electric coil rests. You place soaked wood chunks or chips or an aluminum foil packet of dry wood pellets around but not touching the heating element. The next section of the smoker contains the water pan, which you fill and place on the rack. The top section contains the smoker racks, on which you place the disposable aluminum pans of food to be smoked. Cover the smoker, plug it in, and don't keep checking on it. The more you take the top off to check your food, the longer it will take the smoker to do its job because the temperature will fall. The temperature should remain at a fairly constant 200 to 250 degrees.

KAMADO-STYLE COOKER

This is a replica of an ancient clay oven first discovered in China and later adopted in Japan. It is shaped like an egg, with thick ceramic walls and a tight-fitting dome lid that clamps shut. Place some crumpled newspaper in the bottom of the unit with only a one-inch layer of lump charcoal. Light the paper and the fire will start in about 10 minutes. The charcoal will smoke-cook for several hours. When the cooker is closed, the food inside can smoke or grill very fast, but stays very moist. The fire temperature can reach 600 to 700 degrees Fahrenheit. Smoke fish at 250 degrees and use water-soaked wood chips to enhance the natural flavor of the fish. The lid is always closed when cooking and you never have to use a water pan. There are several manufacturers making this unusual grill/smoker: the Big Green Egg, Grill Dome, and Kamado.

SMOKER BAGS OR STOVETOP SMOKERS

Follow the manufacturer's instructions for using the smoker bag or stovetop smoker. Most of them have wood chips or powder in a bottom compartment of the bag or metal pan. You place the food in the bag or pan, close it, then place the bag or pan in a

SMOKED VEGETABLES

When you have room in your smoker while you are cooking other foods, consider smoking a few vegetables to have on hand for adding a wonderful flavor component to many dishes. Simply place the vegetables in a disposable aluminum foil pan and smoke for at least an hour, until the vegetables have a good, smoky aroma. The vegetables will further soften and can be frozen in resealable plastic bags for later use.

- *Roasted and smoked red bell pepper:* Roast a red bell pepper first under a broiler or on a charcoal or gas grill until it is blackened on all sides. Remove the charred skin, seeds, and white ribs, then smoke.
- *Smoked tomatoes:* Core each tomato, then smoke.
- *Smoked onions:* Peel the onions first, then place them in a microwaveable dish. Microwave on high for 3 minutes to partially cook. Or, place the onions in a steamer basket and steam for about 5 minutes to partially cook. Place the onions in the pan and smoke.
- *Smoked corn kernels:* Blanch the corn for 2 minutes in boiling water, then drain off the water. Place the corn kernels in the pan and smoke.
- *Grilled and smoked Japanese eggplant:* Grill unpeeled whole Japanese eggplant until blackened on all sides. With a paring knife, remove the stem and skin. Place the eggplant pulp in the pan and smoke.

hot oven or over a hot burner on the stove. However, because of the very high cooking temperature, the food cooks fast and doesn't develop the same mellow, smoky flavor as with other methods.

Getting the Flavor

Wood smoke is the flavoring agent for smoked fish and seafood. To get this effect, you need to use hardwoods that will smolder, but not burn; in other words, you want smoke, not heat. That means that hardwood chunks or wood chips will need to be soaked in water for at least 30 minutes before smoking. We usually keep a covered plastic container of soaking wood so we don't have to remember this step; it's already done. The advantage of wood chunks is that you don't have to replace them during smoking. Three wood chunks, the most we recommend for smoking at one time, will last about three hours. Wood chips will have to be replenished more frequently. Follow the manufacturer's directions for using wood pellets or wood chips. And don't overdo it in your enthusiasm—too much wood will create an acrid taste in your food. And, again, only three chunks of soaked wood at a time! More is not better.

TYPES OF WOOD

Throughout the book, we recommend certain types of wood for smoking and grilling recipes. Generally, for a heavier smoky flavor, we recommend mesquite or hickory wood; for a medium smoke flavor, pecan, oak, maple, or alder; and for a mild, sweeter flavor, fruitwoods such as apple, cherry, and pear. Bags of wood chunks, wood chips, and wood pellets are readily available in the Kansas City area and at barbecue and grill shops elsewhere. Also check our mail-order sources for wood in the Source Guide (page 384).

Smoking Temperature

Fish is usually smoked indirectly using a medium to low fire, from 200 to 250 degrees Fahrenheit. Electric smokers keep a constant temperature, but you will need a grill thermometer or a way to judge when the fire is low enough on other types of grills or smokers. The fire is ready when the flames have subsided and the coals are glowing red and just beginning to ash over. You've got a medium-hot fire when the coals are no longer red, but ashen. Another test to gauge the temperature is to hold your hand 5 inches above the heat source. If you can hold it there only for about 2 seconds, your fire is hot; 3 to 4 seconds is a medium-hot fire; and 5 to 6 seconds is a low fire. About 4 to 5 seconds is medium-low, the ideal temperature for smoking. With charcoal bullet smokers and kettle grills, you will need to add more charcoal periodically to sustain the medium-low heat.

Smoking Time

Estimating smoking times will be a challenge, because the time required to cook a fish varies, influenced by such factors as the heat of the fire, the temperature outdoors, and whether the day is windy. With smoking, exact timing is less crucial than with grilling, as smoking is a gentler cooking process. But smoking food for too long will eventually give it a bitter flavor. Use the suggested cooking times given in each recipe but also watch your fish while it's smoking—when the color turns opaque and the flesh just begins to flake when tested with a fork, it's done. We always recommend allowing extra time—an hour perhaps—when smoking any kind of food. You can always wrap it in aluminum foil and keep it warm and moist in a low oven if you are finished well before serving time. But you certainly don't want your guests waiting to eat because your food is not done yet.

Smoking Timetable for Fish and Shellfish

The smoking times given in this chart are approximate, not exact. Several factors influence how quickly or slowly your fish and shellfish will cook over indirect heat.

- *The temperature outdoors.* In hot weather, fish and shellfish will smoke more quickly, as the median hot smoking temperature of 225 degrees Fahrenheit could heat up to 250 degrees. In cold weather, fish and shellfish will smoke more slowly, as the median hot smoking temperature of 225 degrees Fahrenheit could cool down to 200 degrees.
- *The wind.* On a still day, fish and shellfish will smoke more quickly. On a windy day, fish and shellfish will smoke more slowly.
- *The amount of food on the smoker.* The smoking times given in this chart are based on the fish and shellfish being the only food in the smoker. The greater the volume of food in the smoker, the longer it will all take to smoke.
- *The thickness of the fish or shellfish.* Generally, a 1-inch-thick fish fillet (measured at the thickest part) or steak will take about 45 minutes for rare and 60 minutes for well done in the smoker. A 1/2-inch-thick fish fillet will be cooked to rare in about 30 minutes and well done at 45. A whole fish, at least 2 inches thick at the thickest part, will take at least 1 1/2 hours in the smoker.
- *Undercook rather than overcook.* We think it is better to undercook, rather than overcook, your fish and shellfish. You can always finish off undercooked fish in the oven or the microwave; overcooked fish is irretrievable. We recommend checking on your shellfish in the smoker about 10 minutes before the expected finish time; your fish in the smoker about 15 minutes before the expected finish time.

FISH	SMOKING METHODS AND TIMES
VERY SMALL, WHOLE FISH (Smelts, herring, sardines)	30 to 45 minutes over indirect heat
STEAKS OR FILLETS 1 inch thick $\frac{1}{2}$ inch thick	45 to 60 minutes over indirect heat 30 to 45 minutes over indirect heat
WHOLE FISH, ABOUT 2 INCHES THICK 14 to 16 ounces 2 to 3 pounds	$1\frac{1}{2}$ to 2 hours over indirect heat $1\frac{1}{2}$ to 2 hours, planked over indirect heat; 2 hours over indirect heat

SHELLFISH	SMOKING METHODS AND TIMES
WHOLE LOBSTERS	10 minutes over direct heat; 20 to 30 minutes over indirect heat
LOBSTER TAILS	If precooked (which we recommend), 1 hour over indirect heat
SHRIMP AND PRAWNS	If raw, 35 to 45 minutes over indirect heat If cooked, 15 minutes over indirect heat
MUSSELS, OYSTERS, CLAMS	Steam first, then smoke for 30 minutes over indirect heat
SCALLOPS	30 to 45 minutes, planked over indirect heat

Flavor Enhancements

The predominant flavor of smoked fish and shellfish is just that—smoke. But we also like the nuances of flavor that various rubs and marinades can contribute. Each recipe in the smoking section will reveal all kinds of variations on that theme. The recipes in this book have accompanying bastes or marinades, but also see the Sauces chapter on page 271 to experiment and find your favorite flavoring for smoked fish and seafood.

Some dedicated barbecuers like to add herbs or other flavorings to the water pan during smoking. We find that this does not add appreciable flavor to the food, but it certainly does make your backyard smell wonderful, and that is part of the pleasure of smoking. It all adds to the outdoor atmosphere, so if it pleases you, do it!

SIMPLY SMOKED FISH

In the simplest and purest form, fish in the smoker needs little more than olive oil or a liquid, salt, and pepper. The oil adds moisture to the fish so that it won't dry out as easily. It also helps to prevent sticking on the smoker rack. Smoking at 225 degrees Fahrenheit will take approximately 45 minutes to an hour for fish steaks or fillets. Smoking a whole fish takes a little longer, about 1 to 1 1/2 hours. Also, the more fish placed in a smoker, the longer it will take to smoke.

MAKES 2 SERVINGS

One 8-ounce fish fillet or
   steak about 1 inch thick
1 tablespoon olive oil
1/4 teaspoon salt
1/4 teaspoon freshly ground
   black pepper

1. Brush or spray the fish lightly with oil and season with salt and pepper.
2. Prepare a 225 degree Fahrenheit fire in a smoker. Place the fish on the oiled smoker rack. Close the lid and smoke until the fish is opaque and the flesh is just beginning to flake when you test it with a fork, 45 minutes to 1 hour.

The Art of Planking

Wood planking comes from the culinary traditions of Native Americans. Alder and cedar are the most traditional woods used for this kind of aromatic smoking. But any wood that is non-resinous and recommended for regular grilling or smoking can be used. Try fruitwoods, maple, oak, alder, cedar, or hickory.

The most economical place to buy planks is at the lumberyard. You'll need to ask for commercial grade, untreated wood that is 1 inch thick. The size of the plank depends on the size of your smoker or grill. In smaller vertical smoker units, planks should be approximately 8 to 10 inches wide and 10 to 12 inches long. If you'll be planking on a large charcoal or gas unit, there'll be more room for a large plank. A 10 x 18-inch piece of wood will be perfect for a large salmon or halibut fillet.

Retail barbecue stores and kitchen shops that offer grilling utensils may stock cedar planks, too. The choice of aromatic woods will be more limited than the lumberyard's selection. The prices range from five to almost fifty dollars for planks of varying quality. Choose what fits your pocketbook.

Planks must be soaked in water for at least 1 hour prior to using. You'll need to choose what you will soak the plank in when you buy the larger sizes of planks, i.e., a tall bucket or a large rectangular plastic container.

For plank cooking on a grill, the water-soaked plank needs to be heated over direct heat for about 3 to 4 minutes. Then turn the plank and place it on the indirect side of the grill. Place the fish on the plank and close the lid to the grill. Depending on the seafood, cooking time will range from 6 to 10 minutes for scallops or shrimp to 15 minutes or more for fish fillets.

For planking, the lid must be closed and not opened during the cooking time. If the lid is open, heat escapes and it will take longer to cook the fish.

A word of caution—the wood planks are flammable. Have a spray bottle of water handy to douse flare-ups. Do not leave plank cooking unattended.

Planking is a fun way to infuse fish with a lovely aromatic wood taste. Try it once—we think you'll find it much easier than it seems. We think you'll get hooked on plank smoking.

10 TIPS AND TECHNIQUES FOR GREAT PLANKED FISH AND SHELLFISH, EVERY TIME

1. Buy planks of untreated, aromatic wood, available in some gourmet stores and barbecue shops. Or go to a lumberyard and ask for untreated wood 5/8 to 1 inch thick, 8 to 10 inches wide, and 10 to 12 inches long. Make sure the size of plank you purchase fits on your grill so that the lid will close over it.

2. Aromatic wood choices include alder, cedar, fruitwoods, hickory, maple, mesquite, and oak. Do not use resinous wood like Eastern cedar, pine, poplar, or birch.

3. Soak the plank for at least an hour prior to using. This will provide for maximum smoke and it also helps to retard burning.

4. Place the water-soaked plank directly over the fire for 3 to 4 minutes to heat the plank. Place the fish or shellfish on the hot plank and cover the grill immediately. The hotter the grill, the better the smoke.

5. Keep a spray bottle filled with water next to the grill. If the edges of the plank catch fire, douse them with water, move the plank to the indirect side of the grill and close the grill lid.

6. DO NOT LEAVE THE GRILL UN-ATTENDED WHILE PLANK SMOKING.

7. Cooking times will vary depending on whether you are planking fish or shellfish and its size. A rough time estimate is 30 to 60 minutes for most dishes. See specific recipes for exact cooking times.

8. The plank is a natural serving platter. It will be hot and also a little sooty, so place it on another clean plank or a baking sheet covered with an attractive cloth.

9. Planks may be cleaned with hot water and dish soap. Eighty-grit sand paper may be used on the plank, too.

10. Gar à la Plank, adapted from Guy Simpson, The Rib Doctor:

Place the gar on a plank and baste with margarine. Place the plank and gar on the grill and put the lid on. Grill for 12 hours while drinking a bottle of very cheap wine. Remove the gar and plank from the grill. Garnish with lemon and parsley. Remove the gar and eat the plank.

FISH IN THE SMOKER

TARRAGON-INFUSED SMOKED SEA BASS WITH TROPICAL SALSA

Fresh tarragon lends a wonderful aroma and flavor to Chilean sea bass lightly smoked over oak.

MAKES 6 SERVINGS

*3 wood chunks, 1 cup wood
  chips, or 1/3 cup wood
  pellets*
*Six 6- to 8-ounce sea bass
  steaks or fillets*
1/2 cup Dijon mustard
*2 tablespoons white wine
  vinegar*
*1/4 teaspoon red pepper
  flakes*
12 sprigs fresh tarragon
Tropical Salsa (page 330)

1. Place the wood chunks or wood chips in water to soak or wood pellets in a heavy-duty aluminum foil packet with holes poked into it.

2. Prepare an indirect fire.

3. Meanwhile, rinse the sea bass and pat dry with paper towels. In a small bowl, combine the mustard, vinegar, and red pepper flakes. Spread this mixture evenly over one side of each fillet. Place the tarragon sprigs in the bottom of a disposable aluminum pan and lay the fillets on the tarragon, mustard side up.

4. When ready to smoke, place the drained wood chunks or chips or foil packet on the fire if using a kettle grill or charcoal smoker; in an electric smoker, place the wood chunks or chips or packet around the heating element. Fill the water pan and place in the smoker.

5. Place the pan on the grill or smoker rack, cover, and smoke until the fish is opaque and begins to flake when tested with a fork, 45 minutes to 1 hour. Serve with a spoonful of the salsa.

Also good with: monkfish, pink snapper, or tilefish

Suggested wood smoke: oak

THAI-STYLE FISH SOUP WITH COCONUT AND CILANTRO

Plan to have smoked (or grilled) sea bass, red snapper, or halibut leftovers to use in this easy and delicious Thai-style soup. The smokiness adds a third dimension of flavor to the coconut milk and the aromatic seasonings of kaffir lime leaves, which have a pronounced citrus flavor; galangal, with a flavor like that of fresh ginger; and cilantro.

MAKES 4 SERVINGS

2 cups chicken broth
2 kaffir lime leaves (available at Asian markets)
One 1-inch piece fresh galangal (available at Asian markets) or ginger, peeled and thinly sliced
2 tablespoons fish sauce (available at Asian markets)
Juice of 2 lemons
Juice of 2 limes
3 green onions, white part and some of the green, sliced on the diagonal
2 to 3 small red or green Thai chiles, seeded and finely chopped
1 cup canned unsweetened coconut milk
4 ounces smoked fish fillets, cut into pieces (about 3/4 cup)
1/4 cup finely chopped fresh cilantro leaves

1. In a medium-size saucepan, bring the chicken broth, lime leaves, galangal, fish sauce, lemon and lime juices, green onions, and chiles to a boil. Stir in the coconut milk and bring to a simmer.

2. Stir the smoked fish and cilantro into the soup, then ladle immediately into bowls and serve hot.

Also good with: smoked grouper, hoki, tilapia, or tilefish

PECAN-SMOKED CATFISH WITH FIREWORKS RUB AND MISSISSIPPI MOP

Just as flavorful as fried, but minus the fat! Mississippi Mop is the basting mixture, which keeps the catfish moist and delicious while it's smoking. Serve with coleslaw and hushpuppies.

MAKES 6 SERVINGS

1/2 cup Fireworks Rub (page 279)
Twelve 3- to 5-ounce farm-raised catfish fillets
3 wood chunks, 1 cup wood chips, or 1/3 cup wood pellets
Mississippi Mop (recipe follows)

1. Several hours or the night before you're ready to smoke, pat the rub all over the catfish fillets. Place the fillets in a resealable plastic bag and refrigerate until ready to smoke.

2. Place the wood chunks or wood chips in water to soak or wood pellets in a heavy-duty aluminum foil packet with holes poked into it.

3. Prepare an indirect fire.

4. When ready to smoke, place the drained wood chunks or chips or foil packet on the fire if using a kettle grill or charcoal smoker; in an electric smoker, place the chunks, chips, or packet around the heating element. Fill the water pan and place in the smoker.

5. Place the catfish on the oiled grill or smoker rack and baste with the mop, then baste every 20 minutes while the catfish is covered and smoking. The fish is done when it is opaque and begins to flake when tested with a fork, 1 1/2 to 2 hours.

Also good with: sea bass, halibut, or monkfish

Suggested wood smoke: mesquite, oak, or pecan

MISSISSIPPI MOP

2 cups lager or wheat beer
1/4 cup fresh lime juice
1/2 cup corn or canola oil
2 tablespoons Fireworks
  Rub (page 279)

Mix all the ingredients together in a plastic container.

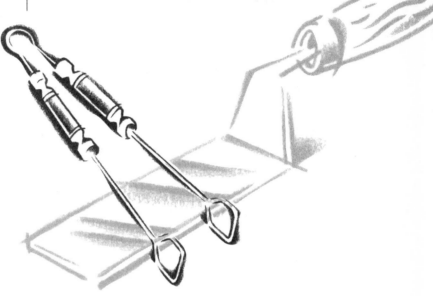

MISSISSIPPI DELTA SMOKED CATFISH SALAD

Blues and B.B. King. Cotton, corn, and catfish. Sultry weather and sweet iced tea. Summer in the Mississippi Delta means stiflingly hot and humid days, when you feel like you're enveloped in a warm, wet blanket when you go outside. This is the salad to eat on those hot days when your appetite flags. It's cool, crisp, and full of flavor.

MAKES 4 SERVINGS

SALAD:

Two 3- to 5-ounce smoked farm-raised catfish fillets (page 194), cut into bite-size pieces

Two 17 1/2-ounce cans corn kernels (about 3 cups), drained

1 large green bell pepper, seeded and finely chopped

1 cup hot pickled okra (available in jars), sliced into thin rounds, or hot pepper rings

4 green onions, white part and some of the green part, chopped

1/2 cup minced fresh Italian parsley leaves

1 cup cherry tomato halves

CREOLE MUSTARD DRESSING:

1 teaspoon sugar

1/4 cup white wine vinegar

1 tablespoon Creole or other mild stone-ground mustard

1. In a large salad bowl, gently combine the smoked catfish, corn, bell pepper, okra, green onions, parsley, and tomatoes.

2. To make the dressing, in a small bowl, whisk the sugar, vinegar, mustard, basil, mayonnaise, pepper, salt, and Tabasco together until smooth. Add the olive oil in a slow, steady stream, whisking constantly, until the dressing has thickened slightly.

3. Toss the salad with the dressing to coat everything evenly and serve immediately.

Also good with: smoked sea bass, halibut, or monkfish

3 tablespoons fresh minced
　basil leaves
2 tablespoons mayonnaise
1/2 teaspoon freshly ground
　black pepper
1/2 teaspoon salt
1/2 teaspoon Tabasco sauce
1/2 cup olive oil

FLY FISHING

We both have taken fly-fishing lessons, with varying results.

Karen puts her training to use whenever she and husband, Dick, catch and release in the American and Canadian Rockies. Karen's first brown trout was on the Eagle River close to Minturn, Colorado. Their friend Darren Williams, who thinks like a fish (one of those trout guys we were talking about), helped her catch it. He could actually see the fish; Karen couldn't. So he told her where to drop the fly. It was on the dime. Fortunately for Darren, his wife, Jennifer, is as avid a fisherman, which makes for marital bliss.

The only thing Judith has reeled in was her fly-fishing instructor for a few dates, a slightly different version of catch and release! In another life (the kind with more free time), however, she would like to go fly-fishing for real. Her dream spot would be in Devon, in southwestern England, where the London Sunday *Times* fish-ing editor has an angler's inn known as the Arundel Arms.

PECAN-PLANKED CATFISH

This goes great with Scalloped Onion Casserole (page 363). For a true Southern feast, serve this with a marinated vegetable salad and hot biscuits.

MAKES 4 SERVINGS

Four 3- to 5-ounce catfish fillets
Lemon pepper to taste

1. Soak two 8 x 16-inch untreated pecan planks in water for at least 30 minutes before smoking.
2. Prepare a medium-hot fire.
3. When ready to smoke, place the planks over direct heat until they begin to smoke and pop, 3 to 4 minutes.
4. Sprinkle the catfish fillets with the lemon pepper.
5. Flip the hot planks over and move to the indirect side of the grill. Immediately place the fillets on the planks, cover, and smoke until the catfish is opaque and begins to flake when tested with a fork, 30 to 35 minutes.

Also good with: salmon, trout, or walleye

CEDAR-PLANKED CHAR

Planking—cooking fish, chicken, or meat on a wood plank over an open fire—is generally done at higher temperatures. However, because the food is separated from the heat by the thickness of the plank, you also get the increased flavor from the wood. Char, a cross between trout and salmon, is best smoked or planked whole. It's easier to fillet and stays moister that way. Whole trout or salmon steaks can also be substituted. Serve the planked char on a bed of aromatic Vegetable Confetti (page 353), perhaps accompanied by a beurre blanc (pages 302–306), Pernod Butter (page 141), or Mustard Cream Sauce (page 321).

MAKES 4 SERVINGS

4 (about 1 pound each) whole Arctic char, cleaned
8 sprigs fresh tarragon
8 sprigs fresh dill
8 sprigs fresh parsley
8 stems fresh chives
Salt and freshly ground white pepper to taste
8 lemon slices

1. Soak two 8 x 16-inch untreated cedar planks in water for at least 30 minutes before smoking.

2. Prepare a medium-hot fire.

3. When ready to smoke, place the planks over direct heat until they begin to smoke and pop, 3 to 4 minutes.

4. Meanwhile, in the cavity of each fish, place 1 sprig each of tarragon, dill, and parsley, and 1 stem of chives. Season with salt and pepper and lay 2 lemon slices over the herbs.

5. Flip the hot planks over and move to the indirect side of the grill, lay the remaining herbs on the plank, and place the fish on the bed of herbs. Cover and smoke until the char is opaque and begins to flake when tested with a fork, about 1 hour.

6. Fillet the char and serve immediately.

Also good with: salmon, sturgeon, or trout

MEDITERRANEAN SMOKED COD ON A BED OF FRESH TOMATO SAUCE

An easy way to enjoy fish in a Caesar-style marinade. Serve with Grilled Red Potatoes, Capers, and Olives (page 368).

MAKES 4 SERVINGS

1 teaspoon anchovy paste
1/2 cup olive oil
Juice of 1 large lemon
2 cloves garlic, minced
1/2 teaspoon sea salt
1/2 teaspoon freshly ground
   black pepper
2 pounds cod steaks or
   fillets, cut into 4 pieces
3 wood chunks, 1 cup wood
   chips, or 1/3 cup wood
   pellets
4 large spinach or leaf
   lettuce leaves
Fresh Tomato Sauce (page
   327)

1. An hour before you're ready to smoke, mix the anchovy paste, olive oil, lemon juice, garlic, sea salt, and pepper together and pour into a large resealable plastic bag. Place the fillets or steaks in the bag, turn to coat with the marinade, and refrigerate until ready.

2. Place the wood chunks or chips in water to soak or wood pellets in a heavy-duty aluminum foil packet with holes poked into it.

3. Prepare an indirect fire.

4. Blanch the spinach or lettuce leaves in a saucepan of boiling water for 1 minute. Carefully remove and pat dry with paper towels. Remove the fish from the marinade and wrap each piece in a spinach or lettuce leaf.

5. When ready to smoke, place the drained wood chunks or chips or foil packet on the fire if using a kettle grill or charcoal smoker; in an electric smoker, place the chunks, chips, or packet around the heating element. Fill the water pan and place in the smoker.

6. Place the fish in a disposable aluminum pan or fish boat and pour the marinade over it. Place the pan on the grill or smoker rack, cover, and smoke until opaque and the thickest part of the fish flakes easily with a fork, about 1 1/2 hours. Serve on a bed of tomato sauce, drizzled with the pan juices.

Also good with: catfish, halibut, or monkfish

Suggested wood smoke: oak or pecan

SMOKED COD BRANDADE WITH SUN-DRIED TOMATOES AND THYME

Traditional French brandade is a simple mixture of soaked and cooked salt cod blended with cooked potato and olive oil into a purée. This version gets a contemporary twist with smoked cod, preserved tomatoes, and fresh thyme.

SERVES 8 AS AN APPETIZER

12 ounces (about 2¼ cups flaked) smoked cod (page 194)

1 medium-size baking potato, baked until tender and flesh scooped out

4 cloves garlic, minced

¼ cup fresh thyme leaves or 2 teaspoons dried

¼ cup sun-dried tomatoes, plumped in hot water to cover and drained

1 cup olive oil

Salt and freshly ground black pepper to taste

1. Preheat the oven to 350 degrees Fahrenheit.

2. Put the cod, potato pulp, garlic, thyme, and tomatoes in a food processor and pulse until smooth, 10 to 15 times. With the machine running, pour in the olive oil in a slow, steady stream through the feed tube until it has all been incorporated into the mixture. Taste and season with salt and pepper. The brandade can be made to this point and kept, covered, in the refrigerator for up to 2 days before serving.

3. Portion out the mixture into eight 8-ounce ramekins or 1 large soufflé dish and bake in the oven: 25 minutes for the ramekins, 1 hour for the soufflé dish.

4. Serve warm with crusty French or artisanal bread.

Also good with: smoked whitefish

BALSAMIC SMOKED HADDOCK

Burnished and fragrant with smoke, this is haddock like you've never had it before! Pair with Fresh Yellow and Red Tomato Salad (page 375) and a good crusty bread. When haddock is not available, use monkfish, halibut, or catfish.

MAKES 4 TO 6 SERVINGS

1/2 cup balsamic vinegar
1/2 cup olive oil
2 cloves garlic, minced
2 pounds haddock fillets or
    steaks
3 wood chunks, 1 cup wood
    chips, or 1/3 cup wood
    pellets

1. An hour before you're ready to smoke, mix the vinegar, olive oil, and garlic together and pour into a large resealable plastic bag. Place the fillets or steaks in the bag, turn to coat with the marinade, and refrigerate until ready to smoke.

2. Place the wood chunks or chips in water to soak or wood pellets in a heavy-duty aluminum foil packet with holes poked into it.

3. Prepare an indirect fire.

4. When ready to smoke, place the drained wood chunks or chips or foil packet on the fire in a kettle grill or charcoal smoker; in an electric smoker, place the wood chunks or chips or packet around the heating element. Fill the water pan and place in the smoker.

5. Remove the haddock from the marinade, place on the grill or smoker rack, cover, and smoke until the fish is opaque and begins to flake when tested with a fork, 1 1/2 to 2 hours.

Also good with: catfish, cod, halibut, or monkfish

Suggested wood smoke: hickory or pecan

SMOKED HADDOCK RISOTTO WITH LEEK AND FENNEL

In England and Scotland, cold-smoked haddock on the bone, or finnan haddie, is the focal point of the famous risotto-like brunch dish known as kedgeree. Our version, using milder hot-smoked haddock or other firm-fleshed fish like catfish, cod, or halibut, is a little more delicate. With a glass of oaky Chardonnay or a peppery young Cabernet, this is a great one-dish supper.

MAKES 4 SERVINGS

3 tablespoons unsalted butter

2 medium-size leeks, white part only, washed well and thinly sliced

1/2 cup chopped fennel bulb

3 to 4 cups chicken broth, as needed

1 cup Arborio rice

8 ounces smoked haddock fillets (page 194), cut into pieces (about 1 1/2 cups)

1/2 cup freshly grated Parmesan cheese, plus more for serving, if desired

Salt and freshly ground black pepper to taste

1. Melt the butter in a large saucepan over medium-low heat. Stir in the leeks and fennel, cover, and cook until the leeks are tender, about 15 minutes. Meanwhile, heat the chicken stock to a simmer in a medium-size saucepan.

2. Add the rice to the leeks and fennel and stir to coat the grains with the buttery juices. Pour in just enough broth to cover the rice and cook, stirring occasionally. Add more of the broth as the rice absorbs the liquid, and continue to cook and stir, about 25 minutes total. The rice should be *al dente*, softened but still slightly chewy.

3. Stir in the fish and Parmesan and cook for 1 more minute to heat through. Season with salt and pepper and serve immediately. Pass more grated Parmesan at the table, if desired.

Also good with: smoked catfish, cod, or halibut

KIPPER-STYLE SMOKED HERRING

The late British food authority Jane Grigson loved lightly cured Northumberland herring that was then cold smoked to become kippers. She preferred, as we do, just a sprinkling of sea salt to help the moisture exude from the fish. Instead of cold smoking, however, we hot smoke over oak wood, basting the fish with a malty ale from a micro-brewery. With the smoked herring, we like to serve Sillsalat (page 371), a relish-like salad that also contains herring.

MAKES 6 TO 8 SERVINGS

Three 12- to 14-ounce
   whole herring, cleaned
1/2 cup coarse sea salt
One 12-ounce bottle dark,
   malty ale
3 wood chunks, 1 cup wood
   chips, or 1/3 cup wood
   pellets

1. In a shallow baking dish, sprinkle the herring all over with the salt, cover, and refrigerate at least 24 hours.

2. The next day, pour off the liquid and rinse the fish in several changes of cold water. Place the fish in a disposable aluminum pan and pour the ale over the fish.

3. Place the wood chunks or chips in water to soak or wood pellets in a heavy-duty aluminum foil packet with holes poked into it.

4. Prepare an indirect fire.

5. When ready to smoke, place the drained wood chunks or chips or foil packet on the fire if using a kettle grill or charcoal smoker; in an electric smoker, place the wood chunks or chips or packet around the heating element. Fill the water pan and place in the smoker.

6. Set the aluminum pan on the grill or smoker rack, cover, and smoke for 30 minutes. Using a spoon, baste the fish with the ale and juices, cover, and continue to smoke until the fish are opaque and flake easily in the thickest part, about 1 hour more.

7. To serve, skin and bone the fish and serve the fillets with sillsalat, horseradish, rye bread, and unsalted butter.

Also good with: bluefish, mackerel, or sablefish (black cod)

Suggested wood smoke: oak

DRIFTWOOD-SMOKED MACKEREL
WITH SAUCE BRETONNE

Vacationers out for a successful fishing trip on the Atlantic can come back to shore, build a fire out of driftwood, and grill whole mackerel until crisp and delicious. Because mackerel are higher in Omega-3 oils, they have a more pronounced flavor and are best eaten very, very fresh. We love them with lots of lemon juice and black pepper, accompanied by the assertive, mustard-flavored Sauce Bretonne.

MAKES 4 SERVINGS

3 wood chunks, 1 cup wood chips, or 1/3 cup wood pellets
Two 1- to 2-pound whole mackerel, cleaned and scaled
3 lemons
8 long sprigs fresh parsley
1/4 cup cracked black peppercorns
Sauce Bretonne (page 320)

1. Place the wood chunks or chips in water to soak or wood pellets in a heavy-duty aluminum foil packet with holes poked into it.

2. Prepare an indirect fire.

3. When ready to smoke, place the drained wood chunks or chips or foil packet on the fire if using a kettle grill or charcoal smoker; in an electric smoker, place the chunks, chips, or packet around the heating element. Fill the water pan and place in the smoker.

4. Rinse the mackerel and pat dry with paper towels. Cut 4 diagonal slashes on each side of the fish. Thinly slice 2 of the lemons and place a half of the slices and 2 parsley sprigs in the cavity of each mackerel. Sprinkle each cavity with 1 teaspoon of the pepper. Place the fish on the grill or smoker rack and drizzle the juice of half a lemon over each fish. Sprinkle the remaining pepper over each fish. Cover and smoke for 1 hour, then drizzle the fish again with the juice of the remaining half a lemon. Cover and continue to smoke until the fish are opaque and begin to flake when tested with a fork, 30 minutes to an hour more.

5. Serve hot with the sauce.

Also good with: bluefish or sablefish (black cod)

Suggested wood smoke: driftwood or oak

ARTICHOKE AND SMOKED MACKEREL PÂTÉ WITH GARLIC-LEMON MAYONNAISE

This is the queen of smoked fish appetizers. Pale green, slightly tart, and just a little bit smoky, this pâté is one of our favorites. This needs to be a made a day ahead of time so it can firm up in the refrigerator. Serve it with Garlic-Lemon Mayonnaise and good, crusty bread such as Life-in-the-Slow-Lane Baguettes in Judith's book *Prairie Home Breads* (Harvard Common Press, 2001). If you use a round springform pan, serve the mayonnaise in a bowl placed in the center of the pâté.

MAKES 8 SERVINGS

2 cups bread cubes (use good-quality bakery or homemade bread, crusts trimmed)

1 cup heavy cream

Three 12-ounce cans artichoke hearts, drained

1/4 cup dry white wine

1 tablespoon Dijon mustard

1/4 cup finely chopped onion

Salt and freshly ground black pepper to taste

2 large eggs

1 cup skinned and flaked smoked mackerel (page 194)

Slices of French bread

Garlic-Lemon Mayonnaise (page 309)

1. Preheat the oven to 325 degrees Fahrenheit. Generously oil a pâté pan or a 10-inch springform pan and set aside.

2. Spread the bread cubes in a shallow baking dish and pour the cream over them. Set aside until the cream is completely absorbed, about 1 hour.

3. Place the cream-soaked bread cubes, artichoke hearts, wine, mustard, and onion in a food processor or a blender and process until smooth. Season with salt and pepper. With the processor running, add the eggs, one at a time, through the feed tube and process until smooth.

4. Spoon half the puréed mixture into the prepared pan, evenly covering the bottom. Sprinkle the flaked fish over the puréed mixture, then spoon the remaining half of the purée over the fish. Gently press down on the pâté with a rubber spatula to remove air pockets. Cover with a sheet of aluminum foil. Then, dampen two tea towels, wrap them around the pan, and place the pan on a baking sheet. Bake until an instant-read thermometer inserted in the middle reads at least 180 degrees Fahrenheit, about 2 hours.

5. Remove from the oven and let cool with the foil still on, but remove the towels. Let cool to room temperature before refrigerating overnight.

6. To serve, remove the pâté from the pan onto a serving platter. Slice the pâté and place on a round of French bread, then top with a dollop of mayonnaise.

Also good with: smoked char, cod, salmon, or trout

OAK-PLANKED SALMON CHARMOULA

We can't think of a better way to enjoy salmon than in this fresh-tasting, healthy Mediterranean recipe. The charmoula, a Moroccan herb-and-spice blend, adds depth to the fresh bite and crunch of the vegetables and the mild smoke and wood flavor of the fish. And this dish looks beautiful as well.

MAKES 6 SERVINGS

1 salmon fillet (about 2 1/2 pounds), with skin on
1/2 cup Charmoula (page 97)

VEGETABLE MEDLEY:

2 tablespoons fresh lemon juice
8 small, ripe Roma tomatoes, diced
2 medium-size cucumbers, peeled, seeded, and diced
1 bunch scallions, chopped
1 red bell pepper, seeded and diced
1 yellow bell pepper, seeded and diced
1 cup chopped fresh Italian parsley leaves
1/2 cup snipped fresh chives
3 tablespoons extra virgin olive oil
1/2 teaspoon sea salt
1/2 teaspoon freshly ground black pepper

Lemon, orange, and lime slices or wedges for garnish

1. Soak one 8 x 16-inch untreated oak plank in water for at least 30 minutes before smoking.

2. Rinse and pat the salmon dry with paper towels. If necessary, trim the fish to fit the plank. Sprinkle the flesh side with the charmoula. Combine the vegetable medley ingredients in a medium-size bowl and mix to blend.

3. Prepare an indirect fire.

4. When ready to smoke, place the plank over direct heat until it begins to smoke and pop, 3 to 4 minutes. Turn the plank over and place the salmon fillet, skin side down, on the hot side of the plank. Top the salmon with the vegetables. Grill over direct heat for about 4 or 5 minutes, then move the plank to the indirect side of the grill. Close the lid and let the salmon plank-smoke until it is opaque and begins to flake with a fork at the thickest part, about 45 minutes.

5. Remove the planked salmon from the grill. Serve directly from the plank with the citrus fruits on the side.

Also good with: char, halibut, or sturgeon

TWO-MARTINI SMOKED SALMON WITH JUNIPER BERRIES

Martini lovers will have most of these ingredients on hand. This recipe is adapted from Karen's *Best Little Barbecue Cookbook* (Ten Speed Press, 2000).

MAKES 4 TO 6 SERVINGS

3 wood chunks, 1 cup wood chips, or 1/3 cup wood pellets

One 3- to 4-pound salmon, cleaned and scaled

1/4 cup gin or vodka

1/4 cup dry vermouth

1/4 cup fresh lemon juice

3 tablespoons unsalted butter, melted

1 tablespoon prepared horseradish

1/2 teaspoon Tabasco sauce

1 clove garlic, minced

2 tablespoons juniper berries (available in the spice section of better grocery stores)

1 lemon, sliced

6 sprigs fresh dill

1. Place the wood chunks or chips in water to soak or wood pellets in a heavy-duty aluminum foil packet with holes poked into it.

2. Prepare an indirect fire.

3. Meanwhile, in a small saucepan, combine the gin, vermouth, lemon juice, butter, horseradish, Tabasco, garlic, and juniper berries, and bring to a boil. Set aside.

4. Rinse the salmon and pat dry with paper towels. Place the salmon on top of a sheet of heavy-duty aluminum foil large enough to hold the fish. Place the lemon slices and sprigs of dill in the cavity of the salmon. Crimp three sides to hold the basting sauce in (the fourth side will fold over). Pour the baste over the salmon, fold over the foil to enclose the salmon, and crimp the edges together.

5. When ready to smoke, place the drained wood chunks or chips or foil packet on the fire if using a kettle grill or charcoal smoker; in an electric smoker, place the wood chunks or chips or packet around the heating element. Fill the water pan and place in the smoker.

6. Place the salmon on the grill or smoker rack, close the lid, and smoke for 1 hour. Open the foil packet, but make sure the edges stay crimped to hold in the baste. Smoke until opaque and the fish begins to flake when tested with a fork, about 1 hour more.

Also good with: whole red snapper or trout

Suggested wood smoke: alder or hickory

SMOKED SALMON AND ASPARAGUS MOUSSE WITH CRÈME FRAÎCHE AND DILL

Both cold- and hot-smoked salmon go into this light, colorful, and delicious appetizer terrine that is surprisingly easy to assemble, as our cooking-class students have remarked. Hot-smoked trout, char, or whitefish are also tender enough to also work in this dish. For a lower-fat version, use lowfat sour cream and Neufchâtel cheese.

MAKES 8 SERVINGS

16 large spinach leaves,
  blanched in boiling
  water for 1 minute,
  drained, and patted dry
Four 1/4-ounce envelopes
  (1 tablespoon) unfla-
  vored gelatin
Juice of 1 lemon
1/2 cup bottled clam juice,
  fish stock, or chicken
  broth
1 large egg white
1/4 cup (1/2 stick) unsalted
  butter
2 tablespoons finely
  chopped onion
8 ounces (about 1 1/2 cups
  flaked) hot-smoked
  salmon fillets (page
  194)
1/2 cup sour cream
One 8-ounce package
  cream cheese, softened
1 teaspoon Maggi
  seasoning
1 teaspoon garlic salt

1. Coat the inside of a 9 x 5 x 3-inch loaf pan with nonstick cooking spray. Line the loaf pan with the blanched spinach leaves. Make sure that the leaves will completely cover the mousse on all sides.

2. Sprinkle the gelatin over the lemon juice in a small dish and set aside to soften. Heat the clam juice in a small saucepan over medium-high heat. When the gelatin has softened, add the mixture to the hot clam juice and stir to dissolve the gelatin.

3. In a medium-size bowl, with an electric mixer, beat the egg white until soft peaks form. Set aside.

4. In a small skillet, melt the butter over medium-high heat, add the onion, and cook, stirring, until softened, about 4 minutes.

5. In a food processor, place the clam juice mixture, sautéed onion, hot-smoked salmon fillets, sour cream, cream cheese, Maggi seasoning, garlic salt, and Tabasco and process until smooth. Spoon the salmon mousse mixture into a medium-size bowl. With a rubber spatula, fold the egg white into the mousse.

6. To assemble the terrine, carefully and evenly spread half the salmon mousse in the bottom of the terrine. Arrange the asparagus spears on top of the mousse, then spread the remaining mousse on top. Cover the mousse with the cold-smoked salmon strips, then fold

¹/4 teaspoon Tabasco sauce

*18 asparagus spears,
steamed just until
crisp-tender*

*4 ounces cold-smoked
salmon, cut into long
pieces*

*Crème fraîche or sour cream
and fresh dill sprigs to
garnish*

over the spinach leaves to completely cover the mousse. Cover with plastic wrap and chill for 4 hours.

7. To serve, slice into 8 portions and garnish each with a dollop of crème fraîche and a sprig of fresh dill.

Also good with: smoked char, trout, or whitefish

NOTE: This dish calls for uncooked egg white. If you have health concerns about using raw egg, you may substitute powdered egg white, reconstituted according to package directions.

OAK-PLANKED ROE-STUFFED SHAD WITH TARRAGON CREAM SAUCE

Poets like Robert Browning might call April "the cruellest month," but shad aficionados rejoice when the calendar flips to that page. April heralds the beginning of the shad run, when the saltwater fish heads to freshwater to spawn.

When the shad are running, everyone gets into the act. The local Rotary Club of Essex, Connecticut, holds an annual Shad Bake. Basted with salt pork drippings, lemon juice, and butter, the shad cooks to perfection under the watchful eye of that year's designated Bakemaster.

Not to be outdone, the Ruritan Club of Wakefield, Virginia, has held their Shad Planking Festival every spring since 1939, luring hundreds with the fragrant smell of wood smoke and the sweet taste of fresh shad. Teams of "plankers," all men, start the seasoned wood and pine branch fire by 5 A.M. Over a ton of fresh shad are scaled, the delicate roe removed, and the fish nailed to oak planks. By 9 A.M., the fish and fire are ready. The planks are lined up around the fire and the fish are basted with a secret sauce. By mid-afternoon, the shad is done to a turn, served with a little more sauce, hushpuppies, coleslaw, and sweet iced tea!

There are shad where we live, too, but they don't seem inclined to run in the Missouri or Kansas Rivers. So, we consulted New England expert Brooke Dojny and adapted her recipe from *The New England Cookbook* (Harvard Common Press, 1999). Shad is naturally very bony, but most eastern markets sell this meaty fish already filleted, and are happy to include the rich roe, for a handsome price. Serve this with sautéed fiddlehead ferns, if you can get them, or steamed asparagus, and boiled new potatoes.

MAKES 4 TO 6 SERVINGS

STUFFING:

2 tablespoons unsalted
    butter
3 tablespoons minced
    shallots
2 pairs shad roe (about 1½
    pounds)
1 cup dry vermouth
1 bay leaf, broken in half

1. Soak one 8 x 16-inch untreated oak or maple plank in water for at least 30 minutes.

2. Prepare an indirect fire.

3. To make the stuffing, melt the butter in a large skillet over medium heat. Add the shallots and cook, stirring, for 1 minute. Add the shad roe, turn to coat it with butter, and add the vermouth and bay leaf. Bring to a gentle simmer and cook, uncovered, until the roe is just barely firm, about 10 minutes. Remove the roe with a slotted spoon to a large plate, reserving the

1 tablespoon fresh lemon
   juice
1/2 teaspoon salt
1/4 teaspoon freshly ground
   black pepper

FISH:

2 large boned sides of shad
   (3 to 4 pounds total)
Salt and freshly ground
   black pepper

TARRAGON
CREAM SAUCE:

1 teaspoon cornstarch
1 cup heavy cream
1 1/2 tablespoons chopped
   fresh tarragon leaves
Salt and freshly ground
   white pepper

poaching liquid. (You can leave the liquid in the pan if you will be finishing the dish right away; otherwise, cover and refrigerate.)

4. Trim off any tough membranes and break the roe into pieces. Add the lemon juice, sprinkle with salt and pepper, and use a large fork to coarsely mash the mixture. (The roe stuffing can be prepared several hours ahead and refrigerated.)

5. Season the shad on both sides with salt and pepper. Place the stuffing under the natural flaps on each side of the fish. Sandwich the stuffed sides together and tie at three intervals with kitchen string.

6. When ready to smoke, place the prepared plank on the hottest part of the fire until it begins to smoke and pop, 3 to 4 minutes. Turn the plank over and place the stuffed shad on the hot side of the plank. Close the lid and cook over direct heat for 10 minutes, then transfer the shad to the indirect heat side. Cover and smoke until the fish is no longer translucent in the thickest part, 30 to 45 minutes more.

7. While the shad is smoking, make the sauce. Boil the reserved roe poaching liquid over high heat until it has reduced to 1/2 cup. Remove and discard the bay leaf. In a small bowl, dissolve the cornstarch in 2 table-spoons of the cream. Whisk the cornstarch mixture and the rest of the cream into the hot poaching liquid and simmer over medium heat, stirring, until lightly thickened. Stir in the chopped tarragon and season with salt and white pepper.

8. To serve, remove the string from the fish and cut horizontally into portions, so everyone gets some of the roe stuffing. Nap each slice with some of the sauce and pass the rest at the table.

Also good with (made without the stuffing):
char, halibut, or salmon

ASIAN LEAF-WRAPPED SNAPPER WITH TAMARIND SAUCE

In tropical countries, large leaves are used to wrap foods for cooking, like we use aluminum foil. Although banana leaves, available at Asian or Hispanic markets, are ideal for this dish, you could also use a moist, tough leaf like chard or mustard greens. Kaffir lime leaves are small, with a pronounced citrus flavor. Galangal is an aromatic root, like fresh ginger. Both add wonderful flavor to this dish. Serve this with Coconut Rice (page 382).

MAKES 4 TO 6 SERVINGS

3 wood chunks, 1 cup wood chips, or 1/3 cup wood pellets

One 4- to 5-pound whole red snapper, cleaned and scaled

1 large banana leaf (available at Asian markets) or several chard leaves or mustard greens

6 kaffir lime leaves (available at Asian markets) or 6 lemon slices

2 thick 6-inch lengths fresh lemongrass (available at Asian markets and larger supermarkets) or 1 tablespoon dried lemongrass (available at health food stores in the loose tea or herb section)

2 cloves garlic, thinly sliced

One 1-inch piece fresh ginger, peeled and thinly sliced

1. Place the wood chunks or chips in water to soak or wood pellets in a heavy-duty aluminum foil packet with holes poked into it.

2. Prepare an indirect fire.

3. Meanwhile, rinse the snapper and pat dry with paper towels. Spread the banana leaf out on a flat surface and place the fish on its side in the middle of the leaf. Place the lime leaves, lemongrass, garlic, ginger, and galangal in the cavity of the fish. Fold the leaf over the fish, like a package.

4. When ready to smoke, place the drained wood chunks or chips or foil packet on the fire if using a kettle grill or charcoal smoker; in an electric smoker, place the wood chunks or chips or packet around the heating element. Fill the water pan and place in the smoker.

5. Place the leaf-wrapped fish folded side down on the grill or smoker rack, cover, and smoke until the fish is opaque and begins to flake when tested with a fork, 2 to 2 1/2 hours.

6. Serve with tamarind sauce.

One 1-inch piece fresh
  galangal (available at
  Asian markets) or more
  fresh ginger, peeled and
  thinly sliced
Tamarind Sauce (recipe
  follows)

TAMARIND SAUCE

Thin, dark, and savory, this Asian-style sauce completes the dish. It is also good as a dipping sauce for other smoked or grilled foods.

MAKES ABOUT 3/4 CUP

1/2 cup Tamarind Liquid
  (page 328)
1 1/2 teaspoons soy sauce
3 tablespoons firmly packed
  brown sugar
2 green Thai chiles or
  jalapeños, seeded and
  finely chopped
4 green onions, white part
  and some of the green
  part, finely chopped

1. Place the tamarind liquid, soy sauce, and brown sugar in a small saucepan over medium-low heat and simmer until slightly thickened, about 5 minutes.

2. Stir in the chiles and green onions and serve.

BEER-BRINED SMOKED SWORDFISH

The elusive flavor and rich color of this hot-smoked fish might persuade you that smoking adds a dimension to food that simple grilling just can't. Serve with Smoked Onions with Thyme Cream (page 364), a baked potato, and a simply dressed green salad. The swordfish needs to be brined for up to 4 hours, so plan ahead.

MAKES 4 TO 6 SERVINGS

2 to 2 1/2 pounds swordfish steaks 1 inch thick, with skin on

BEER BRINE:

4 cups brown ale

1/2 cup coarse sea salt

1/2 cup firmly packed brown sugar

1/4 cup pickling spice

3 wood chunks, 1 cup wood chips, or 1/3 cup wood pellets

1. Rinse the fish, pat dry with paper towels, and place in a deep glass or ceramic bowl or plastic container.

2. In a medium-size saucepan, bring the brine ingredients to a boil over high heat. Stir to dissolve the sugar and salt, then reduce the heat to medium-low and simmer for 15 minutes. Set aside to cool.

3. Strain the brine over the fish, weighting the fish down with a saucer so that it is completely submerged in the brine. Cover and refrigerate for 2 to 4 hours.

4. Place the wood chunks or chips in water to soak or wood pellets in a heavy-duty aluminum foil packet with holes poked into it.

5. Prepare an indirect fire.

6. When ready to smoke, place the drained wood chunks or chips or foil packet on the fire if using a kettle grill or charcoal smoker; in an electric smoker, place the wood chunks or chips or packet around the heating element. Fill the water pan and place in the smoker.

7. Place the onions (if you're making the Smoked Onions with Thyme Cream) on to smoke 30 minutes before the fish.

8. While the onions are smoking, rinse the brine from the fish under cold running water. Remove most of the brine, but not all of it. Place the fish in a disposable aluminum pan, place the pan on the grill or smoker rack, cover, and smoke until the fish is opaque and begins to flake when tested with a fork but is still moist, 45 to 60 minutes.

Also good with: sea bass, bonito, marlin, or tuna

Suggested wood smoke: hickory or pecan

SMOKED SWORDFISH RILLETTES

Rillettes, a specialty of the Loire Valley in France, are usually made from slow-cooked seasoned pork, which is shredded and preserved in pork fat, meant to be spread on good crusty bread. Contemporary French restaurants have stretched the idea of rillettes to include those made with salmon and mackerel. We have found that leftover Beer-Brined Smoked Swordfish (page 224) and Balsamic Smoked Haddock (page 210) also make delicious rillettes, wonderful spread on good artisanal rye or other dark bread, all washed down with a microbrewed beer.

MAKES ABOUT 2/3 CUP

1/2 cup (1 stick) unsalted butter
2 bay leaves
4 ounces (3/4 to 1 cup flaked) smoked swordfish (page 194)
Salt and freshly ground black pepper to taste
Rye, French, or pumpernickel bread

1. In a heavy saucepan, melt the butter over low heat. Add the bay leaf, remove from the heat, cover, and let infuse for 30 minutes.

2. Remove any stray skin or bones from the swordfish. Flake the fish into a bowl. Remove the bay leaf from the butter. With a rubber spatula, blend the flavored butter and swordfish together. Season with salt and pepper.

3. Serve the rillettes in a crock at room temperature, garnished with the remaining bay leaf and surrounded by slices of bread. Cover and chill any leftovers.

Also good with: smoked bonito, marlin, or tuna

APPLE CIDER–SMOKED TROUT WITH HORSERADISH CREAM

Serve this with Spring Onion Spoonbread (page 378) and steamed asparagus or spinach for a delicious spring—or fall—dinner. Taking the skin off the trout first allows the smoke to penetrate more easily. Just about any fish can also be smoked this way. You will get about 8 ounces of fillet from a 14- to 16-ounce whole trout.

MAKES 4 SERVINGS

3 wood chunks, 1 cup wood chips, or 1/3 wood pellets
Four 14- to 16-ounce whole trout, cleaned
1 quart apple cider
1/2 cup Fireworks Rub (page 279)
3/4 cup sour cream
3 tablespoons prepared horseradish
Chopped fresh Italian parsley for garnish

1. Place the wood chunks or wood chips in water to soak or wood pellets in a heavy-duty aluminum foil packet with holes poked into it.

2. Prepare an indirect fire.

3. Meanwhile, bring a large pot of water to a boil. Using tongs, dip each whole trout into the boiling water for 20 to 30 seconds. Remove the trout and peel off the skin. Brush each trout with 1 cup of the apple cider, sprinkle with the rub, and place, cut side down and splayed open, in a disposable aluminum pan.

4. When ready to smoke, place the drained wood chunks or chips or foil packet on the fire if using a kettle grill or charcoal smoker; in an electric smoker, place the wood chunks or chips or packet around the heating element. Fill the water pan with the remaining apple cider, and place the pan in the smoker.

5. Place the pan on the grill or smoker rack, cover, and smoke until the fish are opaque and begin to flake when tested with a fork, 1 1/2 to 2 hours.

6. In a small bowl, mix the sour cream and horseradish together. Serve the fish with a dollop of horseradish cream and a sprinkling of parsley.

Also good with: whole catfish, char, herring, or mackerel

Suggested wood smoke: hickory, oak, or pecan

SMOKED TROUT PÂTÉ WITH DILL AND LEMON

If you don't completely gorge yourself on all the wonderful Apple Cider–Smoked Trout, you can turn the leftovers into this delicious appetizer spread. This pâté can also be made with any tender type of hot-smoked fish, such as salmon, char, or whitefish. Chef Nancy Stark developed this recipe for a "Come Fly with Me" fly-fishing theme dinner featuring wild trout at the Culinary Center of Kansas City.

MAKES ABOUT 2/3 CUP

4 ounces (³/4 to 1 cup flaked) smoked trout fillet (page 194)

¹/2 cup (1 stick) unsalted butter, cubed, at room temperature

1 tablespoon chopped fresh dill, plus more for garnish

1 teaspoon freshly grated lemon zest

Sesame crackers, French bread, or pumpernickel rye

1. Remove any stray skin or bones from the trout fillet. Flake the fillet into a food processor. Add the butter, dill, and lemon zest and process until smooth.

2. Serve the pâté in a crock, garnished with more chopped dill and surrounded by crackers or bread.

Also good with: smoked cod, haddock, salmon, or whitefish

NORTH WOODS SMOKED WALLEYE

For fisherman of the northern Midwestern lakes, late May means walleye season. Marinated in wheat beer and served over mixed greens, this is a fresh-catch meal at its lightest and best. Accompany it with Wild Rice and Dried Cherry Picnic Salad (page 383).

MAKES 4 SERVINGS

BEER MARINADE:

3/4 cup wheat beer

2 cloves garlic, minced

1 tablespoon wildflower or medium-colored honey

1 tablespoon Dijon mustard

1/2 cup balsamic vinegar

2/3 cup olive oil

2 pounds walleye fillets

3 wood chunks, 1 cup wood chips, or 1/3 cup wood pellets

4 cups mixed greens

1. In a medium-size bowl, whisk the marinade ingredients together. Place the walleye fillets in a resealable plastic bag and pour half the marinade over the fish. Close the bag and let marinate in the refrigerator for up to 1 hour. Reserve the remaining marinade in the bowl.

2. Place the wood chunks or wood chips in water to soak or wood pellets in a heavy-duty aluminum foil packet with holes poked into it.

3. Prepare an indirect fire.

4. When ready to smoke, place the drained wood chunks or chips or foil packet on the fire if using a kettle grill or charcoal smoker; in an electric smoker, place the wood chunks or chips or packet around the heating element. Fill the water pan with water and place in the smoker.

5. Remove the fish from the marinade and place in a disposable aluminum pan. Place the pan on the grill or smoker rack, close the lid, and smoke until the fish is opaque and flakes easily in the thickest part of the fillet, 45 to 60 minutes.

6. To serve, place a fish fillet over 1 cup of the greens on each serving plate. Spoon a little of the reserved marinade over the fish and serve.

Also good with: cobia, grouper, hoki, or wolffish

Suggested wood smoke: alder, hickory, or maple

MAPLE-PLANKED WHITEFISH, PEPPERS, AND POTATOES

Native Americans taught the first Great Lakes settlers how to plank their fresh catch by lashing a split and gutted freshwater fish to a piece of driftwood, then stabbing the driftwood into the sand around a roaring beach fire. Our planking method is a little easier and relies less upon chance and more upon your shopping and smoking savvy. Be sure to soak your maple or oak planks in water at least 30 minutes before grilling and smoking.

MAKES 4 SERVINGS

4 large red potatoes

1/2 cup (1 stick) unsalted butter, melted

1/4 cup fresh lemon juice

2 tablespoons fresh lime juice

4 teaspoons sweet Hungarian paprika

2 teaspoons minced fresh thyme leaves

Salt and freshly ground white pepper to taste

One 3- to 3 1/2-pound whitefish, cleaned and dressed

1 red bell pepper, seeded and cut into strips

1 yellow bell pepper, seeded and cut into strips

1 bunch green onions, trimmed

Lemon wedges for garnish

1. Soak three 8 x 16-inch untreated planks in water for at least 30 minutes before smoking.

2. Meanwhile, bring a pot of water to a boil, add the potatoes, and cook for about 10 minutes at a boil. Remove the potatoes from the water and, when cool enough to handle, slice into wedges.

3. In a small bowl, mix together the melted butter, citrus juices, paprika, thyme, salt, and pepper; transfer half of the mixture to a second bowl. Brush the fish inside and out with half the butter mixture from one of the bowls.

4. Prepare a medium-hot fire.

5. When ready to smoke, place the prepared planks over direct heat until they begin to smoke and pop, 3 to 4 minutes. Turn the planks over and move to the indirect side of the grill. Place the fish on one of the hot planks. Place the pepper strips on the second plank and drizzle with half of the butter mixture from the second bowl. Place the potatoes and green onions on the third plank, and drizzle with the remaining half of the butter mixture from the second bowl. Cover and smoke the fish and vegetables for about 1 to 1 1/2 hours. Baste the fish occasionally from the remaining butter mixture in the first bowl. The fish is done when it is opaque and begins to flake when tested with a fork.

6. To serve, fillet the whitefish and place a portion on each plate with the planked vegetables, garnished with lemon wedges.

Also good with: hake, lake perch, or trout

Suggested wood smoke: maple or oak

GREAT LAKES SMOKED WHITEFISH TERRINE

This combination of smoky, creamy, and herby flavors provides the perfect spring or summer appetizer and was adapted from Larry Forgione of The American Place.

TERRINE:

One 1/4-ounce envelope
  unflavored gelatin
1/3 cup cold water
1/3 cup boiling water
1/2 cup mayonnaise
1/4 cup sour cream
2 tablespoons fresh lemon
  juice
2 tablespoons finely
  chopped red onion
1/4 teaspoon cayenne pepper
1/4 teaspoon freshly ground
  black pepper
1/4 cup chopped fresh
  Italian parsley leaves
10 ounces smoked white-
  fish (page 194), skin
  and bones removed and
  finely flaked (2 cups)
2/3 cup whipping cream
2 cups fresh watercress
  leaves

1. To make the terrine, in a large bowl soften the gelatin in the cold water for 5 minutes. Stir in the boiling water and stir until the gelatin has dissolved. Whisk in the mayonnaise, sour cream, lemon juice, onion, cayenne, and black pepper. Fold in the parsley and fish.

2. With an electric mixer, in a medium-size bowl, beat the whipping cream until it just starts to thicken. Fold the cream into the fish mixture.

3. Line an 8 x 4 x 2-inch loaf pan with plastic wrap and pour the fish mixture into the prepared pan. Smooth the top. Cover and refrigerate for 6 hours or overnight.

4. Blend all the sauce ingredients in a medium-size bowl and keep refrigerated until ready to use.

TARRAGON-CHIVE SAUCE:

1/2 cup sour cream

1/2 cup mayonnaise

1/4 cup tarragon vinegar

1 teaspoon chopped fresh dill

1 tablespoon snipped fresh chives

5. To serve, carefully unmold the terrine onto a serving plate and slice with a thin-bladed knife. Arrange the slices on individual plates garnished on the side with the watercress. Top with a dollop of sauce.

Also good with: smoked char, trout, or walleye

SMOKED WHITEFISH BLINIS WITH HERBED SOUR CREAM

This makes a delicious brunch entrée or a light luncheon dish, served with fresh asparagus and a fruit compote. The blini batter needs to rest for an hour before you make the crêpes. You could also make them in advance and freeze them, separated by waxed or parchment paper, in a resealable plastic bag. Smoked trout, salmon, haddock, or cod may also be served this way. Use lowfat sour cream and mayonnaise, if you prefer.

MAKES 4 SERVINGS (ABOUT 8 BLINIS)

HERBED SOUR CREAM:
1/2 cup sour cream
1/2 cup mayonnaise
1/4 cup tarragon vinegar
1 teaspoon chopped fresh
 dill
1 tablespoon snipped fresh
 chives

BLINIS:
1 cup half-and-half
1/2 cup water
1 cup all-purpose flour
1 teaspoon dillweed
2 large eggs, beaten
1/2 cup vegetable oil, plus
 extra for the pan
Salt and freshly ground
 white pepper to taste

1. Combine the herbed sour cream ingredients in a medium-size bowl, cover, and set aside in the refrigerator until ready to use.

2. Whisk all the blini ingredients together in a medium-size bowl until smooth. Cover and let rest for 1 hour, covered, in the refrigerator.

3. Brush an 8-inch nonstick skillet with vegetable oil and heat over medium-high heat. Using a 1/3-cup measuring cup, pour the batter into the hot pan and swirl the pan to make a thin crêpe. Cook until the crêpe can be flipped, about 1 minute. Cook for 30 seconds on the other side, then transfer to a plate to keep warm. Repeat the process with the remaining batter.

10 ounces smoked white-fish (page 194), skin and bones removed and finely flaked (2 cups)
Chopped fresh herbs for garnish

4. Lay each blini out on a flat surface. Place about $1/4$ cup of the smoked fish on each blini and top with 1 tablespoon of the herbed sour cream, then fold in half or roll up. Repeat the process with the remaining fish, blinis, and sour cream. Garnish with chopped fresh herbs.

Also good with: smoked char, trout, or walleye

SHELLFISH IN THE SMOKER

SPICY SMOKED CLAMS

German immigrant Gustav Brunn developed the secret mixture (cloves, pimento, ginger, celery salt, and much more) known as Old Bay seasoning. Originally intended for boiling crab, Old Bay is also delicious for smoking cherrystone, quahog, or little-neck clams. Serve these clams with lots of good crusty bread and unsalted butter, corn on the cob, and coleslaw.

MAKES 4 SERVINGS

4 pounds clams (about 4 dozen)
1 cup dry white wine
2 cloves garlic, minced
1/4 cup fresh lemon juice
1/2 teaspoon red pepper flakes
2 tablespoons Old Bay seasoning or Fireworks Rub (page 279)
3 wood chunks, 1 cup wood chips, or 1/3 cup wood pellets

1. Place the wood chunks or wood chips in water to soak or wood pellets in a heavy-duty aluminum foil packet with holes poked into it.

2. Prepare an indirect fire.

3. Meanwhile, clean the clams under running cold water, scraping away the fibrous bits. Discard any with broken shells or shells that won't close. In a large pot, bring the wine, garlic, lemon juice, red pepper flakes, and Old Bay seasoning to a boil over high heat. Add the clams, cover, and steam until they open, 8 to 10 minutes. Remove the clams from the pot to two disposable aluminum pans, discarding any that won't open; reserve the liquid and keep it simmering.

4. When ready to smoke, place the drained wood chunks or chips or foil packet on the fire if using a kettle grill or charcoal smoker; in an electric smoker, place the wood chunks or chips or packet around the heating element. Fill the water pan and place in the smoker.

5. Place the pans on the grill or smoker rack over indirect heat. Cover and smoke until the clams have a smoky aroma, 20 to 30 minutes.

6. To serve, divide the clams among 4 bowls and pour over the reserved broth.

Suggested wood smoke: hickory

FRESH CORN AND SMOKED CLAM CAKES WITH ANCHO CHILE SAUCE

In the 1950s, we had salmon patties. In the '80s, it was crab cakes. Now it's time for another culinary leap, to these vibrantly flavored cocktail nibbles or light luncheon entrées. Smoked mussels or oysters also taste delicious prepared this way. Ancho chiles are dried, ripened poblano chiles, and their slightly smoky flavor works well in the accompanying dipping sauce.

MAKES 4 MAIN-COURSE SERVINGS OR 12 APPETIZER-SIZE CAKES

12 smoked clams (page
    193), removed from
    their shells and finely
    diced (about 3/4 cup)
3/4 cup fresh corn kernels,
    cooked until tender and
    drained
2 green onions, white part
    and some of the green,
    finely chopped
2 tablespoons finely
    chopped fresh Italian
    parsley leaves
3 tablespoons mayonnaise
1 teaspoon Maggi
    seasoning
1 teaspoon freshly ground
    white pepper
1/4 teaspoon Tabasco sauce
1/2 to 3/4 cup fine dry bread
    crumbs, as needed
Vegetable oil for frying
Ancho Chile Sauce (page
    315)

1. In a medium-size bowl, mix together the diced clams, corn, green onions, and parsley. In a small bowl, mix the mayonnaise, Maggi, white pepper, and Tabasco together. Fold the mayonnaise mixture into the clam mixture with a rubber spatula until everything holds together. Form the mixture into 12 cakes and set aside.

2. Heat 1 inch of vegetable oil in a large skillet over medium-high heat. Place the bread crumbs on a plate or shallow bowl. Dredge each cake on all sides in the bread crumbs. Fry the clam cakes until golden brown, 3 to 4 minutes per side. Drain on paper towels and serve hot with the chile sauce.

LINGUINE WITH SMOKED CLAMS AND PLUM TOMATOES

 delicious remake of the classic.

MAKES 4 SERVINGS

¹/4 cup olive oil

4 garlic cloves, minced

¹/2 cup dry white wine

8 smoked plum tomatoes
(page 190), peeled,
seeded, and diced

2 pounds smoked clams in
their shells (page 193)

¹/2 cup finely chopped fresh
Italian parsley leaves

1 pound linguine, cooked
according to package
directions, drained, and
kept hot

1. In large skillet over medium heat, heat the olive oil and garlic together until the garlic is softened, but not golden, about 3 minutes, stirring. Stir in the wine and chopped tomatoes and simmer for 5 minutes.

2. Remove the clams from their shells and add to the pasta sauce, along with the parsley. Heat through, then toss with the linguine and serve immediately.

PERNOD-SMOKED LOBSTER

We find that the best technique for infusing lobster with a wonderful smoke flavor is threefold: boiling, then grilling, then smoking. The buttery flavor still comes through, so we love this lobster served simply—no sauce, no drawn butter. The lobster should be the star attraction on the plate. A luscious Chardonnay with a hint of oak, a simply dressed green salad, and good crusty bread with unsalted butter is all you need to add.

MAKES 4 SERVINGS

3 wood chunks, 1 cup wood chips, or 1/3 cup wood pellets

3 tablespoons olive oil

3 tablespoons unsalted butter, softened

1 tablespoon Pernod or other anise-flavored liqueur

2 teaspoons lemon pepper

Four 1 1/4- to 1 1/2-pound live lobsters

1. Place the wood chunks or chips in water to soak or wood pellets in a heavy-duty aluminum foil packet with holes poked into it.

2. Prepare an indirect fire.

3. Meanwhile, in a small bowl, mix the olive oil, butter, Pernod, and lemon pepper together and set aside.

4. Bring a large pot of water to a boil. Place the live lobsters in the boiling water, head first, and cook for 5 minutes. Remove the lobsters and drain. Using kitchen shears, remove the membrane from the tail, keeping the tail intact. (This allows more smoke to permeate the lobster.) Brush the lobsters with the butter and olive oil mixture.

5. When ready to smoke, place the drained wood chunks or chips or foil packet on the fire if using a kettle grill or charcoal smoker; in an electric smoker, place the wood chunks or chips or packet around the heating element. Fill the water pan with water and place in the smoker.

6. Place the lobsters on the grill over a hot fire, shell side down, and grill for 10 minutes. Then transfer them to the indirect side, generously brush with the remaining butter and olive oil baste, close the lid, and smoke the lobster until the tail meat is firm and no longer translucent, another 20 to 30 minutes. Serve hot or at room temperature.

Suggested wood smoke: apple or mesquite

SMOKED LOBSTER RAVIOLI WITH SAFFRON CREAM SAUCE

For this recipe, we recommend smoking lobster tails for ease of preparation. You can smoke the lobster and assemble the ravioli a day or two ahead, then finish cooking this decadently delicious main course in minutes. Your guests will rave! The lighter smoke of oak or pecan adds a nuance of flavor without overpowering either the lobster or the saffron sauce. Accompany this dish with a luscious, full-bodied white wine and grilled asparagus. Smoked shrimp is a less pricey choice for the ravioli filling.

MAKES 4 SERVINGS

3 wood chunks, 1 cup wood chips, or 1/3 cup wood pellets

Four 8-ounce rock lobster tails

1/4 cup (1/2 stick) unsalted butter, melted

1 cup dry white wine

8 ounces mascarpone cheese, softened

Salt and freshly ground white pepper to taste

Four 14 x 6 1/2-inch sheets fresh pasta (available at Italian markets)

1 large egg

1 tablespoon water

Saffron Cream Sauce (page 321)

8 asparagus spears, bottoms trimmed and steamed until crisp-tender, for garnish

1. Place the wood chunks or chips in water to soak or wood pellets in a heavy-duty aluminum foil packet with holes poked into it.

2. Prepare an indirect fire.

3. When ready to smoke, place the drained wood chunks or chips or foil packet on the fire if using a kettle grill or charcoal smoker; in an electric smoker, place the wood chunks or chips or packet around the heating element. Fill the water pan with water and place in the smoker.

4. Cut the top membrane from the lobster tails and discard. Loosen the meat from the shell and brush with the melted butter. Place the tails in a disposable aluminum pan cut side up. Pour the wine over the lobster, cover, and smoke over indirect heat until the lobster tails are opaque and have a smoky aroma, about 1 hour.

5. Remove the lobster from the smoker and set aside to cool slightly. Remove the lobster meat from the shells and finely chop. Stir in the mascarpone cheese and season with salt and white pepper. Set aside.

6. Lay out a sheet of the pasta on a lightly floured work surface. Place 1 teaspoon of the lobster filling at 2-inch intervals all over the pasta, leaving a 1-inch border around each spoonful. In a small bowl, whisk the egg and water together to make an egg wash. Brush the border of the pasta and the spaces between the fillings with the egg wash. Carefully lift, then place a second sheet of fresh pasta over the bottom sheet. With your fingers, carefully press the pasta all around the border and between the mounds of filling to seal. Using a pizza wheel or a chef's knife, cut the ravioli into squares and set aside. Repeat the process with the remaining pasta and filling. (The ravioli can be made to this point, placed in single layers separated by waxed or parchment paper in a plastic container, covered, and refrigerated for up to 2 days.)

7. Bring a large pot of water to a boil. Carefully place the ravioli in the water, one at a time. Stir gently and do not overcrowd. The ravioli will float to the top when cooked, 3 to 5 minutes. Remove and drain in a colander.

8. To serve, toss the ravioli in the cream sauce. Place some ravioli and sauce on each plate. Garnish with two asparagus spears placed in a "V" at the bottom of the plate.

Suggested wood smoke: oak or pecan

SMOKED MUSSELS WITH LEMON-GARLIC HOLLANDAISE

We have found that the best way to smoke mussels and other shellfish is to steam them first to snap open the shells, then to smoke them for about 30 minutes. But smoke them any longer, and the mussels could dry out or become leathery. Clams or oysters would also be good this way. Serve with boiled new potatoes and steamed asparagus.

MAKES 4 SERVINGS

3 wood chunks, 1 cup wood chips, or 1/3 cup wood pellets

4 pounds mussels (about 4 dozen)

1 cup dry white wine

2 cloves garlic, minced

1/4 cup fresh lemon juice

2 tablespoons finely snipped fresh chives

Lemon-Garlic Hollandaise (recipe follows)

1. Place the wood chunks or chips in water to soak or wood pellets in a heavy-duty aluminum foil packet with holes poked into it.

2. Prepare an indirect fire.

3. Meanwhile, clean the mussels under running cold water, scraping away the fibrous bits and discarding any that have broken shells or shells that won't close. In a large pot, bring the wine, garlic, lemon juice, and chives to a boil over high heat. Add the mussels, cover, and steam until the mussels open, 8 to 10 minutes. Remove the mussels from the pot to two disposable aluminum pans, discarding any that refuse to open; reserve the cooking liquid.

4. When ready to smoke, place the drained wood chunks or chips or foil packet on the fire if using a kettle grill or charcoal smoker; in an electric smoker, place the wood chunks or chips or packet around the heating element. Fill the water pan with water and place in the smoker.

5. Place the pans on the smoker or grill rack over indirect heat, close the lid, and smoke the mussels until they have a smoky aroma, 20 to 30 minutes.

6. To serve, place a ramekin of hollandaise on each plate, along with a dozen smoked mussels.

Suggested wood smoke: hickory

LEMON-GARLIC HOLLANDAISE

zestier version of the classic sauce.

MAKES ABOUT 1 CUP

1/2 cup reserved mussel steaming liquid (page 244)
3 large egg yolks
1/4 teaspoon cayenne pepper
1/2 cup (1 stick) unsalted butter, melted
Salt to taste

1. While the mussels are smoking, make the hollandaise. Bring the reserved steaming liquid to a boil in a medium-size saucepan and boil for 3 minutes.

2. Place the egg yolks and cayenne in a blender or food processor and process until smooth. With the machine running, pour in the hot wine liquid, then the melted butter.

3. Transfer the mixture back to the saucepan over low heat. Whisk occasionally until the hollandaise coats the back of a spoon, 8 to 10 minutes. Season with salt and keep warm until needed.

WARM SMOKED MUSSEL, POTATO, AND SPINACH SALAD

The market stalls of Bruges, Belgium, provided the inspiration for this recipe. From November through March, you'll see cold-weather greens—chard, spinach, and kale—in stalls that look like Old Masters paintings come to life. To ward off your hunger as you shop in the damp, chilly air, you can buy a bucket of steamed mussels and a paper cone full of French fries topped with a decadent spoonful of mayonnaise. All of those elements come together in this warm and wonderful salad.

MAKES 4 SERVINGS

2 large red potatoes, peeled
    and cut into cubes
2 tablespoons olive oil
Salt and freshly ground
    black pepper to taste
1 pound fresh spinach,
    washed well and heavy
    stems removed
24 smoked mussels (page
    193)
Lemon-Garlic Hollandaise
    (page 245)
Paprika for garnish

1. Parboil the potatoes in a medium-size saucepan full of water for 10 minutes, then drain well.

2. In a large skillet, heat the olive oil over medium heat, then cook the potatoes, stirring occasionally, until golden brown on all sides, about 15 minutes. Season with salt and pepper, then transfer to a bowl to keep warm.

3. Add the spinach to the skillet and stir-fry until the leaves have wilted and turned dark green, about 3 minutes.

4. Place the wilted spinach on each of 4 large salad plates and top with the fried potatoes. Place 6 smoked mussels around the perimeter of each plate and drizzle or spoon the hollandaise over the salad. Sprinkle with paprika and serve warm.

Long a staple of European cuisine, mussels are finally making a statement on American menus. It helps that mussels are now farm-raised—attached to long fiber ropes in saltwater lagoons, so that they never touch the sandy bottom and pick up grit and dirt. Mussels filter up to 15 gallons of seawater a day, consuming anything edible that comes in. Mussel farms carefully monitor water quality and food availability so they avoid seasonal problems, such as the "red tide," that limit the "in the wild" West Coast mussel season from November through April. Farm-raised mussels arrive at the market or in the restaurant much cleaner and fresher than do mussels from the wild.

The most commonly available mussels are:

• Blue mussels (*Mytilus edulis*), which have indigo blue to black shells and tan meat. These are found in the Atlantic from Canada down to the Gulf of Mexico, and especially around Prince Edward Island. In the Pacific, blues are found from Alaska to Baja California. Blue mussels are at their peak from October to May and spawn in May and June.

• Mediterranean mussels (*Mytilus galloprovincialis*), which have black shells and are big and meaty—up to 7 inches long. Although native to Mediterranean waters, they are now farmed in California and Washington, although how they ended up on the West Coast seems like a story out of a pirate movie. Food historians believe these mussels arrived in California firmly attached to the hulls of Spanish galleons and decided to try their luck in a new spot. Mediterranean mussels are at their peak during the summer months and spawn during January and February.

• Green-lipped or New Zealand green mussels (*Perna canaliculus*), which have brown shells edged in emerald green and ivory- or salmon-colored meat. Greens are at their prime in the winter months and spawn during September and October.

Purchase mussels with tightly closed shells or shells that close shut when tapped—otherwise they're not alive and fresh. Discard those with broken shells. Wash mussels in cold water, scrubbing them well. Pull out and discard the fibrous beard that grows between the shell halves.

Mussels and other mollusks require high initial temperatures to cook the mussel and open the shell. We recommend either placing mussels over a hot fire, covering, and letting the mollusks grill-steam for 4 to 5 minutes or steaming the mussels open, then slow smoking for up to 30 minutes.

SMOKED MUSSELS WITH FETTUCCINE

A fresh-tasting pasta dish, simple yet sophisticated.

MAKES 4 SERVINGS

3 wood chunks, 1 cup wood chips, or 1/3 cup wood pellets

4 pounds mussels (about 4 dozen)

1 cup dry white wine

4 cloves garlic, minced

1/4 cup fresh lemon juice

1/2 cup chopped fresh Italian parsley leaves

1/4 cup extra virgin olive oil

1 pound fettuccine, cooked according to package directions, drained, and kept hot

Chopped fresh herbs for garnish

1. Place the wood chunks or chips in water to soak or wood pellets in a heavy-duty aluminum foil packet with holes poked into it.

2. Prepare an indirect fire.

3. Meanwhile, clean the mussels under running cold water, scraping away the fibrous bits and discarding any that have broken shells or shells that won't close. In a large pot, bring the wine, garlic, lemon juice, and parsley to a boil over high heat. Add the mussels, cover, and steam until they open, 8 to 10 minutes. Remove the mussels from the pot to two disposable aluminum pans, discarding any that refuse to open; reserve the cooking liquid and keep it simmering.

4. When ready to smoke, place the drained wood chunks or chips or foil packet on the fire if using a kettle grill or charcoal smoker; in an electric smoker, place the wood chunks or chips or packet around the heating element. Fill the water pan with water and place in the smoker.

5. Place the pans on the grill or smoker rack over indirect heat. Close the lid and smoke the mussels until they have a smoky aroma, 20 to 30 minutes.

6. To serve, toss the pasta with the reserved steaming liquid and the olive oil and apportion the pasta among 4 serving plates. Top with the smoked mussels, garnish with herbs, and serve immediately.

Suggested wood smoke: hickory or oak

HICKORY-SMOKED OYSTERS WITH CAJUN BUTTER BASTE

Sublime! The smoky hickory flavor is sensational with plump juicy oysters.

MAKES 6 SERVINGS

3 wood chunks, 1 cup wood chips, or 1/3 cup wood pellets

CAJUN BUTTER BASTE:

1/2 cup (1 stick) unsalted butter
1/2 teaspoon garlic powder
1/4 cup fine dry bread crumbs
1 teaspoon dried oregano
2 dashes of Tabasco sauce
1 teaspoon chopped fresh Italian parsley leaves
2 tablespoons minced onion

36 oysters on the half shell
Rock salt
1 cup Updated Classic Cocktail Sauce (page 318)

1. Place the wood chunks or chips in water to soak or wood pellets in a heavy-duty aluminum foil packet with holes poked into it.

2. Prepare an indirect fire.

3. Meanwhile, make the butter baste. Melt the butter in a small saucepan. Add the garlic powder, bread crumbs, oregano, Tabasco, parsley, and onion, stir, and set aside.

4. Arrange the oysters on the half shell on a bed of rock salt in a shallow disposable aluminum pan. Spoon 1 teaspoon of the butter baste on each oyster.

5. When ready to smoke, place the drained wood chunks or chips or foil packet on the fire if using a kettle grill or charcoal smoker; in an electric smoker, place the wood chunks or chips or packet around the heating element. Fill the water pan and place in the smoker.

6. Place the pan on the grill or smoker rack over indirect heat, close the lid, and smoke for about 30 minutes. The oysters are done when their edges begin to curl.

7. Serve as an appetizer with the cocktail sauce.

Suggested wood smoke: hickory

Gone are the "R" months. Like not wearing white shoes after Labor Day, the dictum of not eating oysters in months without an "R" in them has faded away. This used to be because oysters spawn in summer months and can have an "off" flavor during that time. Also, bacteria counts in warmer waters made eating oysters undesirable. Now that 75 to 80 percent of oysters are farm-raised, spawning times vary and the consumer gets a cleaner, fresher product all year long. Farm-raised oysters live out their lives in submerged nets in seas with plentiful plankton, the oyster's favorite food. Oyster farmers carefully monitor the size of the oysters as well as the temperature and quality of the water. "Banks" refer to natural oyster beds in the wild; "ponds" refer to farmed oyster beds.

The consumer should beware, however, of any oyster that smells or looks less than fresh from the sea. Oysters can still be contaminated by mercury in the water, along with bacteria, viruses, or improper handling and storage. The best advice: know and trust your supplier. And during the summer months, choose oysters that come from cooler waters in Maine, northern California, Nova Scotia, Prince Edward Island, or British Columbia.

SMOKED OYSTERS ROCKEFELLER

This ultimate version of the classic Oysters Rockefeller from Paul Kirk, the Baron of Barbecue, adds a decadent smoky twist. Betcha can't eat just one! To allow for maximum smoke to circulate, Kirk recommends sitting each oyster in a screwtop canning lid. You could also place the oysters in a disposable aluminum pan.

MAKES 2 DOZEN OYSTERS

3 wood chunks, 1 cup wood chips, or 1/3 cup wood pellets

1/4 cup (1/2 stick) unsalted butter

1/3 cup thinly sliced green onions

2 large cloves garlic, minced

One 10-ounce package frozen chopped spinach, defrosted and patted dry

1 tablespoon dry sherry

1 teaspoon sea salt

1 teaspoon freshly ground black pepper

1/4 cup fine dry bread crumbs

2 dozen oysters on the half shell, drained of their liquor

2 tablespoons fresh lemon juice

Tabasco sauce or other hot sauce

4 strips bacon, fried until crisp, drained on paper towels, and crumbled

Twenty-four 1-inch strips smoked roasted red pepper (page 190) or pimento

1. Place the wood chunks or chips in water to soak or wood pellets in a heavy-duty aluminum foil packet with holes poked into it.

2. Prepare an indirect fire.

3. Heat the butter in a medium-size saucepan over medium-high heat. Add the onions and garlic and cook, stirring, until tender, about 3 minutes. Stir in the spinach, sherry, salt, and pepper and cook for another 3 minutes. Remove from the heat and stir in the bread crumbs.

4. Place each oyster on a screwtop canning lid or on a disposable aluminum tray. Drizzle each oyster with a little lemon juice and a dash of Tabasco. Spoon the spinach mixture over each of the oysters and garnish with bacon crumbles and red pepper strips.

5. When ready to smoke, place the drained wood chunks or chips or foil packet on the fire if using a kettle grill or charcoal smoker; in an electric smoker, place the wood chunks or chips or packet around the heating element. Fill the water pan with water and place in the smoker.

6. Set on the oysters on the grill or smoker rack over indirect heat, close the lid, and smoke until the oysters are opaque, have a mild smoky aroma, and are curled at the edges, 20 to 40 minutes.

Suggested wood smoke: apple or oak

SMOKED OYSTER BISQUE

When chefs Debbie Gold and Michael Smith were at the American Restaurant in Kansas City, Judith begged them for their oyster bisque recipe to include in *Prairie Home Cooking* (Harvard Common Press, 1999). After we tasted how delicious smoked oysters are, we decided they also deserved to be floated at the last minute in this creamy, vichyssoise-like bisque enriched with chicken stock and herbs. A hint of smoke raises this elegant soup to a new level. It's rich enough to be a meal in itself, accompanied by crusty bread and a green salad.

MAKES 8 SERVINGS

3 wood chunks, 1 cup wood chips, or 1/3 cup wood pellets

5 dozen oysters on the half shell, or more, shucked

1/2 cup fresh lemon juice

1/2 cup (1 stick) unsalted butter, melted

2 tablespoons unsalted butter

1 cup finely chopped leeks, whites and part of the green

1 cup finely chopped onions

4 cups peeled and diced baking potatoes

4 cups chicken broth

1 bay leaf

1 sprig fresh summer savory

3 cups heavy cream

Salt and freshly ground black pepper to taste

Homemade croutons and fresh chives for garnish

1. Place the wood chunks or chips in water to soak or wood pellets in a heavy-duty aluminum foil packet with holes poked into it.

2. Prepare an indirect fire.

3. Place each oyster in a screwtop canning lid or on a disposable aluminum pan. Drizzle each oyster with a little lemon juice and melted butter.

4. When ready to smoke, place the drained wood chunks or chips or foil packet on the fire if using a kettle grill or charcoal smoker; in an electric smoker, place the wood chunks or chips or packet around the heating element. Fill the water pan and place in the smoker.

5. Place the oysters on the grill or smoker rack, close the lid, and smoke until they are opaque, have a mild smoke aroma, and are just curled at the edges, 20 minutes to 1 hour.

6. While the oysters are smoking, prepare the bisque. In a large soup pot, melt the 2 tablespoons butter over medium heat. Add the leeks, onions, and 3 cups of the potatoes, and cook, stirring, until the onions are transparent, about 5 minutes. Add the chicken broth, bay leaf, and summer savory. Bring to a boil, reduce the heat to medium-low, and simmer until the potatoes are tender, about 15 minutes. Add the heavy cream and bring to a boil again. Remove from the heat, let cool for 30 minutes, then purée the soup in a blender or food processor. Return the soup to the pot, add the remaining 1 cup potatoes, and simmer until the potatoes are just soft, about 15 minutes.

7. Just before serving, remove the smoked oysters from their shells. Ladle the bisque into bowls and spoon 7 or 8 oysters into each bowl. Serve immediately, garnished with croutons and fresh chives.

Suggested wood smoke: apple, hickory, oak, or pecan

OAK-PLANKED SEA SCALLOPS

This is perfect served with Smoked and Braised Bacon-Wrapped Endive (page 359). In a contemporary French-bistro scallop and endive salad, your taste buds get a work-out from the bitter frisée, seared sweet scallops, smoky chunks of bacon, and tart vinaigrette dressing. Here, we've changed it up just a bit to create an entrée with a hauntingly wonderful aroma and great flavor.

MAKES 4 SERVINGS

2 cloves garlic, minced
2 green onions, finely
   chopped
Juice of 1 lemon
1 teaspoon Dijon
   mustard
¼ cup olive oil
12 large sea scallops,
   rinsed and patted dry

1. Soak one 8 x 16-inch untreated oak plank in water for at least 30 minutes before smoking.

2. In a small bowl, mix together the garlic, green onions, lemon juice, mustard, and olive oil. Dip the sea scallops in this mixture and place on a plate or tray to take outside.

3. Prepare an indrect fire.

4. When ready to smoke, place the plank directly over the fire until it begins to smoke and pop, 3 to 4 minutes. Turn the plank over and move to the indirect side of the grill. Place the scallops on the hot plank, cover, and smoke until they are firm and opaque, 30 to 45 minutes. Serve immediately.

THINGS ARE GETTING FISHY!
(OR WHY YOU NEED A FISHMONGER)

What's in a name? If you're talking about fish names, then you're talking double-talk. Maybe even triple-talk.

Let's begin with the most confusing of all, the sea bass. This wonderfully delicious fish is also known as *loup de mer* in French, which means "sea wolf." (Please don't confuse it with wolffish.)

Nor is the Chilean sea bass a true sea bass, rather it's a Patagonian toothfish. And sometimes the Patagonion toothfish is also called mero, but this mero shouldn't be confused with grouper, which is also known as mero.

Back to wolffish, which is actually a North Atlantic ocean catfish, but not related to channel catfish. Oh well.

Cod is not too bad. Namely, there's rock cod, codling, and scrod cod (cod that weighs in at 2.5 pounds and under). There's also the "Sacred Cod," carved in white pine, that hangs in the Massachusetts Hall of Representatives.

But there's more to the cod family than meets the eye. There's pollock or pollack, which is a member of the cod family regardless how it is spelled. Regional names are where the true confusion comes in. Walleye pollock has no relation to walleyed pike, which is a member of the perch family. Sometimes pollock is called whiting and that's almost okay, because they're both members of the cod family.

Whiting is often interchanged with hake. They are both cod family members, but with a few minor differences.

Salmon are fairly straightforward fish. There's Atlantic salmon. King salmon has several names; chinook is spring salmon, and quinnat is winter salmon. In the Pacific Northwest, you will often hear salmon referred to by its Indian name, tyee. Silver salmon is also known as coho. Sockeye salmon is red or blueback salmon. Chum salmon is known as keta, chub, or dog salmon.

However, dog salmon is not related to dogfish, which is a shark. But dogfish, which is a shark, is sometimes called rock salmon.

Red mullet is sometimes called goatfish.

Stone bass or wreckfish (because they live around wrecked ships at the bottom of the sea) are ugly relatives of the sea bass family. And, don't you know that sea bass are part of the grouper family?

Another ugly-faced fish, John Dory, has a large black spot ringed with yellow in the middle of its very flat body. Lore has it that the spot is St. Peter's thumbprint from when he picked up the fish and found a gold coin in its mouth, which was used to pay the tax collector. Hence John Dory is also known as St. Peter's fish.

And surprise, surprise! Tilapia is also sold under the name of St. Peter's fish.

Sea bream's most popular variety is the gilt-head bream. In Spanish their name is *dorada*.

Oops! That's pretty close to dorado. Mahimahi is known as dorado and dolphinfish. Don't confuse it with the mammal named dolphin.

Enough of this silly fish name business. Let's hit the road, Jack. But, first permit me to introduce you to the jack family, including the permit also known as the pompano, amberjack, and yellowtail.

Holy Mackerel! This nonsense was just for the halibut! So quit your carping!

SMOKED SCALLOPS WITH CITRUS VINAIGRETTE

Steve Cole, the chef-owner of Kansas City's Cafe Allegro, has garnered praise from food critics throughout the country for his "allegro con brio" (lively with brilliance) style. We have adapted his appetizer to include smoked, not seared, scallops. Light and refreshing, these smoked scallops, in a colorful and flavorful citrus vinaigrette, do what all good appetizers do—whet the appetite for what is to follow. Only this dish is so good, you'll be tempted to stop right here. The hardest part is peeling, sectioning, and dicing the various citrus fruits, but you can do this up to 2 days ahead of time, and they will keep, covered, in the refrigerator. The vinaigrette is also delicious with grilled fish that have a slightly sweet flavor, such as cod, haddock, catfish, monkfish, pike, or tilapia.

MAKES 6 SERVINGS

CITRUS VINAIGRETTE:

1 lime
2 lemons
1 orange
1 pink grapefruit
1 cup extra virgin olive oil
2 tablespoons sherry
    vinegar
2 tablespoons soy sauce
1/4 teaspoon cayenne pepper
1/2 teaspoon Tabasco sauce
1/2 teaspoon celery salt
1/2 cup boiling water
30 pink peppercorns (available at gourmet shops)
1/2 cup chopped fresh
    cilantro leaves
1 tablespoon peeled and
    finely grated fresh ginger

1. Peel, section, if necessary, and dice the limes, lemons, oranges, and grapefruit, reserving the juice. Place the diced fruit in a stainless steel bowl with 1/2 cup of the reserved juice. (Use the remaining reserved juice, if any, for smoking the scallops.) Set aside.

2. In a separate bowl, whisk the olive oil, vinegar, soy sauce, cayenne, celery salt, and Tabasco together. Pour in the boiling water, then whisk again to blend. Whisk in the pink peppercorns, chopped cilantro, and ginger. Set aside.

3. Place the wood chunks or chips in water to soak or wood pellets in a heavy-duty aluminum foil packet with holes poked into it.

4. Prepare an indirect fire.

5. When ready to smoke, place the drained wood chunks or chips or foil packet on the fire if using a kettle grill or charcoal smoker; in an electric smoker, place the wood chunks or chips or packet around the heating element. Fill the water pan and place in the smoker.

SMOKED SCALLOPS:

3 wood chunks, 1 cup wood chips, or 1/3 cup wood pellets

18 jumbo sea scallops, rinsed

1/4 cup fresh lemon juice (optional)

1/4 cup (1/2 stick) unsalted butter, melted

Fresh cilantro leaves for garnish

6. Place the scallops in a disposable aluminum pan. Drizzle each scallop with a little lemon juice, if using, or remaining citrus juice and melted butter. Place the pan on the grill or smoker rack over indirect heat, cover, and smoke until the scallops are opaque, have a mild smoky aroma, and are somewhat firm to the touch, 20 minutes to 1 hour.

7. To assemble the appetizer, remove about 1 cup of the combined diced citrus fruit for garnish and set aside. Stir the vinaigrette into the remaining diced citrus fruit until well blended. Place 3 smoked scallops in the center of each plate. Spoon about 1/3 cup of the vinaigrette over and around the scallops. Scatter the reserved diced citrus fruit around the perimeter of the plate and garnish the scallops with cilantro leaves.

Suggested wood smoke: apple, cherry, oak, orange, or peach

PLANKED PRAWNS WITH BÉARNAISE BUTTER

Just as the workplace has gone from suit-and-tie to casual Fridays, so has fine dining gone from Escoffier to Emeril. Escoffier would have served poached crevettes with a classic Béarnaise sauce in the late nineteenth century. Today, the technique of planking provides the Emeril-approved "Bam!" factor for the prawns, while the sauce is simplified to a flavorful butter. Serve this dish with grilled asparagus or other vegetables on the direct heat side of the grill, along with rice cooked in chicken stock and a crisp, dry white wine.

SERVES 8

3 pounds freshwater prawns, shelled and deveined
Béarnaise Butter (recipe follows)

1. Soak two 8 x 16-inch untreated planks in water for at least 30 minutes before smoking.
2. Prepare an indirect fire.
3. When ready to smoke, place the planks over direct heat until they begin to smoke and pop, 3 to 4 minutes. Turn the planks over and move to the indirect side of the grill.
4. Dollop a quarter of the béarnaise butter on each hot plank and top with the prawns. As the butter melts, toss the prawns in it before closing the lid. Smoke until the prawns are firm and opaque with a definite smoky aroma, 20 to 40 minutes. Serve immediately with the remaining butter.

Also good with: lobster tails

Suggested wood smoke: maple or oak

BÉARNAISE BUTTER

2 tablespoons chopped
  shallot
1 tablespoon white wine
  vinegar
1 tablespoon water
2 tablespoons chopped fresh
  tarragon leaves
1/4 teaspoon sea salt
1/2 teaspoon Tabasco sauce
  or to taste
1/2 cup (1 stick) unsalted
  butter, softened

1. In a small saucepan, combine the shallot, vinegar, and water. Bring to a boil, then remove from the heat. Add the tarragon, salt, and hot pepper sauce. Let the mixture cool.

2. In a medium-size bowl, cream the butter and add the cooled ingredients, combining well. (If not using immediately, shape into a roll, wrap in waxed paper, and chill. Slice a pat of butter and place on hot-off-the-grill fish.)

BARBECUED SHRIMP IN THE SHELL

Use whole or headless shrimp for this scrumptious but messy appetizer or very informal main course. You'll want lots of crusty bread to mop up the sauce and juices, and glasses of chilled dry white wine or cold beer. Using hickory or mesquite will give the shrimp a heavier smoke flavor.

MAKES 4 TO 6 MAIN-COURSE SERVINGS OR 8 APPETIZER SERVINGS

MARINADE:

1/2 cup (1 stick) unsalted butter, melted
1 cup smoky, spicy barbecue sauce
1 teaspoon Tabasco sauce
1 teaspoon red pepper flakes
1 teaspoon paprika
1 teaspoon dry mustard
1 teaspoon garlic salt
1 teaspoon dried thyme
1 tablespoon firmly packed brown sugar

2 pounds jumbo shrimp (16 to 25 per pound), deveined and rinsed
1 cup wood chips or 1/3 cup wood pellets

1. Place the marinade ingredients in a resealable plastic bag, seal, then shake to blend. Open the bag and add the shrimp. Again, seal, then shake to coat the shrimp with the marinade. Refrigerate for 3 to 4 hours to marinate the shrimp.

2. Place the wood chips in water to soak or wood pellets in a heavy-duty aluminum foil packet with holes poked into it.

3. Prepare an indirect fire.

4. When ready to smoke, place the drained wood chips or foil packet on the fire if using a kettle grill or charcoal smoker; in an electric smoker, place the wood chips or packet around the heating element. Fill the water pan and place in the smoker.

5. Place the shrimp and their marinade on disposable aluminum pans and place over indirect heat on the grill or smoker rack. Close the lid and smoke until the shrimp are opaque, have a medium smoky aroma, and are somewhat firm to the touch, 20 minutes to 1 hour.

6. Serve the shrimp in their shells with the sauce in individual ramekins or in a large communal pasta bowl, with plenty of napkins to go around.

Suggested wood smoke: hickory, maple, or mesquite

POTTED SMOKED SHRIMP

Serve this smoky and rich spread with a variety of crackers or thin, toasted slices of French bread.

SERVES 10 AS AN APPETIZER

1/2 pound smoked shrimp (page 193), shelled
1/2 teaspoon dry mustard
Juice of 1 lemon
4 ounces cream cheese, softened
1/4 cup bottled chili sauce
2 tablespoons mayonnaise
2 teaspoons prepared horse-radish
1 teaspoon Worcestershire sauce
1/2 teaspoon Tabasco sauce
2 sprigs fresh Italian parsley for garnish

1. Finely chop all but 3 of the smoked shrimp and set aside.

2. In a medium-size bowl, dissolve the dry mustard in the lemon juice. Add the cream cheese and stir to blend. Add chili sauce, mayonnaise, horseradish, Worcestershire, and Tabasco and blend well. Fold in the chopped shrimp. Garnish with sprigs of parsley and the 3 reserved whole shrimp. Chill. (May be prepared 1 or 2 days ahead.) Allow the potted shrimp to come to room temperature for 1 hour before serving.

Also good with: smoked crawfish, lobster, or prawns

A Whole Lotta Smokin' Goin' On

When you cold or hot smoke shellfish, mackerel, whitefish, trout, salmon, bluefish, or char, turn the leftovers into delicious cocktail or first-course fare with these simple recipes.

A Platter of Smoked Fish Appetizers

At Darina Allen's Ballymaloe Cookery School in southeastern Ireland, she sometimes serves a platter of three different kinds of smoked fish—salmon, mussels, and trout— "on tiny rounds of brown yeast bread, topped with a little frill of red leaf lettuce," she writes. With the smoked salmon, she spoons a little marinated cucumber. With the mussels, a dollop of mayonnaise flavored with lemon and dill. With the trout, a mound of mayonnaise flavored with prepared horseradish. Then she garnishes with lemon wedges and sprigs of watercress.

Smoked Fish Cocktail Nibbles

6 ounces smoked fish
2 tablespoons olive oil
4 ounces fresh goat cheese, crumbled
3 pitted green olives, 3 pitted black olives, and 4 radishes for garnish
12 puff pastry shells, prebaked according to package instructions

1. Place the smoked fish, olive oil, and goat cheese in a food processor and process until smooth.
2. Pipe or spoon the mixture into the pastry shells.
3. Thinly slice the olives and radishes, garnish each pastry with a slice of each, and serve.

Carved Angel Smoked Fish Tart

Devon, in southwestern England, is an angler's paradise. In the rolling countryside, you can cast your line into the rushing waters for both brown and salmon trout. At the Carved Angel in Dartmouth, chef-owner Joyce

Molyneux celebrates the local catch with this dish, perfect with a mild smoked fish like trout, char, catfish, or whitefish.

1 sheet puff pastry (from a package)
4 ounces smoked fish fillets
2 large eggs
2 large egg yolks
Juice of 1 lemon
1 cup half-and-half
Salt and freshly ground black pepper to
    taste

1. Preheat the oven to 400 degrees Fahrenheit. Fit the puff pastry into a 9-inch tart pan, prick all over with a fork, and prebake for 15 minutes.
2. In a medium-size bowl, flake the fish, blend with the whole eggs, egg yolks, lemon juice, and half-and-half, and season with salt and pepper. Pour this filling into the tart shell and bake for 20 minutes. Reduce the oven temperature to 325 degrees and bake until the filling is set, about 15 minutes more. Serve warm, accompanied by watercress or a simply dressed salad of field or garden greens.

SMOKED SHRIMP AND GRILLED VEGETABLE GAZPACHO

This is the ultimate gazpacho, with flavors to hit every one of your taste buds. Use leftover smoked shrimp and grill the vegetables or cook everything together using an indirect fire. Garnish with a dollop of lowfat sour cream, several fat smoked shrimp, and a sprinkling of chopped green and red onions.

MAKES 6 SERVINGS

3 wood chunks, 1 cup wood
   chips, or 1/3 cup wood
   pellets
1 large yellow or Vidalia
   onion, cut horizontally
   into 1/2-inch-thick slices
2 medium-size zucchini,
   ends trimmed and cut
   lengthwise into 1/4-inch-
   thick strips
1 yellow bell pepper
1 red bell pepper
2/3 cup olive oil
8 large, ripe tomatoes,
   seeded and diced
3 cucumbers, peeled, seeded,
   and diced
8 cloves garlic, minced
1/2 cup fresh sourdough
   bread crumbs
1/2 cup red wine vinegar
2 cups tomato juice
Salt and freshly ground
   black pepper to taste

1. Place the wood chunks or chips in water to soak or wood pellets in a heavy-duty aluminum foil packet with holes poked into it.

2. Prepare an indirect fire.

3. When ready to smoke, place the drained wood chunks or chips or foil packet on the fire if using a kettle grill or charcoal smoker; in an electric smoker, place the wood chunks or chips or packet around the heating element. Fill the water pan and place in the smoker.

4. Place the onion slices, zucchini strips, and whole peppers on an oiled perforated grill rack and brush with a little olive oil (about 2 tablespoons) on both sides. Grill the vegetables, turning once, until slightly charred and caramelized, 4 to 5 minutes per side. Remove from the grill and set aside to cool.

5. When cool enough to handle, peel the blistered skins from the peppers and remove the seeds and white ribs.

6. Place the grilled onions, zucchini, and peppers in a food processor and pulse several times until coarsely chopped. Transfer the vegetables to a large bowl and add the tomatoes, cucumbers, garlic, bread crumbs, vinegar, and tomato juice, stirring with a wooden

½ cup lowfat sour cream for garnish

18 smoked shrimp (page 193) for garnish

3 green onions, cut thinly on the diagonal, for garnish

2 tablespoons finely diced red onion for garnish

spoon. Gradually add the remaining olive oil, stir, and season with salt and pepper. Cover and chill for 4 to 5 hours before serving.

7. To serve, ladle the gazpacho into 6 shallow soup bowls and garnish each with the green and red onions and 3 smoked shrimp.

Suggested wood smoke: hickory or mesquite

LEAF-WRAPPED SMOKED SHRIMP STUFFED WITH CREAM CHEESE AND FETA

When we prepare and serve this colorful presentation of shrimp as an appetizer platter, people taste one first, then take a plate full. Boursin cheese may be substituted for the cream cheese mixture. Wrap some shrimp with prosciutto, some with spinach, and leave others unwrapped for variety.

MAKES 6 APPETIZER SERVINGS

3 wood chunks, 1 cup wood chips, or 1/3 cup wood pellets

GOAT CHEESE SPREAD:

One 8-ounce package cream cheese, softened

2 ounces fresh goat cheese or feta cheese, softened

2 cloves garlic, minced

1/4 cup snipped fresh chives

2 pounds large shrimp (18-20 count), peeled and deveined

15 medium-size spinach or arugula leaves

5 slices prosciutto (optional), cut lengthwise into strips

Sea salt to taste

Freshly ground black pepper to taste

1 to 2 tablespoons olive oil

1. Place the wood chunks or chips in water to soak or wood pellets in a heavy-duty aluminum foil packet with holes poked into it.

2. Prepare an indirect fire.

3. Meanwhile, combine the cheese spread ingredients in a medium-size bowl with a wooden spoon or in a food processor.

4. With a paring knife, butterfly each shrimp by cutting lengthwise down one side of the shrimp about halfway through. Spoon 1 tablespoon of the cheese mixture into the cut side of each shrimp. Wrap some of the shrimp loosely with either a spinach leaf or prosciutto. Place the shrimp in a disposable aluminum pan. Lightly season with sea salt and pepper, then drizzle lightly with olive oil.

5. When ready to smoke, place the drained wood chunks or chips or foil packet on the fire if using a kettle grill or charcoal smoker; in an electric smoker, place the wood chunks or chips or packet around the heating element. Fill the water pan and place in the smoker.

6. Place the shrimp on the grill or smoker rack, close the lid, and smoke until the shrimp have a pleasant smoky aroma, 35 to 45 minutes.

Suggested wood smoke: hickory or mesquite

SMOKY SHRIMP QUESADILLAS

These quesadillas are delicious as an easy appetizer or a light meal. The barbecue marinade also works well for catfish, trout, salmon, or halibut.

MAKES 4 SERVINGS

2 pounds large shrimp, peeled and deveined

1/2 cup bottled Italian salad dressing

1/4 cup spicy tomato-based barbecue sauce

3 wood chunks, 1 cup wood chips, or 1/3 cup wood pellets

4 flour tortillas

8 green onions, white part and some of the green, chopped

1 cup grated Monterey Jack cheese

1 cup crumbled queso blanco (white Mexican cheese) or grated cheddar cheese

Sour cream, salsa, and chopped fresh cilantro leaves for garnish

1. In a resealable plastic bag, combine the shrimp, Italian dressing, and barbecue sauce. Close the bag and shake to blend everything. Let marinate for at least 30 minutes in the refrigerator.

2. Place the wood chunks or chips in water to soak or wood pellets in a heavy-duty aluminum foil packet with holes poked into it.

3. Prepare an indirect fire.

4. When ready to smoke, place the drained wood chunks or chips or foil packet on the fire if using a kettle grill or charcoal smoker; in an electric smoker, place the wood chunks or chips or packet around the heating element. Fill the water pan and place in the smoker.

5. Pour the marinated shrimp into a round disposable aluminum perforated pizza pan or grill wok over the kitchen sink to drain them. Place the pizza pan on the smoker or grill rack over indirect heat, close the lid, and smoke until the shrimp are opaque and have a good, smoky aroma, about 30 minutes. While the shrimp are smoking, preheat the oven to 350 degrees Fahrenheit.

6. Place a quarter of the smoked shrimp on top of each flour tortilla and top with 1/2 cup of the green onions and 1/4 cup of each cheese. Carefully fold each tortilla into a triangle shape and place on a baking sheet. Bake until the cheese has melted, about 10 minutes.

7. Serve immediately, garnished with sour cream, salsa, and cilantro.

Suggested wood smoke: apple or cherry

PART 3

EVERYTHING ELSE YOU NEED

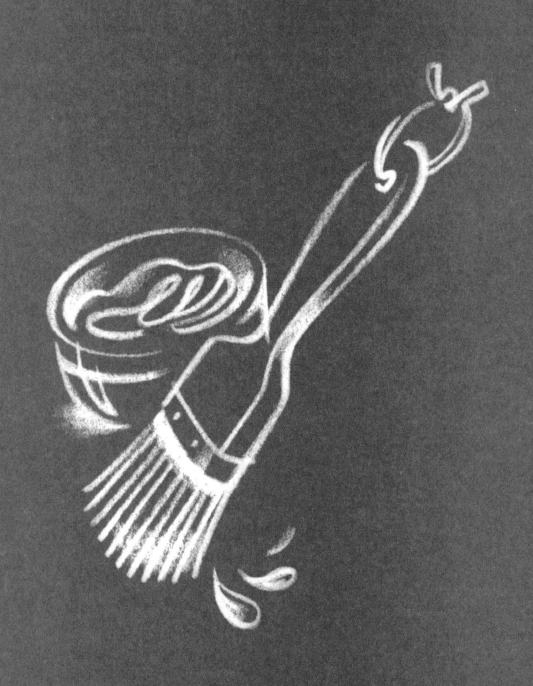

RUBS, MARINADES, BASTES, SAUCES, SALSAS & RELISHES

Grilled *or smoked fish and shellfish are delicious with only the simplest of touches before cooking—a brush of olive oil, a sprinkling of salt and pepper. But when you add a spicy rub, a savory marinade or baste, or a classic sauce, you have a dish that is truly outstanding.*

In this chapter, we have assembled an international array of rubs, marinades, bastes, and sauces to complement the caramelized and smoky flavors of grilled or smoked fish and shellfish. Try a traditional dried herb and spice rub such as Lemon Herb Rub (page 276) or a fresh herb and spice blend like the Moroccan Charmoula (page 94), both applied to the surface of the fish or shellfish before grilling or smoking. Marinate fish or shellfish in heady mixtures that include citrus juice, tequila, toasted sesame oil, or chipotle peppers for up to 45 minutes before cooking. Serve fish and shellfish hot off the grill or smoker, accompanied by a flavorful compound butter, one of the many types of classic French beurre blancs we love, a flavored mayonnaise, or a spoonful of addictive Basil Aioli by Hand (page 311). On the lighter side, dress the fish or shellfish with Four-Herb Chimichurri (page 324), Fresh Orange Sauce (page 320), or Fresh Garden Relish (page 336).

Rubs

Rubs are dry spice mixtures that are sprinkled or rubbed into the surface of fish, meat, or chicken before cooking. Because fish can be bland, we like to use certain spice and herb blends to bring out the most flavor in grilled or smoked fish and seafood.

AUTUMN SPICE HERB RUB

Brush or spray the fish with oil first. Then use about 2 teaspoons of this hearty blend on each fish fillet or steak.

MAKES ABOUT 1/2 CUP

2 tablespoons paprika
1 tablespoon garlic powder
1 tablespoon kosher salt
1 tablespoon lemon pepper
1 tablespoon crushed dried
    thyme
1 tablespoon crushed dried
    parsley
1 tablespoon crushed dried
    tarragon
1/2 teaspoon cayenne pepper

Combine the spice rub ingredients. Will keep in a tightly covered glass jar for several weeks.

LEMON HERB RUB

Lightly oil the fish before coating with this mixture. Use about 1 teaspoon herb mix per serving. The longer the coating remains on the fish, the more pronounced the flavor will be.

MAKES ABOUT 1/3 CUP

1 tablespoon dried lemon
    peel
1 tablespoon dried tarragon
1 tablespoon dried chervil
1 tablespoon dried chives
1 tablespoon garlic powder
2 teaspoons freshly ground
    black pepper
3/4 teaspoon salt
1/2 teaspoon red pepper
    flakes

Combine all the ingredients. Will keep in a tightly covered glass jar for up to several weeks.

SALT-FREE HERB RUB

We like this salt-free rub, which is good on poultry and pork as well as fish and seafood. Start with a teaspoon or two of this rub on a fish fillet or steak, then add more if you find you want more flavor. Leave on the fish about 30 minutes before grilling or smoking.

MAKES ABOUT 1 CUP

1/3 cup instant minced
   onions
1/3 cup dillweed
2 tablespoons dried
   tarragon
2 tablespoons dried oregano
1 tablespoon celery seeds
1 tablespoon lemon pepper
1 tablespoon garlic powder
1 teaspoon red pepper
   flakes

Combine all the ingredients. Will keep in a glass jar with a tight-fitting lid for up to several weeks.

HERBES DE PROVENCE RUB

This is a good blend for fish, meat, and vegetables. We both keep an ever-changing dried herb jar in our kitchens, which receives the addition of a new herb at whim. Customize a jar by combining your favorite dried herbs. Untreated or organic lavender buds are available at health food stores or from your favorite gardener. Use 1 to 2 teaspoons of this rub per fish fillet or steak.

MAKES 3/4 CUP

3 tablespoons dried thyme

3 tablespoons dried
    rosemary

3 bay leaves

2 tablespoons dried basil

2 tablespoons dried
    marjoram

1½ teaspoons fennel seeds

1 teaspoon dried summer
    savory

1 teaspoon untreated dried
    lavender buds

Combine the ingredients, leaving the bay leaf whole. Make the blend at least 1 hour ahead of time so the bay leaf has time to infuse the mixture with its flavor. Don't add the bay leaf when using the blend. Store in a dark cupboard in a jar with a tight-fitting lid; it will keep its punch for up to 6 months.

FIREWORKS RUB

Fireworks Rub—a mixture of herbs, spices, and sugar with medium heat—goes well with firm-fleshed fish, but also smoked brisket, pheasant, and baby back ribs. You can also add this by the tablespoonful to baked beans, cream cheese, or your favorite bread recipe for a savory dash of flavor. Use 1 or 2 teaspoons on each fish fillet or steak.

MAKES ABOUT 1 CUP

1/4 cup chili powder

1/4 cup ground cumin

1/4 cup ground coriander

1 tablespoon ground
    cinnamon

2 tablespoons firmly packed
    brown sugar

1 tablespoon salt

1 tablespoon red pepper
    flakes

2 tablespoons freshly
    ground black pepper

Combine all the ingredients in a jar with a tight-fitting lid. Screw the lid on tightly and shake to blend. Store in a cool, dry place. Will keep for up to 6 months.

BLACKENED SEASONING

In barbecue circles, rubs are spicy combinations of dry seasonings like assorted peppers, paprika, chili powder, garlic, and salt. Sprinkle 1/2 to 1 teaspoon of this mix on a lightly oiled fillet of red snapper, catfish, tuna, or the fish of your choice and grill over high heat to coax a crisp crust.

MAKES ABOUT 1 CUP

2 tablespoons lemon pepper
2 tablespoons paprika
2 tablespoons dried parsley
1 tablespoon garlic powder
1 tablespoon dried basil
1 tablespoon dried oregano
1 tablespoon cayenne
  pepper
1 tablespoon freshly ground
  black pepper
1 teaspoon salt

Combine all the ingredients. Will keep in a tightly covered glass jar for up to several weeks.

BARBECUE SPICE

The spice blend of choice for barbecuers, who put it on everything from ribs to wings to brisket to fish. Use 1 or 2 teaspoons of this rub on each fish fillet or steak. Also delicious with shrimp.

MAKES 1/3 CUP

2 tablespoons paprika
1 1/2 teaspoons ground
    cumin
1 1/2 teaspoons ground
    coriander
1 1/2 teaspoons dry mustard
2 teaspoons red pepper
    flakes
1 teaspoon celery seeds
1 teaspoon ground ginger
1/2 teaspoon ground cloves
1/2 teaspoon ground
    cinnamon
1/2 teaspoon ground allspice

Combine all the ingredients. Will keep in a tightly covered glass jar for up to several weeks.

KITCHEN HERB GARDEN GARNISHES

A kitchen herb garden or *potager* can be as simple as a few pots of your favorite herbs growing on the window sill or in a strawberry pot which can be brought in for the winter. We like to grow our herbs in our edible flower gardens out in our yards and in pots because we cook with them all year long. Between the two of us, our favorites include several kinds of basil, chervil, chives (garlic and onion), cilantro, dill, lavender, lemon balm, lemon verbena, lovage, marjoram, several kinds of mint, oregano, parsley (curly and Italian), rosemary, sage, savory, sweet cicely, tarragon, and thyme.

You'll find our recipes sprinkled with all kinds of herbs because they are a perfect complement to fish. Herb garnishes, in particular, are clever because they can be made ahead of time and will keep refrigerated for up to a week. The garnishes can then be used to finish a simple grilled or smoked fish recipe and also many of the salad, pasta, and side dishes offered.

Here are a few classic herb garnishes. Get creative and make your own signature herb medley. They are flavorful and can be quite colorful, too. Try adding finely minced colored bell peppers and red onions. Edible flowers and flower petals like chive blossoms, marigolds, and nasturtium add great eye appeal. The zest of citrus fruits—lemon, lime, orange, and grapefruit—adds color and packs a wallop of flavor.

PERSILLADE

T his simple French garnish of chopped parsley and garlic is added to dishes just before cooking is complete. Variations include chopped shallot and grated lemon zest. It also works well as a garnish sprinkled to finish a grilled or smoked fish dish.

MAKES 1/2 CUP

1/2 cup packed fresh Italian parsley leaves
1 shallot, peeled
2 cloves garlic, peeled

On a wooden cutting board, combine the parsley, shallot, and garlic and finely chop together. Will keep refrigerated in a resealable plastic bag for up to 1 week.

Gremolata

A garnish consisting of chopped parsley, lemon zest, and garlic, gremolata is traditionally sprinkled over dishes like osso buco and braised short ribs, adding a fresh, bright flavor. It is also a perfect finish to grilled and smoked fish and pasta dishes.

MAKES 1/2 CUP

1/2 cup packed fresh Italian parsley leaves
2 cloves garlic, peeled
1 lemon, zest removed in strips

On a wooden cutting board, combine all of the ingredients and finely chop together. Will keep refrigerated in a resealable plastic bag for up to 1 week.

Citrus Herb Garnish

This variation of gremolata was a hit at one of our cooking classes. The inspiration came from what was available from an early herb garden. Use this as a garnish for fish, seafood, poultry, and pasta dishes.

MAKES ABOUT 2/3 CUP

1/4 cup packed fresh basil leaves
1/4 cup snipped fresh chives
2 tablespoons chopped fresh mint or lemon balm leaves
3 cloves garlic, peeled
1 lemon or lime, zest removed in strips

On a wooden cutting board, combine all of the ingredients and finely chop together. Will keep refrigerated in a resealable plastic bag for up to 1 week.

Marinades and Bastes

Marinades not only add flavor to fish and vegetables, but also keep them moist and soft while grilling and smoking. Most marinades are a combination of an acidic liquid like vinegar, lemon juice, or wine and an oil, with added flavoring agents as varied as garlic, spices, ginger, and mustard. For food safety reasons, never reuse a marinade that has touched raw fish, meat, or chicken, even for basting, unless it has been boiled for several minutes afterwards. We much prefer making an extra batch of marinade or vinaigrette instead of boiling and reusing marinade.

VINAIGRETTE MARINADE

A simple vinaigrette to marinate fish, chicken, or vegetables—or to dress garden greens.

MAKES 1 CUP

3/4 cup olive oil
1/4 cup rice vinegar
2 cloves garlic, minced
1 tablespoon sugar
1 tablespoon Dijon
   mustard
1 teaspoon sea salt
1/2 teaspoon freshly ground
   black pepper

Combine all the ingredients in a glass jar with a tight-fitting lid. Use immediately or store in the refrigerator for up to several weeks.

JALAPEÑO AND CILANTRO MARINADE

This is a lively, vibrant-flavored marinade.

MAKES 1¹/₂ CUPS

1 cup bottled chili sauce

2 tablespoons minced fresh
  cilantro leaves

2 tablespoons minced fresh
  mint leaves

1 tablespoon cider vinegar

1 tablespoon fresh lemon
  juice

4 green onions, minced

1 jalapeño, seeded and
  minced

¹/₄ teaspoon freshly ground
  black pepper

Sea salt to taste

Combine all the ingredients. Will keep, tightly covered, in the refrigerator for several days.

GARLIC-HERB MARINADE

This is a tangy marinade that's infused with fresh thyme and basil.

MAKES ABOUT 1 CUP

1/2 cup extra virgin olive oil
1/4 cup white wine vinegar
Grated zest and juice of 1
*   lemon*
3 tablespoons chopped fresh
*   thyme leaves*
3 tablespoons chopped fresh
*   basil leaves*
4 cloves garlic, minced
1 tablespoon sugar
Sea salt and freshly ground
*   black pepper to taste*

In a small bowl, combine the marinade ingredients. Will keep, tightly covered, in the refrigerator for several days.

THREE CITRUS MARINADE

The lively tartness of fresh citrus cools the cook on a hot summer day. Use this as a marinade (but only let your fish or seafood marinate in it for up to 30 minutes; otherwise it will get mushy) or drizzle it over grilled fish, vegetables, and greens for a delicious dressing.

MAKES 2 CUPS

1/2 cup pineapple juice
1/4 cup fresh lemon juice
1/4 cup fresh lime juice
1 tablespoon chopped fresh basil leaves
1 tablespoon chopped green onion or fresh garlic chives
2 tablespoons chopped red onion
1 cup olive oil
Salt and freshly ground black pepper to taste

1. Place the juices, basil, green onion, and red onion in a blender or food processor and process until smooth. With the machine running, slowly add the olive oil in a steady stream through the feed tube to emulsify.

2. Season with salt and pepper and use immediately or store in a large glass jar with a tight-fitting top or in a plastic container in the refrigerator for up to several days.

LEMON-LIME MARINADE

This is almost like a pesto vinaigrette. It's very refreshing and excellent drizzled over pasta, grilled vegetables, salad, or a plate of sliced tomatoes.

Juice of 2 lemons
Juice of 2 limes
1 cup olive oil
4 cloves garlic, minced
1/2 cup chopped fresh basil
*   leaves*
1/2 cup chopped fresh mint
*   or lemon balm leaves*
Sea salt and freshly ground
*   black pepper to taste*

Combine the citrus juices and olive oil in a medium-size bowl, whisking constantly until thoroughly blended. Add the garlic, basil, and mint and season with salt and pepper. Will keep, tightly covered, in the refrigerator for several days.

CIDER MARINADE

This all-purpose marinade works with just about any fish. For best results, marinate the fish or shellfish for about 30 minutes or up to an hour, refrigerated.

1 1/2 cups cider vinegar
1/2 cup water
3 tablespoons sugar
3 teaspoons celery salt
2 teaspoons dry mustard
1/4 teaspoon freshly ground
*   black pepper*
1/4 teaspoon cayenne pepper

Combine all the marinade ingredients in a medium-size saucepan. Bring to a boil and let boil for 1 minute. Let cool before using. Will keep, tightly covered, in the refrigerator for several days.

MINCED ONION MARINADE

Marinate fish and seafood in acidic marinades for about 30 minutes only or the fish will get mushy.

1 small sweet white onion, minced
½ cup snipped fresh chives
⅓ cup fresh lemon juice
⅓ cup dry white wine
Sea salt and freshly ground black pepper to taste

Combine all the ingredients in a glass jar with a tight-fitting lid. Shake to blend. Will keep in the refrigerator for up to 5 days.

SOY-GINGER MARINADE

We like forgiving recipes and so many marinades are. You can easily substitute a different flavored vinegar, sugar for the honey, garlic powder for fresh, ground ginger for fresh, and sesame seeds or tahini for the sesame oil.

⅓ cup soy sauce
⅓ cup rice vinegar
2 tablespoons honey — *use a little less*
4 cloves garlic, minced
1 teaspoon peeled and grated fresh ginger
1 teaspoon toasted sesame oil

Combine all the ingredients in a small bowl. Will keep, tightly covered, in the refrigerator for several days.

TOASTED SESAME SOY MARINADE

se half of this mixture as a marinade for fish and seafood. Save the other half to drizzle over salad greens or sliced tomatoes served on the side.

MAKES ABOUT 1¹/₂ CUPS

1/2 cup olive oil
1/2 cup grapefruit juice
1/4 cup soy sauce
2 tablespoons toasted
    sesame oil
1¹/2 tablespoons sugar
2 teaspoons peeled and
    grated fresh ginger

Combine all the ingredients in a glass jar with a tight-fitting lid. Shake well to combine and store in the refrigerator for up to 5 days.

TEQUILA-LIME MARINADE

A south-of-the-border flavor dazzler.

MAKES A LITTLE MORE THAN 1 CUP

1/4 cup fresh lime juice
2 tablespoons tequila
3/4 cup extra virgin olive oil
Salt and freshly ground
    black pepper to taste

Combine all the ingredients in a glass jar with a tight-fitting lid. Shake until well combined. Will keep in the refrigerator for up to 5 days.

TAHINI-WASABI VINAIGRETTE

Wasabi comes in either a green paste or a dry powder that can be mixed with water to make a paste. It is often described as Japanese horseradish. You will find it in gourmet or Asian markets.

MAKES ABOUT 1 CUP

1/4 cup tahini
1/4 cup rice vinegar
1/4 cup wasabi powder
1 1/2 teaspoons Dijon
   mustard
1 1/2 teaspoons sugar
1 tablespoon soy sauce

Whisk all the ingredients together until smooth in a medium-size bowl. Will keep, tightly covered, in the refrigerator for up to 5 days.

LIME-GINGER VINAIGRETTE

We dare you to make this recipe only once. Yes, it's that good!

MAKES ABOUT 1 CUP

3 tablespoons chicken broth
3 tablespoons fresh lime
   juice
3 tablespoons peeled and
   grated fresh ginger
2 tablespoons minced
   shallots
1 tablespoon honey
1 tablespoon soy sauce
1 clove garlic, minced
2 tablespoons olive oil

In a small bowl, whisk all the ingredients together. Will keep, tightly covered, in the refrigerator for up to 5 days.

RED WINE SHALLOT VINAIGRETTE

We enjoy making vinaigrettes. So many different varieties can be made by simply changing the citrus juice or the type of vinegar.

MAKES 1 CUP

1/2 cup olive oil
2 tablespoons minced
    shallots
2 teaspoons Dijon mustard
1 tablespoon fresh lemon
    juice
3 tablespoons red wine
    vinegar
Sea salt and freshly ground
    black pepper to taste

Mix together all the ingredients in a glass jar with a tight-fitting lid. Will keep, tightly covered, in the refrigerator for 7 to 10 days.

ANCHO-LIME VINAIGRETTE

This is a flavor-packed vinaigrette!

2 tablespoons freshly grated lime zest

1/4 cup fresh lime juice

1/4 cup firmly packed brown sugar

1/4 cup peeled and grated fresh ginger

1/2 cup finely chopped green onions, white part and some of the green

1 cup packed fresh cilantro leaves

1 teaspoon freshly grated nutmeg

1/4 cup honey

1 teaspoon balsamic vinegar

1 teaspoon Tabasco sauce

1/4 cup olive oil

6 ancho chiles, seeded and cut into thin strips

1. Place the lime zest and juice, brown sugar, ginger, green onions, cilantro, nutmeg, honey, vinegar, Tabasco, and soy sauce in a food processor or blender and process until smooth.

2. With the machine still running, slowly pour in the olive oil through the feed tube in a steady stream. Turn off the machine and stir in the ancho chiles. Will keep, tightly covered, in the refrigerator for up to 5 days.

CHIPOTLE VINAIGRETTE

This is a sublime dressing from author Michael McLaughlin, from among other delicious recipes in his critically acclaimed *The Southwestern Grill* (Harvard Common Press, 2000).

MAKES ABOUT 1 CUP

3 tablespoons sherry
   vinegar
1 tablespoon balsamic
   vinegar
2 cloves garlic, minced
2 canned chipotle chiles in
   adobo sauce, chopped
2 tablespoons adobo sauce
   from the can
1/2 teaspoon salt
2/3 cup olive oil
Freshly ground black
   pepper to taste

In a food processor or blender, combine the vinegars, garlic, chipotles, adobo sauce, and salt and process until smooth. With the motor running, add the olive oil in a slow, steady stream through the feed tube until all the oil is incorporated. Season with the pepper and pulse to blend. Use immediately or pour it into a glass jar with a tight-fitting lid. Will keep in the refrigerator for up to 3 days.

ZESTY LEMON BASTE

Vary this citrus baste with lime, orange, and even grapefruit juice.

MAKES ABOUT 2/3 CUP

1/2 cup (1 stick) unsalted
   butter, softened
1 teaspoon cayenne pepper
Grated zest and juice of 2
   lemons
4 cloves garlic, minced

In a small bowl, combine all of the ingredients and blend. Will keep, well wrapped, in the refrigerator for up to 7 days.

AMARETTO BASTE

This is great with walleye, catfish, orange roughy, monkfish, or trout.

MAKES ABOUT 2/3 CUP

1/2 cup (1 stick) unsalted
  butter
2 tablespoons sliced
  almonds
2 tablespoons Amaretto or
  other almond-flavored
  liqueur

In a small skillet, melt the butter over medium heat, add the almonds, and cook, stirring, until lightly browned. Stir in the Amaretto. Will keep, tightly covered, in the refrigerator for up to 7 days.

ONION BUTTER BASTE

Try making this with softened butter. Whisk in the onion and wine (do not cook). Place the mixture on waxed paper, roll into a log, and put in a resealable plastic freezer bag. Store this compound butter in the freezer for up to several months, using it as needed.

MAKES ABOUT 1 CUP

3 tablespoons unsalted
  butter
1 medium-size onion,
  finely chopped
1/4 cup dry white wine

In a medium-sized skillet, melt the butter over medium heat. Add the onion and cook, stirring, until softened. Add the wine, bring to a simmer, simmer briefly, then remove from the heat and let set until ready to use. Use immediately.

MUSTARD BUTTER BASTE

An assertively flavored baste to use on full-flavored fish such as mackerel, bluefish, and amberjack.

MAKES ABOUT 1 CUP

1/2 cup (1 stick) unsalted
   butter
1/4 cup fresh lemon juice
2 tablespoons coarse-grain
   mustard
2 teaspoons Worcestershire
   sauce
1/2 teaspoon Tabasco sauce
2 cloves garlic, minced
Salt and freshly ground
   black pepper to taste

In a small saucepan, melt the butter over medium-low heat. Whisk in the remaining ingredients. Use immediately or may be stored in the refrigerator for up to 7 days. Reheat before using.

VARIATION: Do not heat the mixture, but rather combine it with softened butter and shape into a roll. Wrap in waxed paper, chill, and use as a compound butter over hot-off-the-grill fish or seafood.

MUSTARD-TARRAGON BASTE

Use for basting fish, seafood, and poultry.

MAKES ABOUT 3/4 CUP

1/2 cup Dijon mustard
2 tablespoons olive oil
2 tablespoons fresh lemon
   juice
8 to 10 sprigs fresh
   tarragon, to your taste

Combine all the ingredients in a glass bowl. Use immediately or will keep in the refrigerator for up to 2 weeks.

Compound Butters

Flavored butters are an easy way to add a last-minute flourish to grilled or smoked fish and seafood. Start with softened unsalted butter, then add whatever flavoring ingredient(s) you wish and mix it all together in a bowl. Shape the butter into a roll, wrap it in waxed paper or plastic wrap, and chill. Slice a pat of butter and let it melt over hot-off-the-grill fish. Compound butters may also be double wrapped, placed in a resealable plastic freezer bag, and frozen for later use, for up to 6 months. Here are some of our favorite flavored butters to serve with your fresh catch.

HERB BUTTER

MAKES ABOUT 1/2 CUP

1/2 cup (1 stick) unsalted butter, softened
1 teaspoon fresh lemon juice
1 tablespoon finely minced fresh herbs or 3/4 teaspoon dried (any combination of chives, thyme, rosemary, basil, or tarragon)

1. Combine all the ingredients in a small bowl.

2. Shape into a roll, wrap in waxed paper, and chill.

3. Slice a pat of butter and place on hot-off-the-grill fish.

TARRAGON BUTTER

3/4 cup (1¹/2 sticks)
  unsalted butter, softened
3 tablespoons white wine
  vinegar
5 tablespoons dry white
  wine
2 tablespoons chopped fresh
  tarragon leaves
Sea salt and freshly ground
  black pepper to taste

1. Place all the ingredients in a blender or food processor and process until smooth.
2. Shape into a roll, wrap in waxed paper, and chill.
3. Slice a pat of butter and place on hot–off–the–grill fish.

CHERVIL BUTTER

¹/2 cup (1 stick) unsalted
  butter, softened
2 tablespoons chopped fresh
  chervil leaves
Freshly ground black
  pepper to taste

1. In a small bowl, combine all the ingredients together well.
2. Shape into a roll, wrap in waxed paper, and chill.
3. Slice a pat of butter and place on hot–off–the–grill fish.

CILANTRO-LIME BUTTER

1 cup (2 sticks) butter,
  softened
1 cup fresh cilantro leaves,
  chopped
Juice from 2 limes

1. In a food processor or a blender, combine the butter, cilantro, and lime juice and process until smooth.
2. Shape the mixture into a roll, wrap in waxed paper, and chill.
3. Slice a pat of butter and place on hot–off–the–grill fish.

PISTACHIO BUTTER

Use this recipe as a template for creating other nut butters. Serve a pat on monkfish, lobster, scallops, or the fish of your choice.

1/2 cup pistachio nuts, shells on
1/2 cup (1 stick) unsalted butter, softened
Kosher salt to taste

1. Shell the pistachios and parboil for 1 minute. Drain, then remove the skins and finely grind in a food processor or by hand.
2. Mix with the softened butter in a medium-size bowl and season with salt.
3. Shape into a roll, wrap in waxed paper, and chill.
4. Slice a pat of butter and place on hot-off-the-grill fish.

HAZELNUT-LIME BUTTER

1/2 cup skinned hazelnuts
Grated zest of 1 lime
Juice of 1 lime
1/2 cup (1 stick) unsalted butter, softened

1. Spread the hazelnuts on a baking sheet and toast in a preheated 350 degree Fahrenheit oven for about 5 minutes. (Watch carefully to avoid burning.)
2. Finely grind nuts in a food processor and combine with lime zest, lime juice, and butter.
3. Shape into a roll, wrap in waxed paper, and chill.
4. Slice a pat of butter and place on hot-off-the-grill fish.

ALMOND BUTTER

Flavorful nut butters remind us of the winter holidays because these make great gifts presented in a ceramic ramekin. Try adding finely chopped dried fruits to this butter for a lovely piquant flavor.

MAKES ABOUT 2/3 CUP

1/2 cup (1 stick) unsalted butter, softened
4 ounces sliced almonds

1. Place the softened butter and almond slices in a small bowl and mix well together.
2. Shape into a roll, wrap in waxed paper, and chill.
3. Slice a pat of butter and place on hot-off-the-grill fish.

GARLIC ANCHOVY BUTTER

A zesty butter best served with full-flavored fish such as bluefish, mackerel, or tuna.

MAKES 1/2 CUP

1/2 cup (1 stick) unsalted butter, softened
1 clove garlic, minced
1 teaspoon anchovy paste
1 teaspoon fresh lemon juice

1. Combine all the ingredients in a bowl and mash together with a fork.
2. Shape into a roll, wrap in waxed paper, and chill.
3. Slice a pat of butter and place on hot-off-the-grill fish.

WHIPPED ONION BUTTER

A luscious flavorful butter that's delectable on fish, meats, vegetables, and crusty bread.

MAKES ABOUT 3/4 CUP

1/2 cup (1 stick) unsalted
   butter, softened
2 tablespoons minced onion
2 tablespoons chopped fresh
   Italian parsley leaves
1 teaspoon Worcestershire
   sauce
1/4 teaspoon dry mustard
1/4 teaspoon coarsely
   ground black pepper

1. Combine all of the ingredients in a small bowl.
2. Shape into a roll, wrap in waxed paper, and chill.
3. Slice a pat of butter and place on hot-off-the-grill fish.

WASABI BUTTER

An assertive butter made with the pale green Japanese horseradish powder known as wasabi.

MAKES 3/4 CUP

1/2 cup (1 stick) unsalted
   butter, softened
1/4 cup wasabi powder
   (available at Asian
   markets)

1. Combine all the ingredients in a medium-size bowl.
2. Shape into a roll, wrap in waxed paper, and chill.
3. Slice a pat of butter and place on hot-off-the-grill fish.

Beurre Blanc

Light, delicate, and buttery, the classic French beurre blanc is a wonderful accompaniment to grilled, planked, and smoked fish and shellfish, spooned over the top or served alongside. The technique for making the sauce is sharply divided into two parts. First, there is the fast reduction of the flavoring ingredients, usually wine, vinegar, shallots, and herbs, over high heat. Then there is the slow whisking of the butter, and perhaps cream, into the reduction to form a silky, smooth sauce heated to barely above a simmer. A finished beurre blanc should never come to a boil or it will separate.

We have experimented with many different beurre blanc variations, and the following are our favorites with grilled fish. Some versions, such as Red Pepper Beurre Blanc and Tarragon Beurre Blanc, are truer to the traditional sauce, with lots of butter and cream. Others, such as Tomato Vermouth Beurre Blanc, are lighter, with less butter and no cream.

RASPBERRY-THYME BEURRE BLANC

MAKES ABOUT 1 CUP

2 tablespoons fresh thyme
    leaves, finely chopped
1/2 cup fresh raspberries
1 cup dry white wine
1/2 teaspoon sugar
2 tablespoons minced
    shallots
1 cup (2 sticks) unsalted
    butter, cut into pieces
Salt and freshly ground
    white pepper to taste

1. Mash the thyme and raspberries together in a small bowl. Stir in the wine and sugar, cover, and let macerate for 1 hour at room temperature.

2. Strain the raspberry mixture through a fine mesh strainer into a medium-size heavy, non–aluminum saucepan and stir in the shallots. Bring to a boil over medium–high heat. Reduce the heat to low and simmer until the mixture has reduced to 1/3 cup, about 15 minutes.

3. Strain the mixture again and return it to the same saucepan. Over low heat, start whisking in pieces of the butter, 1 or 2 at a time, until they just melt into the sauce. Keep whisking in the butter until you have a smooth, buttery sauce. Whisk in salt and white pepper to taste and keep warm. Do not let the sauce boil or bubble. Keep warm until ready to serve.

TARRAGON BEURRE BLANC

3/4 cup dry white wine

1/4 cup tarragon vinegar

1 tablespoon finely chopped
   shallots

1 teaspoon dried tarragon

3/4 cup heavy cream

1 cup (2 sticks) unsalted
   butter, cut into pieces

Salt and cayenne pepper to
   taste

1. In a large, heavy saucepan, bring the wine, vinegar, shallots, and tarragon to a boil over high heat. Continue to boil until the mixture has reduced to about 2 tablespoons.

2. Whisk in the heavy cream and bring to a boil again, whisking until the sauce has thickened and will coat the back of a spoon, about 4 minutes.

3. Reduce the heat to low and whisk in the butter, a little at a time, until you have a smooth, silky sauce. Season to taste with salt and cayenne and serve hot.

SOY-GINGER BEURRE BLANC

2 cups dry white wine

2 tablespoons rice vinegar

2 tablespoons peeled and
   grated fresh ginger

3 shallots, minced

1 cup (2 sticks) unsalted
   butter, cut into pieces

1 tablespoon soy sauce

1. Bring the wine, vinegar, ginger, and shallots to a boil in a medium-size, heavy saucepan over high heat. Reduce until only 2 tablespoons of liquid remain, about 5 minutes.

2. Reduce the heat to low and whisk in the butter, a piece or two at a time, until you have a smooth, emulsified sauce. Whisk in the soy sauce and keep the sauce warm until ready to serve.

CURRY BEURRE BLANC

2 tablespoons dry white
    wine
2 tablespoons white wine
    vinegar
1 tablespoon chopped
    shallots
1/2 pound (2 sticks)
    unsalted butter, cut into
    cubes
1 teaspoon curry powder, or
    to taste
Salt to taste

1. In a large, heavy saucepan, bring the wine, vinegar, and shallots to a boil over high heat. Continue to boil until the mixture has reduced to about 2 tablespoons, about 2 minutes.

2. Reduce the heat to low and whisk in the butter, a few cubes at a time, until you have a smooth, silky sauce. Season with the curry powder and salt and serve hot.

TOMATO VERMOUTH BEURRE BLANC

1 large tomato
1 shallot, finely chopped
1/4 cup (1/2 stick) unsalted
    butter
3 tablespoons dry white
    vermouth
2 tablespoons tarragon
    vinegar
Salt and freshly ground
    black pepper to taste

1. Plunge the tomato into a saucepan of boiling water until you see the skin start to crack and peel away, about 1 minute. Remove the tomato with a slotted spoon and let drain on paper towels. When cool enough to handle, peel, core, and seed the tomato and chop the pulp fine.

2. In a small saucepan, melt 2 tablespoons of the butter over medium heat, add the shallots, and cook, stirring, until softened, about 3 minutes. Whisk in the vermouth, vinegar, tomato, and the remaining 2 tablespoons butter. Season with salt and pepper and serve hot.

EDIBLE FLOWER GARNISHES

Edible flowers add a burst of color and oftentimes a burst of flavor, too. Consider the peppery nasturtium, the fragrant rose petal, and pungent flowering herbs. The beauty of the flowers lends itself to outdoor entertaining and are perfect pairings with many grilled or smoked fish recipes and side dishes. Make sure that the flowers come from pesticide-free gardens or, even better, grow your own. Here is a list of our favorite edible flowers that we grow in our gardens.

- Basil
- Bee balm
- Borage
- Chive
- Daylily
- Dandelion
- Scented geranium
- Hollyhock
- Lavender
- Marigold
- Marjoram
- Mint
- Mustard
- Nasturtium
- Pansy
- Rose
- Rosemary
- Squash blossoms
- Violet
- Winter savory

BEURRE ROUGE

MAKES ABOUT 1 CUP

2 cups Cabernet Sauvignon
1 cup red wine vinegar
2 tablespoons finely
    chopped shallots
1/4 cup heavy cream
1/2 cup (1 stick) unsalted
    butter, cut into pieces
Salt and freshly ground
    black pepper to taste

1. In a large, heavy saucepan, bring the Cabernet, vinegar, and shallots to a boil over high heat. Boil, uncovered, until the mixture reduces to only 3 table-spoons, 8 to 10 minutes.

2. Reduce the heat to low and whisk in the cream and butter all at once until you have a silky, smooth sauce. Season with salt and pepper and serve hot.

RED PEPPER BEURRE BLANC

MAKES ABOUT 3/4 CUP

1/2 cup dry white wine
1 tablespoon tarragon
    vinegar
1 shallot, diced
1 medium-size red bell
    pepper, seeded and
    chopped
1/4 cup heavy cream
1/2 cup (1 stick) unsalted
    butter, chilled
Sea salt to taste

1. In a medium-size skillet, combine the wine, vinegar, shallot, and red pepper. Bring to a slow boil and let boil until reduced to 2 tablespoons of liquid. Add the cream, bring back to a boil, and let boil for 2 minutes.

2. Reduce the heat to low and whisk in the butter a little at a time until all butter is incorporated.

3. Remove from the heat and transfer to a blender or food processor. Process just until smooth. Season with salt. Keep warm in the top of a double boiler until ready to serve.

Mayonnaise

Mayonnaise is the classic accompaniment to poached fish and seafood, so why not grilled and smoked? We love to start with Homemade Mayonnaise and then see how far we can take it flavor-wise. Here are some of our variations that go well with a fresh catch.

A WORD OF CAUTION

To reduce the risk of salmonella, since mayonnaise contains raw eggs, prepare your mayo with great care. Use only the best and freshest eggs that have been kept at a constant temperature in the refrigerator. Also, avoid serving any raw egg product to young children, the elderly, or those with health problems.

HOMEMADE MAYONNAISE

Homemade mayonnaise is a creamy dressing made from emulsifying vegetable oil, egg yolks, lemon juice, and vinegar. It keeps for only three or four days, tightly covered, in the refrigerator, which is why store-bought versions with a shelf life of six months are the more popular choice for most American households.

MAKES ABOUT 2 CUPS

2 large organic eggs
2 large organic egg yolks
1 teaspoon Dijon mustard
1 teaspoon fresh lemon juice
1/4 teaspoon sea salt
1/4 teaspoon freshly ground white pepper
1/8 teaspoon Tabasco sauce
1 3/4 cups olive oil or peanut oil

Combine all the ingredients in a food processor or blender, except the oil. With the motor running, very slowly add the oil in a very thin stream through the feed tube until all of the oil has been incorporated. The mayonnaise should be thick and smooth. Store, tightly covered, in the refrigerator, where it will keep for 3 to 4 days.

SAUCE RÉMOULADE

This classic sauce still tastes wonderful with grilled and smoked fish and shellfish.

1 teaspoon finely chopped
  fresh Italian parsley
  leaves
1 teaspoon grated onion
2 large hard-boiled egg
  yolks
1 teaspoon anchovy paste
1 garlic clove, minced
1 large organic egg
1 cup extra virgin olive oil
2 tablespoons capers,
  drained, rinsed, and
  patted dry
Juice of ½ lemon, or to
  taste

1. Place the parsley, onion, hard-boiled egg yolks, anchovy paste, garlic, and whole egg in a food processor or blender and process into a paste.

2. With the machine running, slowly add the olive oil through the feed tube in a thin stream until the mixture forms a mayonnaise-like consistency.

3. Fold in the capers and add lemon juice to taste. Cover tightly and chill until ready to serve. Will keep, tightly covered, in the refrigerator for up to 3 days.

FLAVORED MAYONNAISE

Whether you make homemade mayonnaise or choose to buy a good-quality brand, here are some ideas and ingredients to titillate your taste buds. Also, try making a quick crème fraîche by combining 1/2 cup mayonnaise and 1/2 cup sour cream or plain yogurt. Then add any of the additional flavorings listed below.

Caviar Mayonnaise: To 1 cup mayonnaise, add 1/4 cup salmon caviar and 3 tablespoons fresh lemon juice.

Dijon Mayonnaise: To 1 cup mayonnaise, add 2 tablespoons Dijon mustard, 2 cloves garlic, minced, and 1 teaspoon fresh lemon juice.

Quick Rouille: To 1 cup mayonnaise, add 6 cloves garlic, minced, 1 tablespoon fresh lemon juice, 1/2 teaspoon salt, 1/4 teaspoon saffron threads, and 1/4 teaspoon cayenne pepper.

Tartar Sauce: To 1 cup mayonnaise, add 1/4 cup sweet pickle relish, 2 tablespoons grated onion, 2 teaspoons fresh lemon juice, 1 teaspoon Worcestershire sauce, and kosher salt and freshly ground pepper to taste.

Fresh Herb Mayonnaise: To 1 cup mayonnaise, add 1/4 cup chopped mixed fresh herbs: chives, parsley, tarragon, and/or basil.

Spicy Chipotle Mayonnaise: To 1 cup mayonnaise, add 1 or 2 canned chipotle chiles in adobo sauce, to your taste, chopped, and 1 teaspoon fresh lemon or lime juice.

Sun-dried Tomato and Basil Mayonnaise: To 1 cup mayonnaise, add 1 tablespoon sun-dried tomato paste and 1 tablespoon chopped fresh basil leaves.

Anchovy Mayonnaise: To 1 cup mayonnaise, add 1 tablespoon anchovy paste and 1 teaspoon Worcestershire sauce.

Orange Mayonnaise: To 1 cup mayonnaise, add 1/4 cup fresh orange juice, 1/2 teaspoon grated orange zest, and 1 1/2 tablespoons heavy cream.

Garlic-Lemon Mayonnaise: To 1 cup mayonnaise, add the juice of half a lemon, 1 teaspoon minced garlic, and freshly ground black pepper to taste.

AIOLI, ROUILLE, AND ROMESCO SAUCES

Say the word *aioli*, and a growing cult of gourmet citizens who read and/or travel to France recognize their "mayonnaise" of choice. It's homemade mayonnaise with a jolt of garlic. Purists say it must be made with a mortar and pestle, slowly adding the oil in a thin stream while using a whisk or hand mixer. Cookbook authors Patricia Wells and Susan Herrmann Loomis, who write about the foods of France, believe that making authentic aioli with a food processor gives it the consistency of glue. We use a light touch with the processor and when the oil is just incorporated—we stop. And our aioli doesn't resemble glue. But we also offer a handmade version for purists.

Serve aioli with seafood. Slather it on sandwiches, preferably on artisanal bread. Use it as a dipping sauce for vegetables. And serve it with *pommes frites* and grilled or smoked mussels for a decadent twist on the traditional.

Aioli's cousin is rouille, a rust-colored mayonnaise spiced with the addition of ground red pepper and saffron. The authentic version of rouille is made with bread crumbs to thicken it instead of egg yolks. Variations of rouille show up in Southwest cuisine with the addition of all kinds of hot peppers, though it isn't usually called rouille. Traditionally, rouille is served on a crouton floating in a bowl of *bourride*, a puréed Provençal fish soup, or with bouillabaisse. It is wonderful with fish, poultry, and as a spread on sandwiches.

If you travel to the Spanish coast from Barcelona to Valencia, you will find a traditional fish stew called *Romesco de Piex*, from whence romesco sauce originates. It is a creamy sauce of red bell peppers, toasted bread, almonds, garlic, parsley, vinegar, and oil. Today the sauce is served with fish or as a dipping sauce alongside a bowl of *alioli* (the Spanish spelling of *aioli*). Sometimes the two sauces are deliciously mixed together.

AIOLI IN THE FOOD PROCESSOR

MAKES ABOUT 1³/₄ CUPS

4 large organic egg yolks
4 to 6 cloves garlic, to your
   taste, minced
1/4 teaspoon sea salt
1/4 teaspoon freshly ground
   black pepper
1 1/2 cups extra virgin olive
   oil

1. In a food processor, combine the egg yolks, garlic, salt, and pepper.
2. While the motor is running, slowly add the olive oil in a thin stream through the feed tube until it all is incorporated. Will keep refrigerated, tightly covered, for 3 to 4 days.

BASIL AIOLI BY HAND

MAKES 1 CUP

2 large organic egg yolks
1 tablespoon fresh lemon
   juice
2 anchovy fillets, minced
2 cloves garlic, minced
2 tablespoons fresh chopped
   basil leaves
1/2 teaspoon Worcestershire
   sauce
1/2 teaspoon red wine
   vinegar
1 cup extra virgin olive oil
Sea salt and Tabasco sauce
   to taste

1. Place the egg yolks in a medium-size glass bowl and microwave for 15 seconds.
2. Whisk the egg yolks together and add the lemon juice, anchovies, garlic, basil, Worcestershire, and vinegar.
3. Slowly drizzle in the olive oil, whisking all the while. When the mixture has thickened, season with salt and Tabasco. If mixture gets too thick, thin with a little warm water. Keep chilled until ready to use. Will keep, tightly covered, in the refrigerator for up to 3 days.

PORTUGUESE AIOLI

Flavored with cayenne pepper, tomato, and orange zest, this salmon-colored aioli is as delicious to eat as it is beautiful on the plate.

MAKES ABOUT 1 CUP

2 large organic egg yolks
2 cloves garlic, minced
1/2 teaspoon cayenne pepper
1/2 teaspoon Tabasco sauce
1 tablespoon tomato purée
Juice of 1 lemon
1/2 teaspoon finely grated
    orange zest
1 cup olive oil
Salt and freshly ground
    black pepper to taste

1. In a food processor or blender, process the egg yolks, garlic, cayenne, Tabasco, tomato purée, lemon juice, and orange zest together until smooth.
2. With the machine running, slowly pour in the olive oil in a steady stream through the feed tube until the sauce thickens. Season with salt and pepper. Will keep, tightly covered, in the refrigerator for up to 3 days.

ROUILLE

Thicker and more garlicky than aioli, rouille is delicious with a grilled fish soup or stew.

MAKES ABOUT 1 1/2 CUPS

4 large organic egg yolks, at
    room temperature
4 to 6 garlic cloves, to your
    taste, minced
1/4 teaspoon saffron threads
1/4 teaspoon sea salt
1/4 teaspoon cayenne pepper
1 cup extra virgin olive oil

1. In a food processor, process the egg yolks, garlic, saffron, salt, and pepper together until smooth.
2. While the motor is running, slowly add the olive oil in a steady stream through the feed tube until the mixture thickens. Will keep, tightly covered, in the refrigerator for 3 to 4 days.

SUN-DRIED TOMATO ROUILLE

In keeping with the rust color of rouille, try this version made with sun-dried tomatoes. It is excellent served alongside grilled seafood, pork, and poultry.

MAKES ABOUT 1¼ CUPS

4 large organic egg yolks

4 to 6 cloves garlic, to your taste, minced

1 fresh serrano chile, seeded and minced

2 teaspoons sun-dried tomato paste

½ teaspoon sea salt

¼ teaspoon freshly ground black pepper

1 cup olive oil

1. In a food processor, process the egg yolks, garlic, serrano, tomato paste, salt, and pepper together until smooth.

2. While the motor is running, slowly add the olive oil in a steady stream until the mixture thickens. Will keep, tightly covered, in the refrigerator for 3 to 4 days.

ROMESCO SAUCE

*1/2 cup blanched almonds,
toasted in a 350°F oven
until light brown*

*1 slice white bread, crust
removed, toasted, and
crumbled*

*2 red bell peppers, roasted
(see below), seeded,
peeled, and cut into
pieces*

*1 tablespoon chopped fresh
Italian parsley leaves*

2 cloves garlic, minced

*1/2 teaspoon red pepper
flakes*

1/4 teaspoon sea salt

*1/4 teaspoon freshly ground
black pepper*

1/3 cup red wine vinegar

2/3 cup extra virgin olive oil

1. In a food processor, finely grind the almonds. Add the toasted bread, peppers, parsley, garlic, red pepper flakes, and salt and process into a smooth paste. Add the vinegar and blend.

2. While the motor is running, slowly add the olive oil in a steady stream through the feed tube until it is all incorporated and the mixture thickens. Adjust the seasonings. Will keep, tightly covered, in the refrigerator for up to several days.

ROASTING PEPPERS

To roast peppers, place them on an oiled baking sheet in a preheated 400-degree-Fahrenheit oven until they blister and burn on all sides, about 15 minutes. Place the peppers in a paper bag or between 2 tea towels to steam. When cool, remove the skin, seeds, and membranes with a paring knife.

Serving Sauces

These quick sauces, which assemble in minutes, go well with all types of fish and seafood, grilled and smoked.

ANCHO CHILE SAUCE

An easy sauce with a slightly smoky, spicy flavor.

MAKES ABOUT 3/4 CUP

1 small ancho chile, halved
    and seeded
1/4 cup mayonnaise
1/2 cup finely chopped fresh
    tomatoes
1 tablespoon finely chopped
    fresh Italian parsley
    leaves

1. Heat a small skillet over high heat until quite hot. Add the ancho chile and "dry fry" until fragrant, about 10 seconds on each side.

2. Transfer the chile to a small bowl and cover with hot water. Let the chile steep for 10 minutes. Drain and pat the chile dry.

3. Place the chile and mayonnaise in a food processor and process until smooth. Stir in the tomatoes and parsley and serve. Will keep, tightly covered, in the refrigerator for 3 to 4 days.

DILLED SOUR CREAM DRESSING

Make this wonderful sauce and serve it with just about any fish or shellfish. It's great to dollop on a baked potato, too. If you *love* capers, double the amount called for in the recipe.

MAKES 3/4 CUP

1/2 cup sour cream
2 tablespoons snipped fresh
    dill
2 tablespoons capers,
    drained
Grated zest and juice of 1
    lemon
Sea salt and freshly ground
    black pepper to taste

1. In a small bowl, combine all of the ingredients.

2. Chill until ready to serve. Will keep, tightly covered, in the refrigerator for 5 to 6 days.

SOUR CREAM CUCUMBER SAUCE

Fresh tasting, this sauce goes well with salmon. Use lowfat sour cream for a lighter version.

MAKES 2 CUPS

*1 cup peeled, seeded, and
    minced cucumber*
1 cup sour cream
*2 teaspoons chopped fresh
    dill*
1/2 teaspoon sea salt

1. Drain the minced cucumber in a sieve for 1 hour. Use a paper towel to blot the moisture out.

2. In a small bowl, blend together the cucumber, sour cream, dill, and salt. Chill until ready to use. Will keep, tightly covered, in the refrigerator for 2 to 3 days.

DILLED CUCUMBER SAUCE

This is an excellent accompaniment to any fish or grilled or steamed vegetables. Try tossing it with some cold pasta to serve alongside your fish as well.

MAKES ABOUT 3 CUPS

*2 cups peeled, seeded, and
    diced cucumber*
*1/2 cup thinly sliced green
    onions*
1/2 cup vegetable oil
*3 tablespoons fresh lemon
    juice*
*4 sprigs fresh dill or 1 tea-
    spoon dillweed*
1/2 teaspoon sea salt
*Freshly ground black
    pepper to taste*

In a blender or food processor, combine all the ingredients and process until smooth. Will keep, tightly covered, in the refrigerator for 2 or 3 days.

TZATZIKI

This is a delicious Greek yogurt sauce. It also makes a superb dressing for fish and shellfish or grilled and steamed vegetables.

1 cucumber, peeled and
    seeded
1 teaspoon sea salt
3 tablespoons finely
    chopped fresh mint
    leaves
1 clove garlic, minced
1 teaspoon sugar
1 cup plain yogurt
Paprika and chopped fresh
    mint leaves for garnish

1. Slice the cucumber thinly and toss with the salt in a medium-size bowl. Set aside for 15 minutes so the cucumbers exude their liquid.

2. Meanwhile, in another medium-size bowl, whisk the mint, garlic, sugar, and yogurt together.

3. Drain the cucumber and rinse well. Pat the cucumber slices dry and stir into the yogurt mixture. Cover and chill. Will keep, refrigerated, for 2 days.

4. To serve, dust with paprika and garnish with mint.

SHRIMP BBQ SAUCE

Drizzle this sauce over a grilled shrimp salad. Add a squeeze of fresh lemon or lime juice for a final taste sensation. Also works great as a marinade.

1/4 cup Vinaigrette
    Marinade (page 284)
1/4 cup of your favorite
    spicy barbecue sauce

Combine all the ingredients in a small glass bowl. Will keep, covered tightly, in the refrigerator indefinitely.

UPDATED CLASSIC COCKTAIL SAUCE

Reenergized with a little more zip, this sauce goes especially well with chilled fish and shellfish.

MAKES 1 CUP

3/4 cup bottled chili sauce
3 tablespoons prepared
   horseradish
1 tablespoon grated onion
1/2 teaspoon Tabasco sauce

Combine all the ingredients in a glass jar and stir to blend. Will keep, tightly covered, in the refrigerator for up to 2 weeks.

TANGY SEAFOOD SAUCE

This is a creamy seafood sauce that combines mayonnaise and chili sauce. If you want to eliminate the mayonnaise, please do so. You will then have a very spicy chili cocktail sauce.

MAKES ABOUT 1 CUP

1/2 cup mayonnaise
1/3 cup bottled chili sauce
1 1/2 tablespoons prepared
   horseradish
1/2 teaspoon dry mustard

1. In a small bowl, combine the ingredients until well mixed.
2. Chill completely before serving. Will keep, tightly covered, in the refrigerator for 3 to 4 days.

Indian dishes that mix spicy and sweet or hot and cool create delicious accompaniments to grilled and smoked fish. Indian cuisine offers the cool, creamy texture and taste of yogurt that complements the spiciness of ginger, garlic, and peppers. Here are a few of our recipe inspirations.

Raita: Combine 1 cup plain yogurt; 1 cucumber, peeled, seeded, grated, and squeezed dry; 4 or 5 cloves garlic, minced; 1 teaspoon chopped fresh mint; and coarse sea salt and white pepper to taste.

Roasted Red Pepper and Cucumber: Roast a red pepper (page 314), remove the skin, white ribs, and seeds, and dice; add the same amount of peeled, seeded, and grated cucumber, squeezed dry.

Indian "Mayonnaise": Combine 1 cup plain yogurt, 3 anchovies, chopped, and 2 or 3 hard-boiled eggs, peeled and chopped.

Coriander Carrot Salad: Combine 2 cups grated carrots and 1 tablespoon coriander seeds that you've toasted in a dry skillet over medium heat until fragrant.

Mint Chutney: In a blender, process together until smooth 4 green chiles, seeded, 1 tablespoon peeled and minced fresh ginger, 1 red bell pepper, seeded, 1 cup packed fresh mint leaves, 1 cup packed fresh cilantro leaves, 2/3 cup white wine vinegar, 1 tablespoon sugar, and 1/2 teaspoon coarse sea salt. (Variation: Add 1 cup plain yogurt instead of the vinegar for a creamy sauce.)

Avocado Relish: Chop each of the following vegetables: 1 ripe avocado, peeled and pitted, 1 small red onion, 1 ripe tomato, 1 jalapeño, seeded. Combine them, then add the juice of 1 lime and coarse salt and freshly ground black pepper to taste.

FRESH ORANGE SAUCE

A wonderful sauce to serve hot over grilled or smoked fish and shellfish from the Gulf of Mexico or warmer waters.

MAKES ABOUT 1¼ CUPS

1 cup fresh orange juice
¼ cup (½ stick) unsalted
    butter, cut into pieces
1 teaspoon Worcestershire
    sauce, or to taste
Salt and freshly ground
    black pepper to taste

1. In a small nonreactive saucepan over high heat, boil the orange juice until reduced by half, about 3 minutes.

2. Remove from the heat and whisk in the butter and Worcestershire. Taste, then season with salt and pepper. Serve hot.

SAUCE BRETONNE

An assertive sauce like this pairs well with full-flavored fish like mackerel, bluefish, and sablefish (blackcod).

MAKES ½ CUP

¼ cup (½ stick) unsalted
    butter
2 large egg yolks
1 teaspoon Dijon mustard
1 teaspoon white wine
    vinegar
1 tablespoon chopped
    mixed fresh herbs,
    such as tarragon, chives,
    parsley, and dill

1. Melt the butter in a small saucepan.

2. Place the egg yolks, mustard, vinegar, and herbs in a blender or food processor and blend well. With the machine running, pour in the hot butter and process until smooth.

3. Transfer the mixture back to the saucepan over low heat. Whisk occasionally until the sauce coats the back of a spoon, 8 to 10 minutes. Serve hot.

SAFFRON CREAM SAUCE

A delicate and delicious sauce perfect for lobster ravioli or mild grilled fish such as char, trout, or tilapia.

1 cup dry white wine
1/2 cup fish broth, bottled
    clam juice, or chicken
    broth
2 tablespoons minced
    shallots
1/4 teaspoon saffron threads
1 cup heavy cream

1. In a medium-size saucepan over low heat, bring the wine, broth, and shallots to a simmer and let continue to simmer for 15 minutes.

2. Whisk in the cream and increase the heat to medium-high. Boil the sauce until it is thick enough to coat the back of a spoon, about 5 minutes. Keep warm until ready to serve.

MUSTARD CREAM SAUCE

A three-mustard sauce that stands up well to full-flavored fish like amberjack, bluefish, and mackerel.

1 cup heavy cream
2 tablespoons whole-grain
    mustard
2 tablespoons Dijon
    mustard
2 teaspoons American-style
    mustard
1 teaspoons sugar
2 teaspoons granulated
    dried onion
1/4 teaspoon freshly ground
    white pepper
1 teaspoon Worcestershire
    sauce

Heat the heavy cream to a simmer in a small saucepan over medium heat. Add the remaining ingredients, bring back to a simmer, reduce the heat to medium-low, and cook until the flavors have blended and the sauce has thickened, about 10 minutes. Keep warm until ready to serve.

HORSERADISH MUSTARD SAUCE

Another delicious option to serve with grilled or smoked shrimp, mussels, clams, or oysters.

MAKES 1¹/₂ CUPS

1 cup heavy cream
¹/₄ cup prepared horseradish
¹/₄ cup whole-grain mustard

In a medium-size bowl with an electric mixer, whip the heavy cream to soft peaks (not standing peaks), then whisk in the horseradish and mustard. Serve chilled.

SHERRIED MUSTARD SAUCE

Sometimes the simplest of ingredients make an exquisite flavor statement.

MAKES ABOUT 2 CUPS

1¹/₂ cups homemade (page 307) or good-quality store-bought mayonnaise
¹/₂ cup Dijon mustard
2 tablespoons dry sherry or dry or sweet vermouth

In a small bowl, whisk all the ingredients together. Chill until ready to serve.

MUSTARD-DILL SAUCE

Make this delectable sauce for holiday gift giving.

MAKES ABOUT 1 CUP

1/4 cup Dijon mustard
2 tablespoons sugar
1/4 cup white wine vinegar
4 sprigs fresh dill
1/2 cup olive oil

In a blender or food processor, combine all the ingredients except the olive oil until smooth. With the machine running, slowly add the oil in a thin stream through the feed tube. Chill completely before serving.

CAPER-PARSLEY SAUCE

This classic sauce is delicious with all shellfish. It also makes a delicious pasta sauce.

MAKES 1 1/2 CUPS

3 tablespoons white wine
 vinegar
1 cup chopped fresh Italian
 parsley leaves
2 cloves garlic, minced
1/4 cup tiny capers, drained
1 tablespoon chopped onion
1 tablespoon Dijon
 mustard
2/3 cup olive oil

Place the vinegar, parsley, garlic, capers, onion, and mustard in a food processor or blender and process until smooth. While the machine is running, add the olive oil slowly in a thin stream through the feed tube to make a thick green sauce. Chill until ready to serve. This will keep, tightly covered, in the refrigerator for several days.

FOUR-HERB CHIMICHURRI

This is a variation of a chimichurri recipe from Karen Adler's *Best Little Marinades Cookbook* (Ten Speed Press, 2000). The white vinegar adds a pronounced tartness to the recipe that we enjoy. To tame it down, substitute red wine vinegar or sherry vinegar.

MAKES ABOUT 3 CUPS

1 cup chopped fresh Italian
   parsley leaves
1/2 cup chopped fresh
   cilantro leaves
1/2 cup chopped fresh mint
   or lemon balm leaves
1/4 cup chopped fresh
   oregano leaves
1/4 cup chopped onion
6 cloves garlic, minced
2 teaspoons cayenne pepper
1 teaspoon coarse salt, or
   more to taste
1 teaspoon freshly ground
   black pepper
1 cup extra virgin olive oil
3/4 cup distilled white
   vinegar, or more to taste
1/4 cup water, or to taste

1. Combine the parsley, cilantro, mint, oregano, and garlic in a food processor and process until finely chopped. Add the cayenne, salt, and black pepper and continue to process until smooth. Add the olive oil, vinegar, and water and process to make a thick sauce.

2. Adjust seasonings and add additional water if needed to achieve the right consistency. The sauce should be packed with flavor. It is best served the same day but will keep, tightly covered, in the refrigerator for up to 5 days.

PESTO

This is a classic pesto. For other flavorful pestos, add different mixes of herbs, like chives, tarragon, mint, lemon balm, oregano, and cilantro. Karen's *Best Little Barbecue Cookbook* series has a nice assortment of pestos, including a spinach and feta cheese pesto. Pesto turns into a luscious marinade when mixed with several tablespoons of oil and vinegar.

MAKES ABOUT 1¹/₂ CUPS

3 cloves garlic, peeled
¹/2 cup packed fresh Italian parsley leaves
1 cup packed fresh basil leaves
¹/2 cup extra virgin olive oil
Salt and freshly ground black pepper to taste
¹/3 cup freshly grated Parmigiano-Reggiano cheese
¹/3 cup pine nuts

1. Place the garlic, parsley, and basil in a food processor and pulse several times until the mixture is a mass of green flecks.

2. With the machine running, pour in the olive oil through the feed tube, then add the cheese and process until you have a smooth mass. Turn the motor off, taste, and season with salt and pepper.

3. Add the pine nuts and pulse again several times, until you have a coarsely grained green pesto.

SPANISH SAUCE

This makes a delicious sauce that is great on fish, pasta, and rice.

2 cups peeled and chopped
   fresh tomatoes
2 tablespoons capers,
   drained
2 tablespoons chopped
   pimentos
1/2 teaspoon sugar
1 teaspoon garlic salt
1 teaspoon Maggi season-
   ing or Worcestershire
   sauce
1/4 teaspoon Tabasco sauce
2 teaspoon paprika
Salt and freshly ground
   black pepper to taste

1. Place the tomatoes, capers, pimento, sugar, garlic salt, Maggi, Tabasco, and paprika in a medium-size saucepan and bring to a boil. Reduce the heat to low and let simmer while you grill the fish.

2. Taste the sauce and season with salt and pepper as needed before saucing the fish.

FRESH TOMATO SAUCE

Fresh-tasting and colorful, this sauce is best made with tomatoes at their peak.

MAKES 2 CUPS

3 tablespoons olive oil
1/4 teaspoon red pepper
   flakes
4 cloves garlic, minced
3 large, ripe tomatoes,
   peeled, seeded, and
   coarsely chopped
3 tablespoons capers,
   drained
Salt and freshly ground
   black pepper to taste
Finely minced fresh Italian
   parsley for garnish

1. Heat the olive oil in a large skillet over medium heat. Add the red pepper flakes and garlic, and cook, stirring, until the garlic just begins to turn golden, about 4 minutes. Stir in the tomatoes and cook, stirring occasionally, until the sauce has thickened slightly, about 15 minutes.

2. Stir in the capers, season with salt and pepper, sprinkle with parsley, and serve hot.

THAI GREEN CURRY AND COCONUT SAUCE

Great with grilled or smoked shrimp as a dipping sauce.

MAKES ABOUT 1 CUP

1 to 2 tablespoons Thai
   green curry paste
   (available at Asian
   markets), to your taste
1 cup canned unsweetened
   coconut milk (not cream
   of coconut)

Blend the ingredients together. Add more Thai green curry paste if you wish. Will keep, covered, indefinitely in the refrigerator.

SPICY TAMARIND DIPPING SAUCE

Tamarind is much used in Middle Eastern cuisine; its sweet-sour note banishes bland flavor.

MAKES ABOUT 1³/4 CUPS

2 tablespoons peanut oil

3 cloves garlic, minced

1 tablespoon Thai red curry paste (available at Asian markets)

²/3 cup Tamarind Liquid (recipe follows)

1/4 cup fish sauce (available at Asian markets)

1/4 cup soy sauce

1/4 cup firmly packed brown sugar

1 tablespoon peeled and grated fresh ginger

6 green onions, thinly sliced on the diagonal

1. Heat a wok or large, heavy skillet over high heat. Add the peanut oil, garlic, and curry paste and cook, stirring, for 1 minute. Add the tamarind liquid, fish sauce, soy sauce, and sugar and cook, stirring, for about 1 minute to dissolve the sugar and slightly thicken the sauce. Add the ginger and scallions and reduce the heat to low. Simmer for 2 minutes.

2. Serve as a dipping sauce for grilled fish.

TAMARIND LIQUID

MAKES ABOUT 2/3 CUP

1/4 cup tamarind pulp (available at Asian markets)

1/2 cup hot water

1. Place the tamarind pulp and hot water in a small bowl. Let soak for about 30 minutes. Mash the pulp several times during the soaking process.

2. Pour the mixture through a fine mesh sieve set over a bowl and use the back of a spoon to extract as much of the juice from the pulp as possible. Discard the pulp that remains in the sieve.

VIETNAMESE DIPPING SAUCE

 dipping sauce with a sour-savory flavor.

1/2 cup water
1/4 cup fish sauce (available
    at Asian markets)
2 tablespoons fresh lime
    juice
1 tablespoon sugar
1 clove garlic, minced
1/4 teaspoon chile oil
    (available at Asian
    markets)

Blend all the ingredients together in a small bowl.
Will keep, covered, in the refrigerator for up to 7 days.

Salsas and Relishes

These salsas and relishes assemble as quickly as it takes to grill a fish—in minutes!

TROPICAL SALSA

This light and fresh salsa, with bite and crunch, is a great foil to buttery smoked sea bass.

MAKES ABOUT 4 CUPS

1 cup peeled fresh pine-
   apple chunks
3/4 cup peeled, pitted, and
   chopped ripe mango
2/3 cup seeded and chopped
   red bell pepper
1/2 cup peeled, seeded, and
   chopped fresh tomato
1/3 cup peeled and chopped
   English cucumber
1/3 cup chopped red onion
3 tablespoons chopped fresh
   cilantro leaves
2 tablespoons chopped fresh
   tarragon leaves
2 tablespoons seeded and
   chopped fresh jalapeño
2 tablespoons fresh lime
   juice
Salt to taste

Combine all the ingredients in a medium-size bowl. Cover and chill for at least 1 hour before serving. Will keep, tightly covered, in the refrigerator for 2 to 3 days.

ISLAND SALSA

This is a forgiving recipe. If mangoes and papayas are not available, substitute cantaloupe, peaches, or nectarines.

1 ripe papaya, peeled,
    seeded, and diced
1 ripe mango, peeled,
    pitted, and diced
1 grapefruit, peeled, seeded,
    and diced
1 orange, peeled, seeded, if
    necessary, and diced
1/2 cup diced red onion
1/2 green bell pepper, seeded
    and diced
1/2 jalapeño, seeded and
    minced
1/4 cup finely chopped fresh
    cilantro leaves
1/4 cup finely chopped fresh
    mint leaves
1 tablespoon fresh lime
    juice
1 tablespoon fresh lemon
    juice
1/2 to 1 teaspoon red pepper
    flakes, to your taste

1. In a large bowl, combine all the ingredients and refrigerate for 1 hour to meld the flavors.

2. Let the salsa come back to room temperature before serving. Will keep, tightly covered, in the refrigerator for 2 to 3 days.

STRAWBERRY SALSA

Prepare this salsa in the late spring or early summer when the best fresh strawberries are available. The peppery flavor is delicious.

2 cups hulled and chopped
    ripe strawberries
2 tablespoons chopped fresh
    mint leaves
2 tablespoons sugar
2 tablespoons dark rum
1/2 teaspoon freshly ground
    black pepper

In a small bowl, combine the ingredients. Serve chilled or at room temperature. Will keep, tightly covered, in the refrigerator for 2 to 3 days.

AVOCADO-CORN SALSA

When fresh picked sweet corn is available, cut the kernels off the cob and mix them with the avocado—this salsa doesn't need to be cooked.

2 large, ripe avocados,
    peeled and pitted
Juice of 1 lime
1 cup fresh or frozen (and
    defrosted) corn kernels
1/4 cup chopped onion
2 cloves garlic, minced
1 tablespoon chopped fresh
    cilantro leaves
1/4 teaspoon red pepper
    flakes
Sea salt to taste

1. Cut the avocados into 1/2-inch cubes and place in a medium-size bowl. Toss with the lime juice to prevent discoloring.
2. Add the remaining ingredients and gently stir together. Let sit for 1 hour at room temperature before serving so the flavors will blend.

ROASTED RED PEPPER AND CORN SALSA

Delicious as a relish with fish or served with blue corn tortilla chips for an appetizer.

2 large red bell peppers
3/4 cup cooked corn kernels
2 tablespoons chopped fresh
basil leaves
2 tablespoons chopped fresh
cilantro leaves
2 tablespoons red wine
vinegar
1/4 cup olive oil
1/2 cup sour cream
1 clove garlic, minced
1/4 teaspoon red pepper
flakes
Sea salt and freshly ground
black pepper to taste

1. Halve and seed the bell pepper. Char the outside skin, either by broiling in an oven or by placing skin side down on the grill over a hot fire. Place the charred peppers in a paper bag for 5 to 10 minutes, then peel off the charred skin and remove the seeds and white ribs. Dice the peppers and place in a large bowl. Add the corn, basil, and cilantro.

2. In a blender or food processor, thoroughly combine the vinegar and olive oil. Add the sour cream, garlic, red pepper flakes, salt, and black pepper and blend with a quick pulse. Add to the roasted pepper mixture and stir to blend. The flavors are best if served at room temperature. Chill if not using right away. Will keep, tightly covered, in the refrigerator for up to a week.

TOMATO SALSA

Add cilantro and mint for some extra oomph of flavor.

2 cups peeled and chopped
ripe tomatoes
1 small onion, diced
3 banana chiles, seeded and
diced
1/4 cup Vinaigrette
Marinade (page 284)
1/4 teaspoon red pepper
flakes

In a medium-size bowl, combine all the ingredients and refrigerate until ready to serve. Serve cold or at room temperature. Will keep, tightly covered, in the refrigerator for 2 to 3 days.

PICO DE GALLO

Colorful and fresh tasting, this is perfect with grilled fish tacos.

3 ripe avocados, peeled,
    pitted, and chopped
2 ripe tomatoes, peeled,
    seeded, and chopped
1 small onion, chopped
2 cloves garlic, minced
1 jalapeño, seeded and
    finely chopped
1/4 cup fresh lime juice
Sea salt and freshly ground
    black pepper to taste

Combine all the ingredients and lightly toss to combine. Chill before serving. Will keep, tightly covered, in the refrigerator for up to a week.

CONFETTI CORN RELISH

A delicious summer relish or salad that's perfect with a patio supper or picnic in the park.

MAKES 6 CUPS

3 cups cooked corn kernels,
    fresh or frozen
1 cup chopped scallions
1/2 cup seeded and diced
    cucumber (don't peel)
1 cup grape tomatoes or
    cherry tomatoes, halved
1/3 cup sour cream
3 tablespoons mayonnaise
1 1/2 tablespoons cider
    vinegar
1/2 teaspoon dry mustard
1/2 teaspoon celery seeds
1/2 teaspoon sea salt

1. In a large bowl, combine the corn, scallions, cucumber, and tomatoes.

2. In a small bowl, combine the sour cream, mayonnaise, vinegar, mustard, celery seeds, and salt, whisking until smooth. Add this to the corn mixture and blend well. Chill in the refrigerator for 1 hour or more. Will keep, tightly covered, in the refrigerator for up to a week.

3. Serve in a pretty glass bowl to show off the salad's colors.

FRESH GARDEN RELISH

Let your own garden be your inspiration in mixing together this medley of vegetables and herbs. It's especially pretty with a variety of red and yellow tomatoes.

4 medium-size, ripe
    tomatoes, chopped
1 green bell pepper, seeded
    and chopped
1 yellow bell pepper, seeded
    and chopped
1/4 cup snipped fresh chives
1/2 cup minced red onions
1 jalapeño, seeded and
    minced
1 1/2 teaspoons sea salt
1/2 teaspoon freshly ground
    black pepper

Combine all the ingredients. Cover and chill until ready to serve. Will keep, tightly covered, in the refrigerator for 2 to 3 days.

ROASTED TOMATO–OLIVE RELISH

We prepared a similar smoked tomato relish for Better Homes and Gardens TV as the 'Que Queens—tiaras and all!

MAKES 4 CUPS

15 ripe Roma tomatoes
1/4 cup extra virgin olive oil
1 tablespoon minced garlic
2 cups Kalamata or niçoise
    olives, drained, pitted,
    and cut in half
1 cup green olives, drained,
    pitted, and diced
2 teaspoons herbes de
    Provence or a mixture
    of dried thyme and
    rosemary
1/4 cup sherry vinegar or
    balsamic vinegar
Salt and freshly ground
    black pepper to taste

1. Preheat the oven to 475 degrees Fahrenheit. Cut the tomatoes in half and place cut side down on an oiled baking sheet. Drizzle 2 tablespoons of the olive oil over the tomatoes and roast until the skins have shriveled, about 15 minutes. Remove from the oven and let cool enough to handle. Skin the tomatoes and set aside.

2. Heat the remaining 2 tablespoons olive oil in a medium-size saucepan over medium heat and cook the garlic, stirring, for 2 minutes, but do not let brown. Stir in the tomatoes and cook until they have stewed and very little liquid remains in the pan, about 10 minutes.

3. Remove from the heat and stir in the remaining ingredients. Let cool, then store in a covered container in the refrigerator. This is best made at least a day ahead of time so the flavors can blend and will keep, tightly covered, in the refrigerator for 4 to 5 days.

MANDARIN ORANGE AND WATER CHESTNUT RELISH

This is a very pretty relish, with its orange, white, and green colors. It's flavorful and refreshing, too.

MAKES ABOUT 2 CUPS

One 8-ounce can sliced
water chestnuts, drained
One 11-ounce can man-
darin oranges, drained
and rinsed
1 1/2 cups very thinly sliced
green onions
3 tablespoons soy sauce
2 tablespoons toasted
sesame oil
3 tablespoons rice vinegar
2 tablespoons sesame seeds,
toasted (page 372)
1 tablespoon honey

1. In a medium-size bowl, combine the water chestnuts, oranges, and green onions. Add the soy sauce, sesame oil, and vinegar, sesame seeds, and honey. Toss well to combine.

2. Refrigerate until completely chilled before serving. Will keep, tightly covered, in the refrigerator for 2 to 3 days.

FRESH PEACH AND ONION RELISH

Substitute nectarines, papayas, or mangoes for the peaches for interesting variations.

MAKES 4 TO 5 CUPS

1/2 cup extra virgin olive oil
3 tablespoons red wine
  vinegar
3 tablespoons fresh lime
  juice
1 tablespoon honey
2 cloves garlic, minced
2 tablespoons chopped fresh
  mint leaves
4 ripe peaches, peeled,
  pitted, and thinly sliced
1 red bell pepper, seeded
  and finely chopped
1 medium-size red onion,
  finely chopped
Sea salt and freshly cracked
  black pepper to taste

1. In a medium-size bowl, whisk together the olive oil, vinegar, lime juice, honey, garlic, and mint. Add the peaches, bell pepper, and onions. Season with salt and pepper.

2. Chill until ready to serve. Will keep, tightly covered, in the refrigerator for 2 to 3 days. Serve chilled or bring back to room temperature.

SIDES

We cannot live by fish and shellfish alone. That's why we've also suggested side dishes that complement the various fish and shellfish recipes in this book. These sides echo the taste, color, and texture of the entrée and match the preparation and cooking times. Our side dishes that accompany grilled foods are quicker to cook or assemble than the sides that go with slower-cooking smoked foods.

With grilled fish and shellfish, we like to use the freshest seasonal vegetables and herbs, often prompted by a trip to the farmers' market. Sometimes the side dishes are an integral part of the entrée—like the light and fresh-tasting cabbage slaw that goes with the Stir-Grilled Fish Tacos (page 60) or the very assertive and lowfat Wasabi Cucumber

Salad that accompanies Teriyaki Catfish (page 39). Tapas-Style Monkfish Skewers (page 72) are naturals with Cumin and Carrot Salad (page 352) , and the Pernod-Buttered Lobster Tails (page 141) wouldn't be the same served without Sautéed Corn and Wilted Lettuce Salad (page 356).

Slower-smoked foods do well with slower cooked side dishes, such as our Oak-Planked Sea Scallops (page 254) with Smoked and Braised Bacon-Wrapped Endive (page 359) and Beer-Brined Smoked Swordfish (page 224) with Smoked Onions with Thyme Cream (page 364). Sometimes an accompanying salad benefits from a little time for the flavors to blend, such as the Wild Rice and Dried Cherry Picnic Salad (page 383) served with North Woods Smoked Walleye (page 229).

Our side dishes also go well with grilled or smoked chicken, pork, or beef. Or they can be enjoyed by themselves. The key, as with the fish and shellfish, is to select the best and freshest produce available in your area.

ARUGULA, SPINACH, AND BERRY SALAD

Arugula is often costly but well worth the price. To soften the ouch on your pocketbook, we've added spinach to stretch this recipe. If money is no object, use 6 cups of arugula only and have a feast!

MAKES 6 SERVINGS

3 cups arugula, stems
  removed
3 cups spinach, washed well
  and stems removed
1 cup fresh raspberries or
  blackberries
1 cup fresh strawberries,
  hulled and sliced
1 cup plain yogurt
2 tablespoons wildflower
  honey
1 tablespoon coarsely
  ground black pepper

1. In a large salad bowl, place the arugula, spinach, raspberries, and half of the strawberries.
2. In a blender or food processor, process the remaining strawberries, the yogurt, and honey together until smooth.
3. Add the dressing to the salad, toss well to combine, and sprinkle with the pepper.
4. Chill for up to 20 minutes in the refrigerator. Toss again before serving.

CHINESE GRILLED ASPARAGUS

Fresh-picked asparagus grill beautifully. If your asparagus is not fresh picked, blanch it in boiling salted water for two minutes prior to grilling for best results.

MAKES 4 TO 6 SERVINGS

1 pound asparagus, bottoms trimmed
1 tablespoon soy sauce
1 tablespoon vegetable oil
1 teaspoon toasted sesame oil
White or black sesame seeds, toasted (page 372), for garnish

1. Place the asparagus in a resealable plastic bag. In a small bowl, whisk the soy sauce, vegetable oil, and sesame oil together and pour over the asparagus. Secure the bag and turn to coat the asparagus in the marinade. Marinate for several hours or overnight in the refrigerator.
2. Prepare a medium-hot fire.
3. Place the asparagus in an oiled grill wok or a hinged grill basket and grill for several minutes on each side until crisp tender.
4. Arrange the asparagus on a serving platter and garnish with sesame seeds.

BLACKENED GREEN BEANS

Adding a little charred flavor to basic green beans greatly enhances their taste. This goes well with salmon.

MAKES 4 TO 6 SERVINGS

1/4 cup olive oil
1 1/2 pounds fresh green beans, ends trimmed
1 cup chopped yellow onions
Sea salt and freshly ground pepper to taste

1. In a large skillet, heat the olive oil over high heat. Add the green beans and cook for about 5 minutes, turning the beans frequently. Add the onions and continue to cook over high heat until half the beans are charred. Add additional olive oil if needed.
2. Season with salt and pepper and serve immediately.

COLD GREEN BEANS AND CRUMBLED QUESO FRESCO

Queso fresco is a delicious Mexican crumbling cheese similar to feta cheese. Another south-of-the-border choice is Chihuahua cheese, similar to Monterey Jack cheese.

MAKES 4 SERVINGS

1 pound green beans, ends trimmed, cooked in water to cover just until tender, and drained

1 small red onion, thinly sliced into rings

1/2 cup minced fresh Italian parsley leaves

2 tablespoons minced fresh mint leaves

1/3 cup crumbled queso fresco cheese

3 tablespoons extra virgin olive oil

1 tablespoon fresh lemon juice, plus more, if needed

1/4 teaspoon sea salt

1/2 teaspoon freshly ground black pepper

1. In a large glass bowl, combine the beans, onion, parsley, mint, and cheese. (The salad can be prepared to this point and refrigerated overnight.)

2. In a glass jar, combine the olive oil, lemon juice, salt, and pepper. Cover and shake to blend.

3. When ready to serve, pour the dressing over the bean salad and toss to blend. Drizzle with extra lemon juice, if needed.

WARM RED LENTILS

Red lentils simmer to a pretty pale golden color. They cook quickly and dissolve into a purée that makes a different and delicious warm side dish.

1 cup dried red lentils, picked over and rinsed
2 cups chicken broth
4 slices bacon
1 cup chopped onions
4 cloves garlic, chopped
2 tablespoons bottled Italian dressing
1/2 cup chopped green onions, white part with some of the green

1. In a large saucepan, combine the lentils and chicken broth and bring to a boil. Reduce the heat to medium-low and simmer until the lentils start to dissolve, about 15 minutes. Turn off heat and set aside.

2. In a medium-size skillet, cook the bacon until crisp, then drain on paper towels. Drain all but 1 tablespoon of the bacon drippings from the pan. Add the onions and garlic and cook over medium heat until softened, 3 or 4 minutes. Reduce the heat to low and add the Italian dressing. (Be careful; the dressing will splatter.) Pour the onion mixture into the lentils and stir to blend.

3. Serve on a platter topped with the crumbled bacon and chopped green onions.

LOW COUNTRY BLACK-EYED PEAS AND SHRIMP

This is our variation on a traditional Low Country bean salad with a hot vinegar and bacon dressing.

MAKES 4 TO 6 SERVINGS

2 cups freshly shelled
   black-eyed peas or one
   10-ounce package
   frozen black-eyed peas,
   defrosted
4 slices smoked bacon
1 large clove garlic, minced
1 small onion, finely diced
1/2 red bell pepper, seeded
   and finely diced
1 tablespoon balsamic
   vinegar
2 teaspoons finely chopped
   fresh chives
2 teaspoons finely chopped
   fresh tarragon leaves
1/2 cup frozen tiny salad
   shrimp, defrosted, or
   canned salad shrimp,
   drained
1 tablespoon freshly ground
   black pepper
Salt to taste

1. Fill a large pot with water and bring to a boil. Add the black-eyed peas and boil until tender, 15 to 20 minutes. Drain in a colander and set aside.

2. Fry the bacon in a large skillet until crisp. Transfer the bacon to paper towels to drain, reserving the bacon fat in the pan. Crumble the bacon. Add the garlic, onion, and bell pepper to the skillet and cook, stirring, over medium heat until softened, about 5 minutes. Stir in the crumbled bacon and black-eyed peas. Stir in the vinegar, herbs, shrimp, and pepper. Season with salt. Serve warm.

ASIAN SLAW

Asian slaw has become one of our favorite side dishes, which we now serve with just about anything.

SLAW:

*5 cups cored and shredded green
   cabbage*
*2 cups cored and shredded red
   cabbage*
*2 red bell peppers, seeded and cut
   into thin strips*
1 cup thin strips peeled jicama
*6 green onions, white part and
   some of the green, chopped*
1/2 cup chopped fresh cilantro leaves

GINGER-PEANUT
DRESSING:

1/3 cup rice vinegar
1/3 cup vegetable oil
5 tablespoons creamy peanut butter
3 tablespoons soy sauce
*3 tablespoons firmly packed brown
   sugar*
*2 tablespoons peeled and grated
   fresh ginger*
1 1/2 tablespoons minced garlic
1 teaspoon toasted sesame oil
1/2 teaspoon red pepper flakes
*Salt and freshly ground black
   pepper to taste*
*1/4 cup sesame seeds, toasted (page
   372), for garnish*

1. In a large bowl, mix together the cabbages, peppers, jicama, onions, and cilantro.
2. To make the dressing, whisk the dressing ingredients together in a medium-size bowl.
3. Right before serving, pour the dressing over the slaw and toss to combine well. Sprinkle the top with the toasted sesame seeds and serve.

AUNT LARETTA'S SLAW

Karen's husband's aunt Laretta was a great cook. This simple slaw is one of Dick Adler's favorites from Aunt Laretta's many recipes. Instead of store-bought Italian salad dressing, we've substituted a homemade vinaigrette. It's great with any grilled foods or summer picnic fare.

MAKES 6 TO 8 SERVINGS

1 medium-size head
   cabbage, cored and
   shredded
1/2 onion, grated
1 1/2 teaspoons salt
1 teaspoon celery seeds
1/2 teaspoon freshly ground
   black pepper
8 slices bacon, fried until
   crisp, drained on paper
   towels, and crumbled
1 cup Vinaigrette Marinade
   (page 284)

1. In a large bowl, combine the cabbage, onion, salt, celery seeds, and pepper. (May be refrigerated for up to several hours at this point.)
2. When ready to serve, add the bacon and toss with the marinade until everything is well coated.

CUMIN AND CARROT SALAD

The cool, sweet flavor of carrots and the warm, somewhat bitter taste of cumin complement each other well in this salad.

MAKES 4 TO 6 SERVINGS

1 pound baby carrots, no
  bigger than 2 inches
  long
3 tablespoons water
2 tablespoons fresh lemon
  juice
2 tablespoons olive oil
1 tablespoon ground cumin
1 garlic clove, minced
1 teaspoon paprika
2 tablespoons minced fresh
  cilantro leaves

1. Put the carrots and water in a medium-size saucepan and bring to a boil. Cover, reduce the heat to low, and let steam until the carrots are crisp tender, 5 to 7 minutes.

2. Drain the carrots, put them in a medium-size bowl with the remaining ingredients, and toss to blend. Cover and let sit at room temperature for at least 15 minutes before serving. This tastes even better made a day ahead, covered, and kept in the refrigerator. Serve at room temperature.

VEGETABLE CONFETTI

A sublimely easy and tasty way to serve a mélange of root vegetables.

1 cup julienned or shredded
  carrots
1 cup julienned or shredded
  celery
1 cup julienned or shredded
  onions
1/2 cup finely chopped
  mixed fresh herbs
  (tarragon, dill, parsley,
  and/or chives)
Fine sea salt to taste
1 teaspoon unsalted butter,
  softened

Combine the carrots, celery, onions, herbs, and salt in a large saucepan. Cut out a piece of parchment or waxed paper to fit over the vegetables and spread it with the butter on one side. Place the paper, butter side down, on top of the vegetables. Cook over low heat until the vegetables are tender, about 30 minutes. Serve hot.

SPICY CAULIFLOWER

For tapas-style or Indian fish dishes, serve this cauliflower as a worthy accompaniment.

MAKES 6 TO 8 SERVINGS

1 medium-size head
   cauliflower, cut into
   3/4-inch florets
2 tablespoons toasted bread
   crumbs
2 cups plain yogurt (not
   lowfat)
1/2 cup chopped fresh
   cilantro leaves, plus more
   for garnish
1 tablespoon fresh lemon
   juice
1 tablespoon peeled and
   grated fresh ginger or
   1/2 teaspoon ground
   ginger
4 cloves garlic, minced
1/2 teaspoon cayenne pepper
1/2 teaspoon ground cumin
1/2 teaspoon ground
   coriander
Sea salt to taste

1. Place the cauliflower florets in a large pot and cover with water. Bring to a boil, reduce the heat to medium-low, and simmer until crisp-tender, about 5 minutes. Drain the cauliflower and set aside.

2. In a large bowl, combine the remaining ingredients and stir to blend. Add cauliflower to the yogurt mixture. Serve immediately.

We especially like the uncooked vegetable appetizers and side dishes from France and Belgium as delicious accompaniments to grilled or smoked fish and seafood.

Belgian Endive Leaves with Assorted Spreads: Endive leaves with Smoked Trout Pâté (page 228).

Red Cabbage Slaw: Core and shred one 1-pound head red cabbage, then heat 1 1/2 cups cider vinegar and 2 tablespoons sugar, pour the mixture over the cabbage, tossing to coat evenly, and refrigerate to chill. Toss with 1/2 cup vegetable oil and 1 teaspoon chopped fresh thyme leaves, season with sea salt and freshly ground black pepper, and serve.

Stuffed Tomatoes: Trim and core a large, ripe tomato and discard some of the flesh and all the seeds with a small spoon. Lightly season the inside of the tomato with salt and freshly ground black, fill the tomato with grilled lobster meat (page 241) mixed with Homemade Mayonnaise (page 307) or Aioli (page 311).

Fresh Beet Salad: Combine 4 beets, peeled and grated, and 1/4 teaspoon cumin seeds toasted in a dry skillet over medium heat until fragrant. Toss with 2 to 3 tablespoons Three Citrus Marinade (page 287). This is also good prepared with grated carrots.

Chickpea Salad: Combine one 15-ounce can chickpeas, drained, 6 green onions, chopped, and 2 to 3 tablespoons Vinaigrette Marinade (page 284). Substitute white beans for the chickpeas to make White Bean Salad.

SAUTÉED CORN AND WILTED LETTUCE SALAD

Summertime means fresh vegetables, and this simple salad makes the most of two farmers' market standouts.

MAKES 6 SERVINGS

6 cups tender salad greens
1/4 cup Vinaigrette
    Marinade (page 284) or
    bottled Italian dressing
2 ears fresh sweet corn,
    kernels cut from the cob

1. Place salad greens in a large bowl.
2. In a small skillet over medium-high heat, cook the vinaigrette and corn together for 3 to 4 minutes.
3. Pour the mixture over the salad greens, toss well, and serve immediately.

GRILLED CORN IN THE HUSK

This corn is so sweet, spicy, and delicious, you may want to double the recipe to provide two ears per person at least!

MAKES 4 SERVINGS

4 ears fresh sweet corn
1/4 cup Zesty Lemon Baste
    (page 294)

1. Peel back the corn husks and remove the silks. Soak the corn with their husks in cold water to cover for 30 minutes. Remove one ear of corn at a time as you proceed.
2. Brush 1 tablespoon of the butter baste over each ear. Pull the husks back up over the corn.
3. Prepare a medium-hot fire.
4. Place the corn directly over the fire and grill for 10 to 15 minutes, turning the corn often.
5. To serve, pull the husks back and tear off a thin piece of husk. Use it to tie the husks back for a pretty presentation.

HERBED CREAMED CORN

In the heat of summer, just-picked sweet corn varieties such as Purdue Super Sweet, Peaches and Cream, or Silver Queen are sold at farmstands. Make this side while the grill is heating up.

MAKES 4 TO 6 SERVINGS

2 tablespoons unsalted
    butter
1 shallot, finely chopped
2 cloves garlic, minced
1 teaspoon ground
    coriander
1/2 teaspoon dried thyme
1/2 cup dry white wine
3 cups fresh or frozen (and
    defrosted) corn kernels
1 cup heavy cream
Salt and freshly ground
    white pepper to taste

1. Melt the butter in a heavy saucepan over medium-high heat, add the shallot, garlic, coriander, and thyme, and cook, stirring, until the shallot and garlic are translucent, 2 to 3 minutes.

2. Pour in the wine and deglaze the pan, stirring with a wooden spoon. Stir in the corn and heavy cream, cover, and let cook until the corn is just done, 5 to 8 minutes. Season with salt and white pepper and serve immediately.

TRI-COLOR CUCUMBER SALAD

For extra vinegar flavor, soak all of the vegetables in straight vinegar for about 30 minutes. Then drain the vinegar and combine it with the marinade ingredients and mix the salad together again.

MAKES ABOUT 8 SERVINGS

SALAD:

1 large, ripe beefsteak tomato, peeled and cut into wedges

1 cucumber, peeled, quartered lengthwise, seeded, and chopped

1 red or yellow bell pepper, seeded and chopped

1 small red onion, cut into thin wedges

1 jalapeño, seeded and finely minced

HERBED MARINADE:

1/2 cup tarragon vinegar

1/2 cup white wine vinegar

1 cup olive oil

1/4 cup sugar

4 cloves garlic, minced

3 tablespoons snipped fresh chives

1 tablespoon chopped fresh basil leaves

1/2 tablespoon dry mustard

2 1/2 teaspoons kosher salt, or to taste

1/2 teaspoon freshly ground black pepper

1. In a large-size glass bowl, combine the salad ingredients.

2. In a large glass jar, combine the marinade ingredients. Cover with the lid and shake to blend. Pour the marinade over the vegetables.

3. Cover tightly and refrigerate for several hours or overnight to let the flavors blend.

SMOKED AND BRAISED
BACON-WRAPPED ENDIVE

If you're serving this with the Oak-Planked Sea Scallops (page 254), prepare it first, then start smoking the scallops after the endive has smoked for one hour.

MAKES 6 TO 8 SERVINGS

8 small heads Belgian
    endive, trimmed
4 slices smoked bacon, cut
    in half lengthwise
1 tablespoon honey
Garlic salt and freshly
    ground black pepper to
    taste

1. Prepare an indirect fire, adding 3 water-soaked oak chunks to the charcoal in a kettle grill or charcoal smoker. Fill the water pan and place the pan in the smoker.

2. Blanch the endive in a large saucepan of boiling water for 3 minutes. Drain and pat dry with paper towels.

3. Wrap a strip of bacon around each endive and place in a disposable aluminum pan. Brush the endive with the honey and sprinkle with garlic salt and pepper. Place on the bottom rack of the smoker and smoke until the endive is tender and has a smoky aroma, about 1 1/2 hours.

ITALIAN FENNEL SALAD

This is a refreshingly crisp salad that pairs well with seafood.

1 medium-size fennel bulb,
    trimmed (keep some of
    the feathery fronds for
    garnish)
4 ounces Parmesan cheese,
    very thinly sliced
8 ounces button mushrooms,
    thinly sliced
1/4 cup extra virgin olive oil
Fresh lemon juice to taste
Salt and freshly ground
    black pepper to taste

Thinly slice the fennel bulb from the top to the base. Lay the slices out on a serving plate and top with the Parmesan and mushroom slices. Drizzle with the olive oil and lemon juice, season with salt and pepper, and serve immediately.

JICAMA STICKS

Cool and crisp, jicama sticks go well with grilled fish and shellfish of all kinds.

2 or 3 jicamas
1/4 cup Chipotle
    Vinaigrette (page 294)

1. Peel and cut the jicama into thin 2-inch-long sticks. Place in a medium-size food storage bowl with a tight-fitting lid. Add the vinaigrette, cover with the lid, and shake well.
2. Refrigerate for several hours to chill and shake well again before serving.

SAVORY LEEK AND HERB CUSTARD

This crustless quiche can be served hot from the oven or just warm.

2 tablespoons unsalted
   butter
1 cup chopped leeks, white
   part only, rinsed well
   and patted dry
1/2 cup finely diced onion
4 large eggs
1 cup half-and-half
2 tablespoons freshly grated
   Parmesan cheese
1 tablespoon chopped fresh
   Italian parsley leaves
1 teaspoon fresh rosemary
   leaves

1. Preheat the oven to 350 degrees Fahrenheit. Coat the inside of a 1-quart casserole dish with nonstick cooking spray and set aside.

2. Melt the butter in a skillet over medium-high heat, add the leek and onion, and cook, stirring, until transparent, about 5 minutes.

3. In a large bowl, whisk the eggs, half-and-half, Parmesan, and herbs together. Whisk in the sautéed leek mixture and pour the mixture into the prepared dish. Bake until a knife inserted in the center comes out clean, 40 to 45 minutes.

SKEWERED SCALLIONS

Skewering the green onions keeps these slender treats from falling through the grill grates. We like them charred.

MAKES 2 TO 4 SERVINGS

1 bunch scallions or green onions, 8 to 12
1 tablespoon extra virgin olive oil
Sea salt and freshly ground black pepper to taste

1. Clean the scallions or green onions. Thread 2 or 3 onions onto 2 toothpicks, pushing one toothpick through the white part of the onions and the second toothpick about an inch lower through the white part as it begins to turn green. Repeat the threading procedure until all the onions are secured.
2. Place the onions flat on a baking sheet. Drizzle with the olive oil and season with salt and pepper. Set aside.
3. Prepare a hot fire.
4. When ready to grill, remove the onions from the sheet and grill until charred, about 5 minutes per side.

GRILLED GARDEN ONIONS AND LEMON HALVES

The warmed lemons come off the grill very juicy and are luscious with grilled fish. I serve the onions charred and whole so they stay hot. It is easy to cut them in half on your plate and then devour the sweet white flesh.

MAKES 4 TO 6 SERVINGS

4 to 6 medium-size yellow or white onions, preferably fresh from the garden
2 to 3 lemons, halved

1. Prepare a hot fire.
2. When ready to grill, place the onions, with their outer skins intact, on top of a hot grill for 10 to 15 minutes. The outer skin will char, but the inside flesh will be soft. Remove from the grill and, when cool enough to handle, remove the charred outer skin.
3. Place the lemon halves directly over the hot fire and grill until charred on all sides, 4 to 5 minutes. Serve immediately.

SCALLOPED ONION CASSEROLE

This pairs beautifully with Pecan-Planked Catfish (page 206), but it's also great as an accompaniment for Thanksgiving turkey.

MAKES 8 SERVINGS

5 tablespoons unsalted
   butter
4 celery stalks, chopped
1 cup small frozen pearl
   onions (about 4 ounces),
   defrosted
1 cup chopped yellow
   onions
4 green onions, white part
   and some of the green,
   chopped
1/4 cup all-purpose flour
1 teaspoon salt
1/2 teaspoon freshly ground
   white pepper
1/2 teaspoon Tabasco sauce
2 tablespoons sour cream
2 cups half-and-half
1/3 cup sliced almonds, plus
   1/4 cup for garnish
1/2 cup freshly grated
   Parmesan cheese, plus
   1/2 cup for garnish

1. Preheat the oven to 350 degrees Fahrenheit. Lightly butter a 1-quart casserole and set aside.
2. Melt the butter in a large skillet over medium heat, add the celery, and cook, stirring, for 5 minutes. Stir in the pearl, yellow, and green onions. Sprinkle the flour over the vegetables, stir until combined, and cook for 3 to 4 minutes. Stir in the salt, pepper, Tabasco, and sour cream. Pour in the half-and-half and stir until the sauce slightly thickens, about 5 minutes. Fold in 1/3 cup of the almonds and 1/2 cup of the Parmesan.
3. Transfer the onion mixture to the prepared casserole and sprinkle with the remaining 1/4 cup almonds and 1/2 cup Parmesan. Bake until the casserole is bubbling and browned on top, about 15 minutes.

SMOKED ONIONS WITH THYME CREAM

For a colorful platter, choose an assortment of white, yellow, and red onions.

3 wood chunks, 1 cup wood chips, or 1/3 cup wood pellets
1/2 cup heavy cream
3 sprigs fresh thyme or 1 teaspoon dried thyme
Salt and freshly ground black pepper to taste
3 large Vidalia or other sweet onions, peeled and cut in half horizontally

1. Place the wood chunks or chips in water to soak or wood pellets in a heavy-duty aluminum foil packet with holes poked into it.

2. Prepare an indirect fire.

3. Meanwhile, in a small, heavy saucepan, bring the cream and thyme to a boil. Cover, remove from the heat, and let infuse for 20 minutes.

4. When ready to smoke, place the drained wood chunks or chips or foil packet on the fire in a kettle grill or charcoal smoker; in an electric smoker, place the wood chunks or chips or packet around the heating element. Fill the water pan and place the pan in the smoker.

5. Place the onion halves, cut side up, in a disposable aluminum pan. Drizzle each onion half with 1 tablespoon of the flavored cream, then season with salt and pepper. Place the pan on the smoker or grill rack, cover, and smoke until the onions have softened and have a smoky aroma, 1 to 1 1/2 hours.

Suggested wood smoke: pecan

ORANGE AND RED ONION SALAD

This is a favorite of the Adler household any time of year.

MAKES 4 SERVINGS

2 oranges, peeled and
    sectioned
4 thin slices red onion,
    pulled apart into rings
4 cups torn lettuce
1/4 cup orange juice
1/4 cup olive oil
2 tablespoons chopped
    mixed fresh herbs
    (chives, basil, and/or
    parsley)
1 teaspoon Dijon mustard
1/2 teaspoon capers (option-
    al), drained and mashed
1/2 teaspoon red pepper
    flakes
Sea salt to taste

1. Place the oranges, onion, and lettuce in a large salad bowl.

2. In a small bowl, whisk together the orange juice, olive oil, herbs, mustard, capers, if using, and red pepper flakes, and season with salt.

3. Pour the dressing over the salad mixture and toss. Serve immediately.

MANDARIN ORANGE SALAD

This refreshing salad is based on a recipe by the irrepressible food authority Shirley Corriher from her book *Cookwise* (William Morrow, 1997). Marinating the canned oranges briefly in ginger and sugar water removes the canned taste.

MAKES 6 TO 8 SERVINGS

1 cup hot tap water
One 1-inch piece fresh
    ginger, peeled and cut
    into thin slices
2 tablespoons sugar
4 ice cubes
Two 11-ounce cans
    mandarin oranges,
    drained and rinsed
4 cups mixed salad greens
    (including bitter
    varieties such as frisée
    and radicchio)
Brandied Tomato Cream
    (page 146)

1. In a medium-size stainless-steel bowl, stir the hot water, ginger slices, and sugar together. Place the bowl in the freezer for 5 minutes, then remove and stir in the ice cubes for further cooling. Stir in the mandarin oranges and marinate for 5 minutes.

2. Place the salad greens in a large serving bowl. Remove the mandarin oranges from the marinade with a slotted spoon and place on the greens. Toss the salad greens and oranges together, then drizzle with the tomato cream and toss again. Serve immediately.

GRILLED POTATO WEDGES

Grilled potatoes are delicious. They can be served hot, at room temperature, or cold with your favorite flavored mayonnaise (page 309) on the side.

MAKES 6 TO 8 SERVINGS

4 large baking potatoes
1/4 cup olive oil
Sea salt

1. Place the potatoes in a large saucepan and cover with water. Place over high heat and parboil the potatoes for 15 minutes. Drain, then cut the potatoes into wedges and toss with the olive oil in a large bowl.
2. Prepare a hot fire.
3. When ready to grill, place the potatoes in an oiled grill wok and stir-fry, turning occasionally with wooden paddles, until the potatoes are soft and browned, 5 to 10 minutes. Season with salt and serve immediately.

CHEDDAR-ROMANO POTATO SLICES

Mellow and cheesy, with a hint of smoke.

MAKES 6 TO 8 SERVINGS

3 large russet potatoes
2 tablespoons olive oil
Sea salt and freshly ground
 black pepper to taste
1 cup shredded sharp
 cheddar cheese
1/2 cup shredded Pecorino
 Romano cheese
1 cup crumbled fried bacon
 (4 to 5 strips)

1. Slice the potatoes lengthwise about 3/8 inch thick. Place the potato slices in a large pot of boiling salted water and parboil for about 7 minutes. Drain and pat dry.
2. Prepare a hot fire.
3. Place the drained potatoes in a disposable aluminum pan. Lightly drizzle with the olive oil and season with salt and pepper. Turn the potato slices over and evenly top with the cheeses and bacon.
4. When ready to grill, place the pan on the grill and cook until the cheeses begin to melt and the bottom of the potato slices begin to brown, 5 to 7 minutes. Potatoes are done when they can be pierced with a fork.

GRILLED RED POTATOES, CAPERS, AND OLIVES

A colorful and delicious side dish, perfect with full-flavored grilled fish or beef.

6 medium-size red
    potatoes, cut into sixths
1/4 cup capers, drained
1/2 cup Kalamata olives,
    drained, pitted, and
    chopped
4 cloves garlic, minced
1/4 cup olive oil

1. In a large saucepan of boiling salted water, parboil the potatoes for about 10 minutes, drain, and pat dry. Place the potatoes in a disposable aluminum pan.

2. Mix together the capers, olives, garlic, and olive oil, crushing the capers as you mix. Spoon this mixture over the potatoes.

3. Prepare a hot fire.

4. When ready to grill, place the pan on the grill, cover, and grill until the potatoes are tender, about 25 minutes. Serve warm.

FRIED POTATOES

Whether you cube them or slice them, whether they're red or russet, home-fried potatoes are pure comfort food.

1/2 cup olive oil
4 medium-size russet
    potatoes, peeled and
    cubed
8 large garlic cloves, peeled
2 teaspoons chopped fresh
    rosemary leaves
Salt and freshly ground
    black pepper to taste

1. Heat the olive oil in a large skillet over medium-high heat, then add the potatoes. Spread them out in the pan in a single layer and leave to form a golden crust on the bottom, about 5 minutes.

2. Turn the potatoes carefully and scatter the garlic cloves on top of them. Cook until the bottoms are browned, about 4 minutes more, without stirring.

3. Add the rosemary and stir the potatoes. Continue to fry, turning the potatoes and garlic, 6 to 8 minutes more. Season with salt and pepper and serve hot.

WARM NEW POTATO AND WATERCRESS SALAD

Spring watercress gathered from a creek bank with tender baby new potatoes make an unforgettable French-style potato salad drizzled with a lemony vinaigrette. If watercress isn't available, substitute curly cress or curly endive.

MAKES 4 TO 6 SERVINGS

1 pound small new red
    potatoes, rinsed and
    scrubbed
2 large bunches watercress,
    stems trimmed away and
    rinsed
Juice of 2 to 3 lemons, to
    your taste
1 clove garlic, minced
1/2 cup extra virgin olive oil
Salt and freshly ground
    black pepper to taste

1. Place the potatoes in a large saucepan with enough water to cover and bring to a boil over high heat. Reduce the heat to medium-high and boil until the potatoes are cooked through, 10 to 15 minutes. Drain and, when cool enough to handle, cut each potato into quarters.

2. Place the watercress in a large salad bowl. Whisk the lemon juice, garlic, olive oil, and seasonings together to make a vinaigrette. Toss the watercress with the warm potatoes and vinaigrette. Serve immediately.

TAPAS-STYLE POTATO SALAD

This has become our favorite potato salad, with tapas-style fish and with burgers, chicken, or steak.

MAKES 4 SERVINGS

1/2 cup homemade (page 307) or good-quality store-bought mayonnaise

3 cloves garlic, minced

4 medium-size baking potatoes, baked until tender and cooled

2 tablespoons chopped fresh Italian parsley leaves

1. In a large bowl, blend the mayonnaise and garlic together.

2. Cut the potatoes in half and cut the baked potato flesh into pieces. Gently blend the potatoes with the garlic mayonnaise using a rubber spatula. Blend in the parsley and serve.

SILLSALAT

The pickled herring in this relish-like salad gives a clean and salty flavor, much like anchovy does in Italian recipes. The ruby color of the salad, so brilliant at holiday time, deserves a cut-glass bowl for serving.

MAKES 6 TO 8 SERVINGS

1 pickled herring
1 cup pickled beets, drained
   and cut into small dice
1 1/2 cups peeled potatoes
   boiled in water to cover
   until tender, drained,
   and cut into small dice
1 1/2 cups Granny Smith
   apples cored and cut into
   small dice
1/4 cup onion cut into small
   dice
1/3 cup bread-and-butter
   pickles cut into small
   dice
1/4 cup cider vinegar
2 tablespoons water
1/4 teaspoon freshly ground
   white pepper

1. Soak the herring in water to cover for 30 minutes, then drain, skin, and fillet.

2. Cut the herring fillet into very small pieces and place in a large bowl. Add the remaining ingredients and mix well.

3. Cover and let marinate in the refrigerator for at least an hour before serving.

SESAME SEED SPINACH SALAD

We always get requests for this recipe, which goes well with anything!

1 pound spinach leaves,
   washed well and heavy
   stems removed
1 tablespoon unsalted
   butter
1/2 cup sesame seeds
1 cup sour cream
1/2 cup mayonnaise
1/4 cup shredded Parmesan
   cheese
1/4 cup seeded and finely
   chopped green bell
   pepper
2 green onions, green part
   only, finely chopped
1 tablespoon tarragon
   vinegar
1 tablespoon sugar
1/2 teaspoon sea salt
1/4 teaspoon garlic salt

1. Place the spinach in a large salad bowl. Set aside.

2. Melt the butter in a small skillet over medium heat. Add the sesame seeds and cook, stirring, until golden brown. Transfer to a small bowl to cool.

3. In a small bowl, combine the sour cream, mayonnaise, Parmesan, green pepper, green onions, vinegar, sugar, and salts. Add the toasted sesame seeds and mix well. Toss with the spinach greens and serve immediately.

PANZANELLA SALAD

We both remember our parents' stories about our grandparents' "victory gardens" from World War II. That American pride is still "growing" strong in our own Midwest gardens. We both have gardens and grow lots of tomatoes, red and yellow, big and small. So, whenever we make a tomato platter or a salad like this one, we use all different colors and shapes. It makes quite a fetching display of vibrant garden color.

MAKES 8 TO 10 SERVINGS

2/3 cups extra virgin olive oil

1/3 cup red wine vinegar

1/3 cup fresh lemon juice

1/3 cup finely chopped fresh Italian parsley leaves

1 teaspoon sea salt

6 cups cubed Italian bread with crusts removed, toasted in the oven

6 large, ripe tomatoes, cut into wedges

4 ripe Roma tomatoes, cut into wedges

2 cups cherry and yellow pear tomatoes

1 large red onion, cut into slivers

1 cup cured olives, drained, pitted, and chopped

1 cup loosely packed fresh basil leaves

1 cup freshly grated Parmesan or pecorino cheese

1. In a large salad bowl, whisk together the olive oil, vinegar, lemon juice, parsley, and salt.

2. Add the bread cubes, tomatoes, onion, and olives and toss to coat. Add the basil and cheese, lightly toss again, and serve.

PARMESAN-CRUSTED TOMATOES

We love sliced garden tomatoes. But after your taste buds are sated with fresh tomatoes, try this baked recipe for a flavor change. This is a great recipe to use with store-bought tomatoes.

MAKES 6 SERVINGS

3 large, ripe tomatoes,
   halved
3 tablespoons dry sherry
1 1/2 teaspoons chopped
   fresh dill or 3/4 teaspoon
   dillweed
3/4 teaspoon freshly ground
   black pepper
1/4 cup mayonnaise
1/4 cup freshly grated
   Parmesan cheese

1. Preheat the broiler.
2. Pierce the tomato halves several times with a fork on the cut side. Sprinkle 1/2 teaspoon of the sherry, 1/4 teaspoon of the fresh dill (or 1/8 teaspoon of the dill-weed), and 1/8 teaspoon of the pepper over each tomato half.
3. Combine the mayonnaise and Parmesan and spoon this over each tomato half. Broil for 3 to 4 minutes to lightly brown. Serve hot.

GRILLED GOAT CHEESE TOMATOES

Serve these piquant grilled tomatoes as a side dish with a salad of mixed greens and black olives.

MAKES 4 TO 8 SERVINGS

Eight 1/2-inch-thick slices
   beefsteak tomatoes
1 tablespoon extra virgin
   olive oil
Sea salt and freshly ground
   pepper to taste
Eight 1-ounce slices goat
   cheese, feta, mozzarella,
   or blue cheese

1. Prepare a hot fire.
2. Meanwhile, place the tomato slices in a disposable aluminum pan or on an oiled grill rack. Lightly coat with the olive oil and season with salt and pepper. Turn the tomatoes over and lightly season with salt and pepper again. Top each tomato with a slice of goat cheese.
3. When ready to grill, place the pan of tomatoes on the grill rack and grill until warmed though and the cheese has melted, 6 to 8 minutes. Serve hot.

FRESH YELLOW AND RED TOMATO SALAD

Serve this with a good crusty bread to soak up the summery juices.

MAKES 4 SERVINGS

2 cups mixed salad greens
2 large, ripe red tomatoes,
    coarsely chopped
1 cup yellow pear tomatoes
1/4 cup crumbled blue
    cheese
2 tablespoons olive oil
2 tablespoons balsamic
    vinegar

1. Place the salad greens to the side of each plate and top with the red and yellow tomatoes. Sprinkle with the blue cheese.

2. In a small bowl, whisk the olive oil and balsamic vinegar together. Drizzle 1 tablespoon of dressing on each salad and serve.

GRILLED MEDITERRANEAN VEGETABLES

This recipe is like a salsa. Serve it as a side dish or spoon it on top of a grilled fish steak or fillet. It would also be delicious to toss it with toasted bread cubes for a panzanella-style warm salad.

MAKES 8 TO 10 SERVINGS

2 tablespoons unsalted
    butter, softened
2 cups chopped fresh
    tomatoes
2 cups chopped onions
1 cup cured black olives,
    drained
1 cup chopped fresh Italian
    parsley leaves
3/4 cup Vinaigrette
    Marinade (page 284)

1. Prepare a medium-hot fire.

2. Grease a large sheet of heavy-duty aluminum foil with the butter and place the tomatoes, onions, and parsley on top of it. Fold and seal the foil into a packet and poke several holes in the top. (Or butter a disposable aluminum pan or fish boat and place the vegetables in the pan. Cover with aluminum foil and poke several holes in the foil.)

3. When ready to grill, place the foil packet of vegetables directly on the grill grate. Grill the vegetables for 8 to 10 minutes and serve hot.

ZUCCHINI CASSEROLE

One of Dee Conde's (Karen's mother) most delicious summer dishes is made with vine-ripened tomatoes and garden zucchini. All of her daughters keep this casserole in their repertoire. It's a great dish to prepare in the morning and refrigerate until ready to bake in the evening. It is fun to vary the colors in the casserole, too. Try it with red and yellow tomatoes, yellow crookneck squash, and green zucchini. Also, experiment with the cheese by trying Parmesan or goat cheese for a variation.

MAKES 6 TO 8 SERVINGS

6 medium-size zucchini, ends trimmed and sliced 1/4 inch thick

Sea salt and freshly ground black pepper to taste

24 saltine crackers

6 medium-size, ripe tomatoes, sliced 3/8 inch thick

1 large onion, finely chopped and sautéed in the bacon grease

1 pound sliced bacon, fried until crisp, drained on paper towels, and crumbled

2 cups shredded sharp cheddar cheese

1. Preheat the oven to 350 degrees Fahrenheit.

2. Meanwhile, butter a 3-quart deep-dish glass casserole. Cover the bottom with one-third of the zucchini slices and lightly season with salt and pepper. Crush 8 saltine crackers over the squash. Layer in one third of the tomato slices and lightly season with salt and pepper. Layer in one third of the sautéed onion, top with one-third of the crumbled bacon, then one-third of the shredded cheese. Repeat these layers 2 more times.

3. Bake until the vegetables are tender, about 1 hour. (For crisper vegetables, reduce the cooking time to 35 to 45 minutes.) Serve hot.

PARMESAN GRITS

We're not southern ladies, but we both love grits. If you want to spice up this recipe, add one or two chopped jalapeños or other hot peppers and a dash of hot sauce or a sprinkle of cayenne pepper for heat.

MAKES 6 TO 8 SERVINGS

4 cups water

1 cup grits (not quick-
    cooking)

1 teaspoon sea salt

1/2 cup (1 stick) unsalted
    butter, cut into pieces

1 1/2 cups freshly grated
    Parmesan or Romano
    cheese

1/2 cup shredded sharp
    cheddar cheese

1/2 teaspoon garlic salt

1/2 teaspoon freshly ground
    white pepper

1. In a large saucepan, bring the water to a boil. Slowly add the grits and salt, stirring constantly. Stir until thick, 20 to 30 minutes.

2. Meanwhile, butter a shallow baking dish and set aside.

3. Reduce the heat under the saucepan to low and stir in the butter, 1 cup of the Parmesan, the cheddar, garlic salt, and white pepper.

4. Transfer the grits to the prepared dish. Sprinkle the remaining 1/2 cup Parmesan cheese evenly over the top. At this point, you may keep the grits warm by putting them outside on the hot grill, in a preheated 300-degree-Fahrenheit oven, or you may microwave the grits for 3 to 5 minutes before serving.

SPRING ONION SPOONBREAD

A taste of the South, delicious with grilled or smoked trout and catfish.

MAKES 4 TO 6 SERVINGS

2 1/2 cups milk

1 cup stone-ground yellow
cornmeal

6 tablespoons (3/4 stick)
unsalted butter, cut into
cubes

1 teaspoon salt

1 teaspoon freshly ground
white pepper

1 1/2 teaspoons baking
powder

3 large eggs, separated

1 bunch green onions, white
part and some of the
green, chopped

1. Preheat the oven to 350 degrees Fahrenheit. Grease a 1-quart soufflé dish and set aside.

2. Bring the milk almost to a boil in a large saucepan. Gradually pour in the cornmeal, whisking constantly. Reduce the heat to a simmer and cook, whisking occasionally, until the mixture has thickened to a porridge, about 10 minutes.

3. Whisk in the butter, salt, white pepper, baking powder, egg yolks, and green onions.

4. In a large bowl with an electric mixer, whip the egg whites until soft peaks form. Fold the cornmeal mixture into the egg whites, using a wooden spoon.

5. Pour the batter into the prepared soufflé dish and bake until a toothpick inserted in the center comes out clean, 25 to 30 minutes. Serve hot.

PEPPERY COUSCOUS

A lowfat side dish sure to pique tired taste buds.

MAKES 6 TO 8 SERVINGS

4 cups chicken broth

3 cups instant couscous

1/2 cup dried currants

1 bunch green onions, white
part and some of the
green, thinly sliced

1 teaspoon freshly ground
black pepper

Sea salt to taste

1. In a medium-size saucepan, bring the broth to a boil. Remove from the heat and stir in the couscous. Cover and let stand for 5 minutes.

2. Fluff the couscous with a fork. Stir in the currants, green onions, pepper, and salt. Serve immediately.

MEDITERRANEAN ORZO SALAD

Orzo salad is a great company dish because it can be prepared a day ahead. If you are doing so, reserve a cup of the pasta water to hydrate the pasta as needed before serving.

1/2 pound (1 cup) orzo, cooked in boiling water until al dente and drained

1 bunch green onions, white part and some of the green, chopped

1 cucumber, peeled, seeded, and diced

8 ounces feta cheese, crumbled

1/2 cup pitted and chopped Kalamata olives

1/3 cup extra virgin olive oil

1/3 cup fresh lemon juice

2 cloves garlic, minced

2 tablespoons chopped fresh dill or 2 teaspoons dill-weed

1/4 teaspoon dried oregano

Salt and freshly ground black pepper to taste

1. In a large bowl, combine the drained orzo, green onions, cucumber, feta, and olives.

2. In a small bowl, whisk together the olive oil, lemon juice, and seasonings.

3. Pour the dressing over the orzo and toss to blend well. Refrigerate until ready to serve.

LEMON RICE

For a pretty presentation, sprinkle some Gremolata (page 283) over the rice for color and extra flavor.

MAKES 6 SERVINGS

2 tablespoons unsalted
   butter
1 cup long-grain white rice
2 cups chicken broth
1/2 cup dry white wine
Grated zest and juice of
   1 lemon
1 teaspoon sea salt

1. Melt the butter in a medium-size saucepan over medium heat. Add the rice and cook, stirring, until the rice is opaque, about 5 minutes. Add the broth, wine, and salt. Bring to a boil, reduce the heat to low, cover, and simmer until the liquid is absorbed, about 40 minutes.

2. Add the lemon juice and zest and fluff with a fork.

SAVORY RISOTTO CAKES

High-style risotto cakes for when you want to impress your guests.

4 cups chicken broth
1/4 cup (1/2 stick) unsalted
    butter
1/4 cup chopped onion
1 cup Arborio rice
1/2 cup smoked Gouda
    cheese, cut into small
    dice
1/2 cup peeled, seeded, and
    chopped fresh tomato
Salt and freshly ground
    white pepper to taste

1. About 3 hours before serving, pour the chicken broth into a medium-size saucepan and bring to a simmer.

2. Melt the butter in a large, heavy saucepan over medium-high heat, add the onion, and cook, stirring, for 2 minutes. Stir in the rice, until it is coated with the butter. Add 2 cups of the hot broth to the rice and stir with a wooden spoon until the rice has absorbed the liquid. Add another cup of broth and continue to stir, adding more broth as the rice absorbs it, about 20 minutes total.

3. Stir in the Gouda and tomato and season with salt and pepper. Let the risotto cool to room temperature.

4. Lay a sheet of waxed or parchment paper on a flat work surface and spoon the cooled risotto onto the paper. Smooth the risotto to make a rectangle about 1 inch thick. Coat the inside of a 3-inch donut or biscuit cutter with nonstick cooking spray and cut out 4 risotto cakes. Cover and chill until ready to serve.

5. Five minutes before serving, coat the inside of a large nonstick skillet with nonstick cooking spray. Gently heat the risotto cakes over medium-high heat until just warmed through, turning them once.

COCONUT RICE

A fragrant and slightly crunchy rice to serve with Indian- and Asian-style fish and shellfish dishes.

1 tablespoon vegetable oil
1 green Thai chile or
   jalapeño, seeded and
   finely chopped
4 green onions, white part
   and some of the green,
   finely chopped
1/2 cup unsweetened flaked
   coconut (available at
   Asian markets and
   health food stores)
1 cup long-grain rice
3 cups chicken broth

Heat the vegetable oil in a large saucepan over medium heat. Add the chile, green onions, and coconut and cook, stirring, for 3 to 4 minutes. Stir in the rice until coated with the oil, then pour in the chicken broth. Bring to a boil, reduce the heat to low, cover, and simmer until the rice can be fluffed with a fork, about 15 minutes.

WILD RICE AND DRIED CHERRY PICNIC SALAD

Dried Michigan cherries rank high on our list of favorite pantry items. They are delicious in sweet breads or bread puddings, tangy in southwestern salsas, and they make exquisite dessert sauces.

MAKES 8 TO 10 SERVINGS

1 1/2 cups long-grain rice, cooked according to package instructions

1/2 cup wild rice, cooked according to package instructions

1/3 cup dried cherries, plumped in hot water to cover and drained

1/3 cup pine nuts, toasted

1/2 yellow bell pepper, seeded and chopped

1/2 red onion, chopped

3 tablespoons chopped fresh Italian parsley leaves

3 tablespoons balsamic vinegar

3 tablespoons extra virgin olive oil

Salt and freshly ground black pepper to taste

Combine all the ingredients in a large salad bowl until well mixed. Serve immediately at room temperature or refrigerate and serve cold.

SOURCE GUIDE

FISH PURVEYORS

50 FATHOM LINE
P.O. BOX 532
VASHON ISLAND, WA 98070
800-569-2124
A gourmet source for wild king salmon from the icy, nutrient-rich waters of Alaska and the Pacific Northwest. Their troll-caught albacore tuna is caught on hooks and lines and pose no threat to other marine mammals. Orders for wild king salmon fillets, alder-smoked salmon, and albacore tuna loins may be placed via e-mail (*crbc@wolfenet.com*) or via telephone or fax at 206-463-7715.

ATLANTIC SEAFOOD DIRECT
21 MERRILL DRIVE
ROCKLAND, ME 04841
800-227-1116
Providers of live lobster and fresh seafood from the Atlantic. Call for additional information and to find out what fresh catch is available.

DUCKTRAP RIVER FISH FARM
RR 2, BOX 378
LINCOLNVILLE, ME 04849
800-828-3825
Summer vacations spent in Maine, a stint on an Alaskan salmon-fishing boat, a biology degree from Harvard, and a

desire to open a trout farm all prompted Washington, D.C., born and bred Des Fitzgerald into trying his luck in a small coastal town 100 miles north of Portland, Maine.

Although the fish farm didn't work out, the smoking techniques he developed for fish definitely did. Fitzgerald uses a curing rub of brine, herbs, spices, and dehydrated natural sugar cane juice (Sucanat). Then he cold smokes local Cape Split mussels, Snake River (Idaho) farm-raised trout, and local farm-raised salmon over smoldering fires of sugar maple, wild cherry, red oak, and apple—the combinations of wood chips unique to each kind of fish.

EMPRESS INTERNATIONAL LTD.
IRVINE, CA
800-645-6244
WWW.EMPFISH.COM

EMPRESS INTERNATIONAL OF
    CALIFORNIA, LTD.
PORT WASHINGTON, NY
949-789-6720
WWW.EMPFISH.COM
Wholesalers of Xcellent whole shrimp (head on)—white, brown, pink, and Black Tiger farm-raised shrimp—harvested by net at night during cooler temperatures. The shrimp are then carefully sorted and graded by size before going to the processor. From pond to freezer takes less than 4 hours.

FRESH CHOICE SEAFOOD.COM, INC.
P.O. BOX 2070
KEY WEST, FL 33045
877-554-3737
FRESHCHOICESEAFOOD@YAHOO.COM
Fresh from the Florida Keys—yellowtail snapper, mahimahi, grouper, and more. Captain Ryon and Carter Logan, who are brothers, have been commercial fishing for the most of their lives in South Florida. "We deal specifically with individuals who demand a higher standard for the seafood they require. Our seafood products are completely domestic to insure the quality of your product," the brothers say. All seafood orders are packaged in a Styrofoam cooler with frozen gel packs and shipped overnight via Federal Express.

GEORGE'S ULTIMATE SEAFOOD
112 GREEN STREET
WORCESTER, MA 01604
800-951-CLAW (2529)
WWW.ULTIMATESEAFOOD.COM
Great source for shellfish and more. Lobster, clams, mussels, oysters, tuna, swordfish, halibut, and salmon come overnight to your door nestled in seaweed.

INLAND SEAFOOD
1222 MENLO DRIVE
ATLANTA, GA 30318
800-883-FISH (3474)
WWW.INLANDSEAFOOD.COM
Wholesale distributor to restaurants,

caterers, and retail markets. Over 1,000 fish, shellfish, and gourmet specialty items are available. Orders are shipped via overnight delivery.

KEY WEST SEAFOOD
P.O. BOX 6676
KEY WEST, FL 33041
800-292-9853
WWW.KEYWESTSEAFOOD.COM
This company claims "from sea to door in 24." They provide never-frozen Key West pink shrimp, Florida lobster tails, stone crab claws, mahimahi, mangrove snapper, yellowtail snapper, grouper, wahoo, and tuna.

LEGAL SEA FOODS
33 EVERETT STREET
BOSTON, MA 02139
800-343-5804
WWW.SENDLEGAL.COM
Legal Sea Foods is a top-ranked seafood company based in Boston. They operate over 25 restaurants along the Eastern seaboard from Massachusetts to Florida. The mail-order division offers a substantial list of items including live lobster, littleneck clams, oysters, shrimp, smoked salmon, bluefish pâté, clam chowder, fish chowder, and all the makings for an authentic New England fish boil.

LEO'S LIVE SEAFOOD
4098 LEGOE BAY ROAD
LUMMI ISLAND, WA 98262
360-758-7318
WWW.LEOSLIVE.COM
Leo's family-operated live holding facility is located in North Puget Sound near the San Juan Islands. They reef net fish for wild salmon which ensures safe handling. Overcatch or undesirables are returned to the sea unharmed. Shrimp and Dungeness crab are available, too.

MAINE LOBSTER DIRECT
849 FOREST AVENUE
PORTLAND, ME 04103
800-556-2783
Live lobsters are shipped anywhere in the country. The Down East Feast is a basket filled with lobsters, steamer clams, lemons, corn on the cob, and a big enameled pot for a New England fish boil.

OHANA SEAFOOD MARKET
168 LAKE STREET SOUTH
KIRKLAND, WA 98033
WWW.FISH2GO.COM
Ohana is a Hawaiian word that translates to "family" or "kin." This family-owned business offers a large variety of fish including Alaskan halibut, salmon, red snapper, cod, orange roughy, sea bass, sole, and flounder and smoked fish, too.

PURE FOOD FISH MARKET
PIKE PLACE MARKET
SEATTLE, WA 98100
206-622-5765
WWW.FRESHSEAFOOD.COM
Founded in 1911 by Jack Amon, sons Sol and Irving run the family business at Seattle's Pike Place Market. Their catch is Pacific Northwest wild salmon and halibut and the delicious and popular Copper River Salmon.

TASTE FOR SEAFOOD
1222 MENLO DRIVE
ATLANTA, GA 30318
404-352-0829
WWW.INLANDSEAFOOD.COM
This company is a full-line distributor to the consumer of fresh, frozen, and smoked specialty seafood items. They also offer specialty gourmet products including foie gras. Orders are shipped overnight.

TIDELAND
P.O. BOX 145
ROUND POUND, ME 04564
800-562-8649
TideLand ships live lobsters. Market prices change weekly so it is best to call first.

WOODSMOKE PROVISIONS
1240 MENLO DRIVE
ATLANTA, GA 30318
404-355-5125
MGALLANT@WOODSMOKE.COM
President Mitch Gallant sums it up by saying, "Our product is fresh, never frozen from start to finish. Our deep culinary roots using all natural ingredients add depth, character, and complexity to our products." This micro-smokery produces cold- and hot-smoked fish including cold-smoked Atlantic salmon, gravlax, and fresh boneless rainbow trout fillets that are first cured in brown sugar, gently rinsed, washed in Jack Daniels, and smoked with cracked pecan nut shells. Call or e-mail for a brochure.

GRILL AND SMOKER MANUFACTURERS
ALFRESCO GOURMET GRILLS
7039 EAST SLAUSON AVENUE
COMMERCE, CA 90040
323-722-6115
WWW.ALFRESCOGRILLS.COM
High-performance commercial stainless-steel grills for the home.

ARCTIC PRODUCTS
P.O. 104293
JEFFERSON CITY, MO 65110-4293
800-325-8157
WWW.ARCTICPRODUCTS.COM
Arctic's Fire Ring is a rugged cast-iron

ring with cooking grid, perfect for shore lunches and campfires. It also complies with National Forestry rules that all campfires must be contained. The company also manufactures a Kettle Cart B-B-Q Grill that includes an easy-to-light charcoal system that's shaped like a charcoal chimney and lights with a single match. It comes in stainless steel or porcelain enamel coating. The three-leg design is built with a lower storage rack that doubles as extra leg support for greater stability.

BARBEQUES GALORE
15041 BAKE PARKWAY, SUITE A
IRVINE, CA 92618
949-597-2400
WWW.BBQGALORE.COM
Manufacturers of LP, natural gas, and charcoal grills, including the Turbo and the Bar-B-Chef. Retail division includes over 60 stores nationwide.

BIG GREEN EGG
3414 CLAIRMONT ROAD
ATLANTA, GA 30319
800-939-EGGS (3447)
WWW.BIGGREENEGG.COM
The largest producer of a ceramic Kamado-style combination charcoal smoker/grill that cooks with a tight-fitting lid and produces juicy flavorful food. They also provide covers, replacement parts, and wooden carts.

BIG JOHN GRILLS & ROTISSERIES
P.O. BOX 5250
PLEASANT GAP, PA 16823
800-326-9575
WWW.BIGJOHNGRILLS.COM
A large assortment of commercial and consumer equipment including several varieties of large rectangular flatbed grills that range in size up to 6 feet long. Great for feeding a crowd, these units come in gas, charcoal, and rotisserie, with or without lids. Several models can be towed, too.

BRINKMAN CORPORATION
4215 McEWEN ROAD
DALLAS, TX 75244
972-770-8521
Manufacturers of bullet-shaped charcoal and electric smokers and grills. Accessories are also available.

CAJUN GRILL
204 WILSON STREET
LAFAYETTE, LA 70501
800-822-4766
WWW.CAJUNGRILL.COM
Manufacturer of The Cajun Grill and The Cajun Smoker. They offer a line of gourmet Cajun products, too.

CALIFORNIA FIREPIT
P.O. BOX 1047
FRESNO, CA 93714
888-486-FIRE (3473)
WWW.FIREPIT.COM
The Tahoe Firepit converts into a super grill with cooking space large enough to hold 2 or 3 fish fillets, several kabobs, and a grill wok. The grill gate is adjustable for easy heat control. They have a portable version, too.

CALIFORNIA OUTDOOR CONCEPTS
135 WEST SUMNER STREET
LAKE ELSINORE, CA 92530
877-274-6773
Stylish granite-topped patio tables include a removeable centerpiece that unveils a stainless-steel multipurpose well. The well contains a gas burner that can be used for grilling-in-the-round. It can be converted to a fireplace for warmth. Or it may be used as an iced drink tub.

CHAR-BROIL
P.O. BOX 1240
COLUMBUS, GA 31993
706-571-7000
WWW.CHARBROIL.COM
Manufacturers of charcoal, electric, and gas barbecue grills; accessories; and replacement parts.

COOKSHACK, INC.
2340 NORTH ASH STREET
PONCA, OK 74601
580-765-3669
WWW.COOKSHACK.COM
Manufacturer of smoker ovens for home use and commercial food service. They also have a line of barbecue seasonings, sauces, and woods.

DCS—DYNAMIC COOKING SYSTEMS, INC.
5800 SKYLAB ROAD
HUNTINGTON BEACH, CA 92647
714-372-7000
WWW.DCSAPPLIANCES.COM
DCS offers a full line of innovative professional-style cooking products for the home. Outdoor products include stainless-steel gas and infrared grills and rotisseries.

DUCANE COMPANY
1241 AMBASSADOR BOULEVARD
ST. LOUIS, MO 63132-1705
800-379-5719
WWW.DUCANE.COM
Ducane produces stainless-steel free-standing kitchens with rotisseries and warming drawers. Side burners have been a hallmark of this industry leader. The warming rack can double as a cooking rack for additional cooking space.

DYNASTY RANGE
7355 EAST SLAUSON AVENUE
COMMERCE, CA 90040
800-749-5233
WWW.DYNASTYRANGE.COM
Manufacturer of the "ultimate" commercial-quality, high-performance outdoor gas grill kitchen.

EUROPEAN OUTDOOR CHEF
5207 QUARRYSTONE LANE
TAMPA, FL 33624
813-962-2414
WWW.OUTDOORCHEF.COM
Manufacturers of portable gas grills and campfire units for the outdoors.

GRAND HALL USA, INC.
10280 MILLER ROAD
DALLAS, TX 75238
214-349-1097
WWW.GRANDHALL.COM
Manufacturers of the Globe Café and Grand Café line of premium gas grills. They manufacture all of their own parts, too.

GRILL DOME
6303 PEACHTREE INDUSTRIAL
   BOULEVARD
DORAVILLE, GA 30360
770-454-6797
WWW.GRILLDOME.COM
Manufacturer of a Kamado-style ceramic charcoal barbecue and smoker. They also offer accessories, carts, wood chips, and tool sets.

GRILLS TO GO
37140 MARCIEL AVENUE
MADERA, CA 93938
559-645-8089
WWW.GRILLSTOGO.COM
Manufacturer of towable commercial charcoal, wood, and gas barbecue grills.

HASTY-BAKE
7656 EAST 46TH STREET
TULSA, OK 74145
918-665-8220
WWW.HASTYBAKE.COM
Versatile charcoal-fired barbecues for grilling, baking, and smoking, both built-in and portable. These units have an easy-to-adjust cooking rack making them a premier unit for heat control. They also offer natural hardwood charcoal and other accessories.

HOLLAND COMPANY, INC.
600 IRVING PARKWAY
HOLLY SPRINGS, NC 27540
800-880-9766
WWW.HOLLANDGRILL.COM
The Holland Company manufacturers and distributes a combination gas grill/smoker. It has a patented system that prevents flare-ups. It can grill,

smoke, or steam. Stainless-steel construction includes a built-in thermometer and smoker drawer.

KAMADO OF ATLANTA
3100 HARTRIDGE DRIVE
ATLANTA, GA 30022-6102
770-664-0999
WWW.KAMADO.COM
The Kamado is a ceramic charcoal grill, a gas grill, or a combination of both! It is also available with an electric heating element for use in areas where open flames are prohibited.

LYNX PROFESSIONAL KITCHEN
    PRODUCTS
6023-25 EAST BANDINI BOULEVARD
COMMERCE, CA 90040
888-289-5969
Manufacturer of Lynx Grill-Pro and Lynx Professional Grills.

MAGMA PRODUCTS, INC.
3940 PIXIE AVENUE
LONG BEACH, CA 90712-4136
800-86-MAGMA (62462)
WWW.MAGMAPRODUCTS.COM
Magma has been building barbecues for use on the open seas for over 25 years. The Del Mar model is an attractive stainless-steel pedestal gas grill. It takes up very little room, making it a perfect choice for yachts and condominiums with small balconies or patios. The unit uses inexpensive, lightweight, disposable canisters for fuel.

MASAGRIL, LLC
9570 PATHWAY, SUITE C
SANTEE, CA 92071
619-596-4745
WWW.MASAGRIL.COM
The Masagril is an all-in-one barbeque and fire pit entertaining unit. The inner circle is the fire pit or grill, while the tiled tabletop is an entertainment unit. So you can cook and dine at the table.

MASTERBUILT MANUFACTURING, INC.
450 BROWN AVENUE
COLUMBUS, GA 31906
706-327-5622
WWW.MASTERBUILT.COM
Outdoor cooker manufacturer of charcoal, gas, and electric smokers. Portable grills, deep fryers, and camping units are made with the outdoorsman in mind.

MODERN HOME PRODUCTS CORP.
150 SOUTH RAM ROAD
ANTIOCH, IL 60002
888-647-4745
WWW.MODERNHOMEPRODUCTS.COM
Home to several brands of barbecues including MHP, BBQer's Choice, Flavor Master, Infra Roast, and Sear Magic.

NAPOLEON APPLIANCE CORPORATION
214 BAYVIEW DRIVE
BARRIE, ON L4N 4Y8
CANADA
888-329-2220
WWW.NAC.ON.CA
High-end gas grills, rotisseries, and smokers are produced by this manufacturer. Brushes, cookware, covers, flavored wood chips, flavored wood pellets, gloves and mitts, replacement parts, and tool sets are sold through specialty dealers only.

NEW BRAUNFELS SMOKER COMPANY, INC.
1903 NORTH AUSTIN STREET
SEGUIN, TX 78155
888-895-9672
WWW.NBSMOKER.COM
Manufacturers of heavy-gauge steel smokers, grills, and fryers.

PITTS & SPITTS, INC.
14221 EASTEX FREEWAY
HOUSTON, TX 77032
281-987-3474
Manufacturer of "the finest Texas cookers you'll ever see."

SOLAIRE INFRARED GRILLING SYSTEMS
12028 EAST PHILADELPHIA STREET
WHITTIER, CA 90601
562-696-8718
WWW.RIWINC.COM
Stainless-steel gas grills with the modern technology of infrared cooking over

27,500 BTUs. The high-heat searing power of these units locks in flavor and juices in less than half the time of traditional grills.

THE ISLANDS
LAS VEGAS, NV
888-227-5399
WWW.ISLANDSBBQ.COM
The Islands manufactures custom barbecue units primarily for custom-built outdoor kitchens. Everything is high-grade stainless steel. They manufacture the storage drawers, refrigerators, side burners, and ice chests, too.

TRAEGER INDUSTRIES, INC.
P.O. BOX 829
MT. ANGEL, OR 97362
503-845-9234
WWW.TRAEGERINDUSTRIES.COM
The original and best wood pellet barbecues and smokers manufactured for over 40 years. There is no open flame making it almost impossible to burn your food. Wood pellets are a clean burning, renewable resource and they are 100% natural. The pellet grill is three appliances in one: It grills, bakes, and smokes, all with the flip of a switch.

VERMONT CASTINGS
MAJESTIC PRODUCTS DIVISION
410 ADMIRAL BOULEVARD
MISSISSAUGAU, ON L5T 2N6
CANADA
800-525-1898
Manufacturers of high-end gas grill smoker ovens. The porcelain on cast-iron cooking grates are extremely easy to clean. More important, they are excellent heat conductors. A large smoker box is built into the gas burners. An infrared rear rotisserie burner and a stainless-steel oven burner are included so you can roast and smoke.

VIKING RANGE CORPORATION
111 FRONT STREET
GREENWOOD, MS 38930
888-845-4641
WWW.VIKINGRANGE.COM
Viking's gas grill offers professional cooking power and exceptional features such as a smoker system and heavy-duty rotisserie. Gas side burners and collapsible side shelves offer extra cooking space. The corporation also offers state-of-the-art cooking schools throughout the United States.

WEBER-STEPHEN PRODUCTS COMPANY
200 EAST DANIELS ROAD
PALATINE, IL 60067
847-934-5700
WWW.WEBERBBQ.COM
Weber-Stephen manufactured the famous Weber kettle-shaped charcoal grill in 1951. Their bullet-shaped smoker is the Smokey Mountain Cooker Smoker. They also produce the Genesis and Summit gas grills. They produce barbecue covers, flavored wood chips, gloves and mitts, replacement parts, tool sets, charcoal, firestarters, and cookbooks. They have their own Weber restaurants, too.

CATALOGS

CHARCOAL COMPANION
7955 EDGEWATER DRIVE
OAKLAND, CA 94621
800-521-0505
Manufacturers and suppliers of gourmet grill accessories for the outdoor cook.

CHEF'S
P.O. BOX 620048
DALLAS, TX 75262-0048
800-338-3232
WWW.CHEFSCATALOG.COM
Purveyors of professional restaurant equipment for the home chef. Items we like for the grill include the line of Lodge Cast Iron, heavy-weight cast-iron cooking skillets and griddles that are perfect for pan grilling fish outdoors. They carry grill woks, baskets, and racks, too.

FRONTGATE CATALOG
5566 WEST CHESTER ROAD
WEST CHESTER, OH 45069
800-626-6488
WWW.FRONTGATE.COM
This lifestyle catalog offers high-end outdoor stainless-steel kitchens including the Viking Grill. They also offer an array of outdoor home products for the pool and patio.

GRILL LOVER'S CATALOG
P.O. BOX 1300
COLUMBUS, GA 31902-1300
800-241-8981
WWW.GRILLLOVERS.COM
The Char-Broil grill is manufactured by the parent company that produces this full-line barbecue and grill catalog.

NORDIC WARE OUTDOOR PRODUCTS
5005 HIGHWAY 7 AT 100
MINNEAPOLIS, MN 55416-2274
800-328-4310, EXT. 500
WWW.NORDICWARE.COM
Nordic Ware is known for wonderfully designed cookware including the original Bundt cake pan. They also offer barbecue and grill accessories. Their fish boat is a versatile accessory for grilling or smoking delicate fish.

OSCARWARE, INC
749 PRICEVILLE ROAD
BONNIEVILLE, KY 42713-0040
270-531-2860
WWW.OSCARWARE.COM
Reasonably priced grill racks, pizza grill pans, and grill woks are offered from this manufacturer.

OUTDOOR COOKING STORE
2225 4TH STREET
WHITE BEAR LAKE, MN 55110
651-653-6166
WWW.OUTDOORCOOKINGSTORE.COM
This is a multipurpose company located outside of the St. Paul/Minneapolis area. It includes a retail store, the online catalog, the mail-order catalog, and a barbecue cooking school, too.

HARDWOOD CHARCOAL, WOOD PELLETS, AND PLANK SUPPLIERS

AMERICAN BBQ WOOD PRODUCTS
9540 RIGGS
OVERLAND PARK, KS 66212
913-648-7993
A large assortment of wood products are available here from wood chips and chunks to logs. Wood flavors include mesquite, hickory, oak, pecan, maple, grape, apple, cherry, and alder. They also carry mesquite and hardwood lump charcoal.

APPLE CREEK TIMBER
4010 MERIDIAN EAST
EDGEWOOD, WA 98371
253-770-9561
From the beautiful state of Washington comes a supply of apple wood chips and chunks. Other varieties are available, too. Call for information.

B & B CHARCOAL COMPANY
P.O. BOX 230
WEIMAR, TX 78962
WWW.BBCHARCOAL.COM
Oak and mesquite lump charcoal, wood chunks and chips, and mini-logs are available in 10-pound to 1,250-pound bags!

BAR B Q WOODS, INC.
800 EAST 14TH STREET
NEWTON, KS 67114
316-284-0300
This wood company offers commercial and consumer wood chunks, chips, and logs in a variety of flavors.

BBQR'S DELIGHT
P.O. BOX 8727
PINE BLUFF, AR 71611
877-275-9591
WWW.BBQRSDELIGHT.COM
This company offers one of the most extensive lines of barbecue wood pellets. Flavors include apple, black walnut, cherry, hickory, Jack Daniels, mesquite, mulberry, oak, orange, pecan, sassafras,

and sugar maple. A 1-pound bag is enough for approximately 10 uses and the bag has a resealable closure.

BIRCH CREEK
8880 BABCOCK ROAD
BURTCHVILLE, MI 48059
WWW.SMOKINGWOOD.HOMESTEAD.COM
Apple, hickory, oak, and maple wood are available in large chunks and chips.

BRAZOS MESQUITE
P.O. BOX 9009
COLLEGE STATION, TX 77842
979-229-7868
WWW.BRAZOSMESQUITE.COM
Brazos offers mesquite, hickory, and pecan wood chunks in quantities from 12 pounds to truckloads.

CHIGGER CREEK WOOD PRODUCTS
409 EAST 2ND STREET
SEDALIA, MO 65301
660-826-0702
Barbecue wood chips, chunks, and logs in 14 different wood varieties are offered here. Retail and bulk packaging plus hardwood lump charcoal is also available.

COWBOY CHARCOAL COMPANY
P.O. BOX 3770
BRENTWOOD, TN 37024
615-661-6882
Natural wood and wood products including hardwood lump charcoal are available from this company.

FAIRLANE BAR B Q WOOD
12502 3RD STREET
GRANDVIEW, MO 64030
816-761-1350
Fairlane specializes in mesquite, pecan, hickory, oak, apple, cherry, and sassafras. They will ship anywhere.

HEARTLAND FRAGRANCE &
    HERB COMPANY
2909 EAST INDUSTRIAL DRIVE
SPRINGFIELD, MO 65081-0855
417-831-7510
Cowboy Gourmet flavored wood chips for grilling and smoking on the barbecue are produced here. Call for additional information.

HUMPHREY CHARCOAL CORPORATION
P.O. BOX 440
BROOKVILLE, PA 15825
814-849-2302
Manufacturers of premium hardwood charcoal products in lump, briquette, and granular form.

INDIAN CREEK MESQUITE, INC.
P.O. BOX 1644
BROWNWOOD, TX 76804
915-646-0393
Indian Creek offers mesquite wood chunks and chips.

MA'S SMOKIN CHIPS
P.O. BOX 433
PALOUSE, WA 99161
503-778-5642
WWW.SMOKINCHIPS.COM
Apple, peach, cherry, grape, pear, pecan, hickory, mesquite, alder, oak, and apricot chips and chunks are available from Ma's. They also carry grills, sauces, rubs, and lots more.

OUTDOOR HOME
1661 EAST ST. LOUIS STREET
SPRINGFIELD, MO
888-869-EGGS
WWW.OUTDOORHOME.COM
Fourteen flavors of wood chunks, chips, and hardwood lump charcoal are offered by Outdoor Home. They have an assortment of grills, accessories, and a large assortment of barbecue cookbooks, too.

PACIFIC NORTHWEST FINE WOOD
    PRODUCTS
P.O. BOX 935
BELFAIR, WA 98528
800-881-1747
The Cedar Baking Plank from this company is top-notch. It is about 2 inches thick. To prevent the wood from splitting, there are heavy bolts in the plank that can be tightened when small cracks

appear. It is very attractive and can be used for aromatic wood smoking on the grill and presentation on the table. It is available in upscale gourmet and kitchen shops.

PEOPLES WOODS
75 MILL STREET
CUMBERLAND, RI 02864
800-729-5800
WWW.PEOPLESWOODS.COM
Nature's Own natural lump charcoal charwood contains chunks of kiln-fired, virgin sugar maple trees harvested from a government-owned 3,000-square-mile forest in Quebec. The trees are selectively cut there under a strict government reforestation program.

WEST OREGON WOOD PRODUCTS, INC.
P.O. BOX 249
COLUMBIA CITY, OR 97018
503-397-6707
WWW.WOWPELLETS.COM
Lil' Devils barbecue pellet flavors include hickory, mesquite, alder, and apple wood.

WW WOOD, INC.
P.O. BOX 398
PLEASANTON, TX 78064
830-569-2501
WWW.WOODINC.COM
Manufacturer and supplier of a full line of aromatic wood products for the barbecue. Mesquite and hickory wood chunks are available. Chips come in apple, cherry, hickory, Jack Daniels, maple and mesquite. They also offer a metal wood smoker box.

INDEX